China's Climate-Energy Policy

China's recent climate-energy policy, an outcome of contemporary challenges, has generated conflict of interest amongst major stakeholders. Coupled with a boost in demand for oil, gas and coal, as well a rapid growth in wind and solar power, it has not only affected domestic fossil fuel and renewable energy providers, but has also provoked a resource boom, affecting development pathways internationally.

This book therefore seeks to examine the economic, social and ecological effects associated with China's climate-energy policy. Assessing how the policy has been and will be formulated and implemented, it analyses the changing use of energy, CO_2 emissions and GDP, as well as social and environmental impacts both domestically and internationally. It presents in-depth case studies on specific policies in China and on its resource exporting countries, such as Indonesia, Australia, Myanmar and Mongolia. At the same time, using quantitative data, it provides detailed input-output and applied computable general equilibrium analyses. Arguing that China has actively advanced its climate-energy policy to become a leader of global climate governance, it demonstrates that China ultimately relocates the cost of its climate-energy policy to resource exporting countries.

This book will be of great interest to students and scholars of energy, the environment and sustainability, as well as Chinese Studies and economics.

Akihisa Mori is an Associate Professor of Kyoto University, Japan, and the Director and Secretary General of the East Asian Association of Environmental and Resource Economics. His recent publications include *Green Growth and Low Carbon Development in East Asia* (Routledge, 2015) and *The Green Fiscal Mechanism and Reform for Low Carbon Development* (Routledge, 2013).

Routledge Contemporary China Series

China's Hydro-politics in the Mekong
Conflict and Cooperation in Light of Securitization Theory
Sebastian Biba

Economic Policy Making in China (1949–2016)
The Role of Economists
Pieter Bottelier

The Power of Relationalism in China
Leah Zhu

China's Financial Opening
Coalition Politics and Policy Changes
Yu-Wai Vic Li

Urbanization, Regional Development and Governance in China
Jianfa Shen

Midwifery in China
Ngai Fen Cheung and Rosemary Mander

China's Virtual Monopoly of Rare Earth Elements
Economic, Technological and Strategic Implications
Roland Howanietz

China's Regions in an Era of Globalization
Tim Summers

China's Climate-Energy Policy
Domestic and International Impacts
Edited by Akihisa Mori

For more information about this series, please visit: www.routledge.com/
Routledge-Contemporary-China-Series/book-series/SE0768

China's Climate-Energy Policy

Domestic and International Impacts

Edited by Akihisa Mori

Routledge
Taylor & Francis Group

LONDON AND NEW YORK

First published 2019 by Routledge

2 Park Square, Milton Park, Abingdon, Oxfordshire OX14 4RN

52 Vanderbilt Avenue, New York, NY 10017

Routledge is an imprint of the Taylor & Francis Group, an informa business

First issued in paperback 2019

Copyright © 2019 selection and editorial matter, Akihisa Mori; individual chapters, the contributors

The right of Akihisa Mori to be identified as the author of the editorial material, and of the authors for their individual chapters, has been asserted in accordance with sections 77 and 78 of the Copyright, Designs and Patents Act 1988.

All rights reserved. No part of this book may be reprinted or reproduced or utilised in any form or by any electronic, mechanical, or other means, now known or hereafter invented, including photocopying and recording, or in any information storage or retrieval system, without permission in writing from the publishers.

Notice:
Product or corporate names may be trademarks or registered trademarks, and are used only for identification and explanation without intent to infringe.

British Library Cataloguing-in-Publication Data
A catalogue record for this book is available from the British Library

Library of Congress Cataloging-in-Publication Data
Names: Mori, Akihisa, 1970– editor.
Title: China's climate-energy policy : domestic and international impacts / edited by Akihisa Mori.
Description: Abingdon, Oxon ; New York, NY : Routledge, 2019. | Series: Routledge contemporary China series ; 194 | Includes bibliographical references and index.
Identifiers: LCCN 2018013408 | ISBN 9781138489424 (hardback) | ISBN 9781351037587 (ebook)
Subjects: LCSH: Energy policy – Environmental aspects – China. | Environmental policy – Economic aspects – China. | Climatic changes – Government policy – China.
Classification: LCC HD9502.C62 C4956 2019 | DDC 333.790951 – dc23
LC record available at https://lccn.loc.gov/2018013408

ISBN: 978-1-138-48942-4 (hbk)
ISBN: 978-0-367-89452-8 (pbk)

Typeset in Times New Roman
by Apex CoVantage, LLC

Contents

Illustrations

Figures

Tables

Map

Contributors

Hikari Ban is a professor and Dean of Faculty of Economics, Kobe Gakuin University, Japan.

Le Dong holds a PhD from the Graduate School of Global Environmental Studies, Kyoto University, Japan.

Kiyoshi Fujikawa is a professor at the Applied Social System Institute of Asia, Nagoya University, Japan.

Nobuhiro Horii is an associate professor at Graduate School of Economics, Kyushu University, Japan.

Akihisa Mori is an associate professor at Graduate School of Global Environmental Studies, Kyoto University, Japan, and a director and the secretary general of the East Asian Association of Environmental and Resource Economics.

Mika Takehara is a senior researcher at the Japan Oil, Gas and Metals National Corporation (JOGMEC), Japan.

Lynn Thiesmeyer is a professor at Faculty of Environment and Information Studies, Keio University, Japan.

Zuoyi Ye is an associate professor at Shanghai University of International Business and Economics, China.

Acknowledgements

I am indebted to a number of people and organizations for the preparation of this book. First, I appreciate the host institutions of the co-authors and myself who enabled us to access much of our materials, as well as our staff (in particular, Hiromi Odaguchi and Kana Fujita) who supported the administrative work for this research at each host institution.

We benefitted from the feedback we received at the Congress of the East Asian Association of Environmental and Resource Economics (EAAERE), especially from Shiqiu Zhang, Budy Resosudarmo and Meiyu Guo. We also benefitted from the feedback from seminars at the Crawford Public School of Australian National University; the Indonesian Institute of Sciences (LIPI); the Asian Energy Studies Centre of Hong Kong Baptist University; the Japan Oil, Gas, Metals National Corporation (JOGMEC); and the Research Center for Sustainability and Environment of Shiga University; as well as from lectures at the Faculty of Economics and Business of Universitas Indonesia and talks at the School of International Studies of Jawaharlal Nehru University. We express a special thanks to Ross McLeod, Max Corden, Raghbendra Jha, Maxensius Tri Sambodo, Daphne Mah, Alie Damayanti, Katsuya Tanaka and Nandakumar Janardhanan who hosted these seminars and lectures, and gave us precious opportunities to deepen our analysis.

We would also like to express our gratitude to the Japan Society for the Promotion of Science (JSPS), which provided financial support to research projects on "energy and climate change policy in China and its impacts on energy exporting Asian countries" (Grant No. 26281061).

We are grateful to Routledge for its excellent editorial work. In particular, we would appreciate Georgina Bishop for her indispensable assistance and patience in producing this work, as well as the anonymous reviewers for their productive comments and suggestions.

A big final great thank to our team of co-authors, for their precious work, patience and exchanges of research. Their great contributions and different perspectives allowed us to extend our understanding of the climate-energy nexus and domestic-international linkage of China's climate-energy policy.

Akihisa Mori

Part I

Why China's carbon-energy policy matters

1 Climate-energy policy

Domestic policy process, outcome and impacts

Akihisa Mori

Emergence of climate-energy policy

States have implemented energy policies to meet the needs of multiple stakeholders at multiple levels of governance. In general, they address the "four As of energy security" (availability, accessibility, affordability and acceptability) (APERC 2007), considering environmental and social concerns, vulnerability of vital energy systems (Cherp and Jewell 2014).

Climate change poses an additional challenge to the state. Given the increasing pressure on the food and energy systems, as highlighted in the assessment reports of the Intergovernmental Panel on Climate Change (IPCC) (IPCC 2007, 2014), climate change appears as a matter concerning the survival of human beings. To effectively combat climate change, policy sectors that affect and will be affected by climate change are required to integrate or mainstream climate change into their policy process and policy output (Dupont 2016). Among them, the energy sector receives special attention, as it contributes at least two-thirds of global greenhouse-gas (GHG) emissions (IEA 2017). While carbon dioxide (CO_2) emissions (the majority in the GHG emissions) became flat between 2014 and 2016, they are far above the 450 ppm scenario for the global 2 °C climate change target[1] (IEA 2017). In this regard, tackling energy-related CO_2 emissions is crucial for climate change mitigation.

To move the energy sector toward a low CO_2 emissions pathway, additional energy-related climate policy measures are required besides those already existing and planned. Among them, increasing energy efficiency and scaling up the use of renewables in power generation and beyond are listed as cost-effective measures in the marginal abatement cost schedule (McKinzey & Company 2009). They are estimated to account for an 80 percent of the reduction in the 450 ppm scenario (IEA 2017).

Coherence with concerns about energy security

Climate policy can clash with energy security. While it enables energy-importing countries to increase energy security by reducing fossil fuel consumption, energy dependency on unstable or hostile regions, or over-dependence on few suppliers, it can weaken energy security of energy-exporting countries by reducing demand, political security and bargaining power vis-à-vis importers (Sharples 2013).

Energy-importing countries also face difficulties in effectively integrating climate concern into energy policy for a transition toward a low CO_2 pathway. Energy systems are featured by suck investments, long operating lifetimes and complementary capital investments (Schmidt et al. 2017). They are also strongly path-dependent and deeply embedded in society in terms of norms, values, laws, modes of governance, social relations and culture (Verbong and Geels 2010). These features make energy systems prone to technological and institutional lock-in, and become so economically, institutionally and politically entrenched that reconfiguration becomes difficult (Fouquet 2016).

This is why climate change is reframed as a discourse that is acceptable by the regime and the society. Reframed as a decarburization discourse that gives priority to nuclear power in countries where nuclear power prevails, it becomes compatible with the prevailing sense of energy security. However, liberalization of the energy market renders the cost of nuclear highly uncertain, making private investors and energy companies hesitant to invest (Toke 2013). In addition, the Fukushima nuclear disaster raises concerns over the safety and security of the nuclear reactors, forcing the state to give up the decarburization discourse (Szarka 2013). In fact, the discourse loses support even where a vertically integrated monopolistic or oligopolistic supply system of electricity is justified, and incumbent suppliers can capitalize on the excess rents to gain comparably large power and resources to pursue regulatory capture (Mori 2017b).

Climate change is reframed as a green economy or ecological modernization in Germany and to a less extent the United States. While both countries have succeeded in emerging renewable energy industries and diffusing renewable energy, they show contrasting results in the amount of diffusion and emissions reduction. In Germany, high concern about over-dependence on one supplier, coupled with a social structure that accepts necessary changes including higher electricity price, drives diffusion of renewables (Hillebrand 2013).

In contrast, climate change is reframed to justify policies conceived to protect what are seen as energy security objectives in Brazil (Vieira and Dalgaard 2013). The main driver of Brazil's energy security policies continues to be strategic concerns over the availability and reliability of supplies. This revitalizes biofuel and hydroelectricity as climate-energy programs for energy security.

These observations indicate that policy process and outcomes to tackling energy-related CO_2 emissions vary by how a country reframes climate change to attain energy security at the same time. They also suggest that coverage of energy security differs by domestic imperatives (Grundmann et al. 2013).

This book defines policy outcomes to tackling energy-related CO_2 emissions as climate-energy policy and analyzes their impacts on CO_2 emissions as well as energy demand and supply, economic growth and society.

Domestic impacts

Climate-energy policy can exert influence on emitters' decisions through direct intervention, change in market price and discourses. In particular, accelerating renewables can potentially break institutional lock-in and reconfigure the prevailing energy regime for several reasons (Mori 2017a). First, it can increase competition and diversify monopolistic or oligopolistic markets. This will eventually alter prevailing market dynamics within the energy sector as the generation cost approaches grid parity through technological feedback effects. Second, such competition and diversity squeeze excess rent to the incumbent suppliers, making them incapable of compensating opposing stakeholder groups and of propagating the population. Third, it can foster emerging local industries poised to benefit from increased renewable energy growth. Fourth, decentralized or distributed energy technologies offer greater flexibility and can therefore more readily organize and enable distributed political and economic power, generating a policy feedback effect.

However, attempts to reconfigure the prevailing energy system open up frictions and develop into struggles of power (Stirling 2014). Reconfiguration threatens the economic interests and political influence of incumbent energy suppliers, and entails additional burden. Incumbent suppliers have comparably large power and resources not only because states depend on them to secure a stable supply, but also because they can exert influence in three ways: through relational networks and close contacts with senior policymakers; internalization of the ideas and interests of the incumbents; and corporate political strategies such as information strategies, financial incentives, organized pressure and direct lobbying (Geels 2014). Once policymakers and incumbents form an alliance, a stable and hegemonic "historical bloc" (Levy and Newell 2002) emerges to stabilize and reproduce existing paradigms and structures, thus reinforcing the current regime. Reconfiguration becomes hard-fought inter- and intra-scalar contestations between old and new institutions, agents and technologies (Rock et al. 2009). It can make struggles last several decades before being settled (Lockwood 2015), posing limitations on rapid change (Smith and Raven 2012).

Attempts at reconfiguration can also clash with the affordability of energy – the priority in the existing energy, industrial and military policies (Aldy et al. 2010). A resultant rise in energy price can hit the middle class most severely because they are required to pay both higher gasoline prices and higher electricity tariffs (Blobel et al. 2011). In particular, carbon pricing causes two side effects: unequal impacts on industrial competitiveness, and regressive impacts on income distribution (Andersen and Ekins 2009; Ekins and Speck 2011). These side effects are likely to hinder social acceptance of climate change mitigation and instead motivate people to vote for the political parties that prioritize affordability over sustainability.

There are several possible ways to get out of this climate-energy conundrum. One is to create, maintain and fund a long-term policy framework. This can allow incumbents to take flexible measures to address climate change while sustaining momentum toward reconfiguration (Mazzucato 2015).

Second is to secure relatively cleaner energy at an affordable price. This includes the exploration of domestic oil and gas fields, development of oil and gas pipelines and acquisition of oil and gas fields in foreign countries. This option, however, can raise a conflict of interest with energy security, unless energy security can be farmed as reducing reliance on energy imports. Development of domestic non-traditional oil and gas fields through fracking enables the United States to take this option at the expense of modest progress in renewables (Vezirgiannidou 2013).

Third is displacement of carbon-intense industries. Carbon pricing sparks concern over industry and country competitiveness, incentivizing carbon-intense industries to displace plants to countries without high abatement policies. This results in carbon leakage (Andersen and Ekins 2009).

Obviously, the second and third options can have adverse economic and environmental impacts on energy-exporting countries and host countries for investments, including a resource curse as well as disruptions to livelihood and ecology.

International impacts

Resource curse

The resource curse is defined as less economic growth, less democracy and worse development outcomes than countries with fewer natural resources. It can be explained by the Dutch disease and volatile resource revenue. Dutch disease refers to the contraction of the traded goods sector and growth in non-trade sectors in response to a resource boom and the resultant appreciation of real exchange rate. As the traded goods sector, namely the manufacturing sector, is the engine of growth and is beneficial in terms of learning by doing and other positive externalities, the contraction of the sector makes it difficult for resource-rich countries to fully recover their productivity once resources run out and they lose their competitive edge (van der Ploeg 2011). This further increases domestic consumption and imports while decreasing non-resource exports, the savings rate, wealth, and social welfare, thus locking the country into the vicious cycle of the resource curse. In addition, highly volatile commodity prices make their resource revenue and economic growth highly volatile and cyclical to the commodity price, generating adverse growth effects (van der Ploeg and Poelhekke 2009).

The Dutch disease can be mitigated if a country uses a "park fund" for resource revenue so as not to ramp up spending too rapidly; the economy is flexible in terms of openness to trade, ease of market entry by new firms and labor market flexibility; and the country addresses the potential bottleneck of infrastructure and labor skills for wealth creation (Venables 2016). This implies that the right set of institutions is the key to whether countries will fall into the curse or not.

However, the existence of a resource wealth can worsen the quality of institutions. It allows governments to pacify dissent, avoid accountability and resist modernization (Isham et al. 2005), while encouraging productive entrepreneurs and politicians to shift activities toward rent-seeking (Torvik 2002), destroying institutions as a result (Ross 1999). Actual political decisions depend on how resource rents affect the leader's probability of survival. If a resource boom raises the value of staying in office, the political leader will shift resource revenue from productive to unproductive activities. But if the leader responds to the windfall gain by offering better and more outside opportunities to rebel groups, the windfall will become a blessing (Caselli and Cunningham 2009).

The extent of the curse can vary by resource. "Point source" resources that have limited socioeconomic linkage can cause a greater curse and result in weaker institutions (Isham et al. 2005; Auty 2006). As mining requires a huge amount of capital and advanced technologies, a few large, often transnational companies tend to operate under a concession contract with a host country's government. While the government obtains resource revenue through tax, this structure prompts concentration of resource wealth to a limited number of people, causing an uneven distribution. In addition, where the host country favors imports over domestic production in input supplies, backward linkage is constrained while forward linkage is stunted, as the resource-processing industry is too internationally competitive to rapidly develop. As a result, taxation becomes a dominant resource flow, which amplifies the probability of predatory behavior, policy failure and economic distortion resulting from clumsy rent-seeking.

From this point of view, oil can be identified as a resource that is most likely to cause the curse. A few countries have managed the resource rent wisely to competitively diversify the economy, and in effect, mitigate the constraints on widening backward and forward linkage. Coal can be defined as a resource that causes less of a curse. It is scattered around the country and easily accessible to a wider set of economic agents. Moreover, it is easier to create many socio-economic linkages with coal than with oil, although wealth from coal mining can be concentrated in specific patronage networks, where a small number of large companies are given concessions to large mining areas or small mining companies are merged.

Still, a varied extent of the curse can be observed within oil- and gas-rich countries. Luong and Weinthal (2010) refute that it is the structure of ownership by which resource-rich states choose to manage their mineral wealth that plays the decisive role. State ownership and control enable political elites to derive income exclusively from resource rents, freeing them from developing the state's capacity for effective taxation and increasing social expectations for wide distribution of the state's resource income to the population. Private ownership and control, on the other hand, increase transaction costs for the government in exploiting resource rent. This provides political elites with no choice but to seek a broad-based tax regime while reducing social expectations for distribution.

The authors also highlight the fact that political elites in resource-rich countries can change ownership and management. Uzbekistan and Turkmenistan have maintained state ownership and control since their independence, causing political leaders to perpetuate authoritarian regimes, and lead the states as rentier and distributive with increasing reliance on resource rent. This situation widens the wealth gap and worsens the level of human development represented in the UNDP's Human Development Index. In contrast, Russia implemented comprehensive tax and expenditure reforms and increased its accountability to the population after it shifted toward private ownership and control.

These arguments suggest to us that the resource curse that might have been intensified by China's quest for resources can vary by the structure of ownership of resources in energy-exporting countries as well as by the type of energy they export.

Disruption of livelihood and ecology

Foreign direct investment (FDI) and the environment became a hot debate at the end of the 1990s. Despite the relatively small share of mining in world investment flows, FDI in this sector represents a substantial part of capital formation and GDP in many developing and emerging economies (Kondo 2002). FDI flow into the resource extractive sector, including oil and gas, surged in the late 1990s after it had gone through liberalization and deregulation in the structural adjustment package that aimed at attracting FDI to boost export. However, the sector, particularly in sub-Saharan Africa, was criticized for labor abuse; livelihood and ecological disruption by extensive logging, mining and hydropower development; blood resources; proliferation of dictatorships; inefficient state of enterprises (SOEs) that are not held accountable (Moyo 2012); and eroding of transparency and human rights (Serge and Beuret 2010). Several projects have also been suspended by fierce local protests over concerns of serious ecological impacts (Grumbine 2010).

Competition for FDI between countries and gaps in national environmental standards are regarded as underlying causes for ecological disruptions, creating pollution havens and propelling a global race to the bottom in terms of social and environmental regulation. Decrees and regulations that set environmental standards often lag behind the FDI surge, giving concessions without preparing consideration to environmental and social safeguards. Lobbying by investors and their home countries – in addition to a lack of institutional capacity, finance and in some cases political will – hampers efforts of some host country governments to implement effective environmental regulation (Boocock 2002). Under an unfavorable investment climate such as in Russia and Kazakhstan, only investors seeking quick returns and injecting high-risk capital are attracted to projects without regard to ownership, despite posing a risk of adverse impacts on the environment and the society (Henzler 2002).

On the other hand, global market forces and political pressures can create pollution halos in developing countries, pulling them towards environmental policy convergence (Zarsky 2002). Companies from developed countries can push to promote the establishment of higher environmental standards and management practices through the transfer of technology and management expertise under appropriate framework conditions (Borregaard and Dufey 2002).

While pollution "havens" cannot be statistically proven, there are clearly "pollution zones" inhabited by poorer people, both within and across countries, where firms perform worse and where regulation is less effective (Zarsky 1999: 66).

To address this deficiency, multilateral organizations have initiated multi-lateral guidelines and agreements. International financial institutions (IFIs) such as the World Bank Group, including International Finance Corporation (IFC) has stipulated social and environmental safeguard policies that go far beyond national regulations, requiring foreign investors to comply as lenders or equity holders. Underpinned by the United Nations, the Kimberley Process Certification Scheme was established that safeguards the shipment of "rough diamonds" and certifies them as conflict free. The OECD drafted *Guidelines for Multinational Enterprises* that include environmental considerations, requiring member countries to convince their investors to follow them. The Equator Principles were prepared to provide financial institutions with a minimum standard for due diligence and monitoring to support responsible risk decision-making. The Extractive Industries Transparency Initiative (EITI) was set up by governments, companies and civil society organizations to ensure benefits from the extractive industries to citizens through high standards of transparency and accountability; for this, it requires countries to publish timely and accurate information on the number of licenses, as well as the revenue from extractive industries and its allocation (EITI 2017).

Nonetheless, these countermeasures have two imitations. First, due to their voluntary nature, they can work effectively only when the private investors can gain by replacing existing practices to safety countermeasures, or when there is sufficient external pressure to make initiatives work (Gunningham 2002). Second, non-OECD investors can avoid these guidelines and agreements to make investments as long as they can self-finance or are backed by non-IFIs financial institutions that do not mind international reputations. Besides there are a number of loopholes in host countries that can all cause harmful ecological impacts, such as different legal requirements by size and type of mining activity, inter-ministerial conflicts, a lack of enforcement capacity and political will on which FDIs can capitalize to obtain mining concession that can cause harmful impacts (Boocock 2002).

China

China's reframing of energy security

China's notion of energy security has evolved along with its transition from a planned to socialist market economy, with consequences borne by state enterprises and the environment.

In the planned economy period, energy security was defined as ensuring proper and smooth domestic supply. In the transition to a socialist market economy, the Communist Party of China and the state came to perceive economic growth, poverty alleviation, social stability, nationalism and patriotism as the foundation for their legitimacy (Chen 2012; Wang 2012). The resultant high-speed economic growth turned China into a net oil importer in the mid-1990s and net energy importer in the early 2000s (Figure 1.1). This raises a concern about the

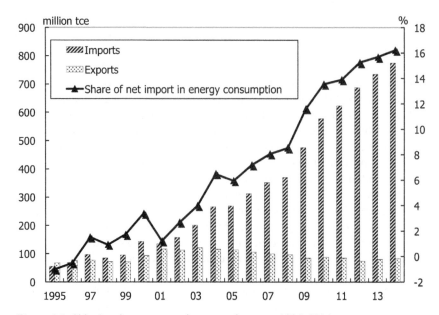

Figure 1.1 China's primary energy import and export, 1995–2014

Sources: Author compilation based on China Statistics Press, *China Energy Statistics Yearbook 2009*, *2015*.

appropriate mix of energies and about the way to access these energies, both from a geopolitical and technological standpoint (Di Meglio and Romano 2016b).

However, the country's macroeconomic reform has swung the priority of energy security back and forth, restricting the Chinese government to implement a coherent energy policy or strategy designed to enhance energy security (Yao and Chang 2015). This has generated a trilemma between expansion of supply capacity, a structurally heavy reliance on and inefficient use of coal, and air pollution (Hatch 2003; Mori and Hayashi 2012).

In the coal-mine industry, town and village coal mines (TVCMs) were stimulated for expansion in order to meet the increasing energy demand of the early 1990s. But in the late 1990s when the Asian economic crisis slowed it down, TCCMs became a target of closure, and state coal mines fell into financial distress due to overstaffing and high welfare costs. State coal mines were transformed into limited liability companies with the state retaining a controlling interest in the companies.

In the power sector, construction of thermal plants was preferred over hydroelectric ones from the perspective of cost, time, reliability of operation, and the constraints of hard foreign currency (Lieberthal and Oksenberg 1988). Local governments and foreign companies were encouraged to invest in and to have their own plants. However, these plants became the targets for shut down in the late 1990s to protect the State Power Corporation of China (SPCC) and to enhance control of most of the electricity-related assets.

Still, these consolidated state companies had insufficient capacity to meet the skyrocketing demand in the early 2000s, resulting in severe blackouts in eighteen out of the thirty-one provinces in 2003. In response, local governments and companies revived the TVCMs, coal power and industrial plants that had been officially closed; but the abolishment of the ministries in charge weakened the administrative capacity to oversee and provide funding for energy conservation. The fiscal and SOEs reforms discouraged local governments and SOEs to invest in clean coal technology and other environmental protection activities that required longer time to generate return. All of this made it difficult to enforce environmental and safety regulations, causing severe disasters,[2] inefficient energy use, air pollution, health damage and an increase in carbon emission (especially embodied carbon emission; see Chapter 2). Stringent air pollution controls simply reduced investments in coal power and industrial plants as pollution abatement technologies often brought them little profit and the SOEs reforms constrained the state from offering financial support that could mitigate hard budget constraints.

In response, the Hu administration attempted to accelerate economic transformation in order to resolve the negative effects of China's rapid economic growth, including energy-related environmental degradation (Yao and Chang 2015). The administration accelerated the re-distribution of state-owned assets and the regrouping of SOEs on the basis of market principles, and the SPCC was vertically and horizontally unbundled to increase competition. State coal mines were consolidated into thirteen production bases to gain competitiveness amid gradually expanding and accelerating price reform for marketization (Chapter 4). These reforms created the industrial structure in the coal mine and power sectors consisting of a few conglomerates with a number of small, inefficient private companies that often had market competitiveness due to cheap labor and externalized environmental costs. Coupled with local governments' impulse toward economic growth and protection of local companies, the industrial structure posed another difficulty in getting out of the trilemma.

To address these difficulties, the state shifted the notion of energy security to address the appropriate mix of energies as well as the way to access them, both from a geographical and technological point of view (Di Meglio and Romano 2016b). It accepted the need for flexibility and realism to secure easy access. It justified additional development of oil and gas around the world as a means to enhance domestic energy security through increasing global energy security, and reframed renewable energy as industrial policy to foster new competitive edge. This provided profit and personal career building opportunities for the main national oil companies (NOCs) to improve their performance through competition and vertical integration, while assuring an equal guarantee to the population and price controls to be consistent with its energy security concerns.

In principle, when implementing climate-energy policy, the Chinese government reframes climate change to be consistent with the flexible notion of the energy security, and employs the same instruments and agencies (Chapter 3). Xi administration took a further step into the appropriate mix of energies, setting the coal consumption target in the 13th Five-Year Plan (FYP) and the coal dependency target of below 50 percent by 2035.

Possible domestic impacts

Previous research suggests a variety of domestic impacts from the implementation of China's climate-energy policy. Among these are regressive distributional effects on urban areas through a carbon tax (Brenner et al. 2007; Ye et al. 2016). Climate-energy policy also increases coal imports, which intensify conflicts of interest between the China National Coal Association and state-owned power utilities that fell into financial distress: 70 percent of them tuned into the red and more than half owed wages despite consolidation (Wong 2014). Conflicts of interest will also intensify between the government's climate and energy security concerns, and NOCs' profit motives. Two-thirds of NOCs' foreign investments are break-even and only a tenth of their extracted oil is directly imported into China: the majority of their oil is sold in the world market to secure a profit (Di Meglio and Romano 2016b).

Finally, climate-energy policy will generate renewable curtailment through rapid and large expansion of renewable energy generation capacity. China has gone through large curtailment since 2010 under the electricity infrasystem, which is characterized by a prohibition against direct provision to end-users, sluggish grid connectivity, priority to fossil fuels in grid connection, and the overcapacity of coal power (Fang et al. 2012). Although the rate of idle wind power capacity dropped to 17 percent in 2012 and to 11 percent in 2013, about 16 TWh was still wasted due to curtailment (REN21 2014). Solar photovoltaic (PV) also encountered curtailment of 12 percent of its national average in 2015 owning to huge investments in large-scale plants (REN21 2016).

Possible international impacts

China's aggressive quest for resources has been criticized for causing or intensifying livelihood and ecological disruption in resource-exporting countries. Aside from this, it has been criticized for cutting Western countries' monopoly over political presence, market and resources, in addition to allegations of unfair competition, and corruption (Burgis 2015). China's infrastructure financing has also criticized for the dominant acquisition of development projects by Chinese companies (Copper 2016), the tying with labor and intermediary goods imports from China, and less contribution to economic diversification (Cáceres and Ear 2013), although the oil-for-infrastructure scheme is viewed as a practical way of mitigating the resource curse in Africa (Brautigam 2009).

China is increasingly becoming a key player in gas and some other commodities prices, at least for the region spanning from Central to East Asia (Di Meglio and Romano 2016a). The direct investments from China have been criticized for their livelihood and ecological disruptions as found in logging in Cambodia (Cáceres and Ear 2013), mining in Myanmar (Cockett 2015), hydropower dam development in the upper Mekong river basin (Lyu 2015) and coal power in Indonesia (Hervé-Mignucci and Wang 2015). Increasing dependency on China is blamed for shrinking local manufacturers (Serge and Beuret 2010), decreasing the number of skilled jobs in Thailand (Pupphavesa et al. 2013) and depriving workers of opportunities to develop skill and capacity in Cambodia (Chandarany et al. 2013). While several projects have been suspended by fierce local protests over concerns of serious ecological disruptions (Grumbine 2010), the Chinese government often places pressure on the governments in host countries to remedy such situations.

The Chinese government uses the leverage of its banking system to encourage Chinese companies to improve their environmental and social practices in foreign business. The China Development Bank adopted a guideline in 2005 to require all firms seeking loans to implement environmental impact assessment and to include environmental costs and standards in loan contracts. In its guideline, the Export-Import Bank of China (CEXIM) also requires several sets of environmental and social requirements for its loans. However, the Chinese government has limited will and ability to strictly monitor and enforce the compliance of Chinese companies. Along with insufficient laws, regulations and the weak governance in host countries, the stance of the Chinese government remains weak and lets Chinese companies ignore local laws and regulations, raising concerns about social and environmental impacts to local communities – thus triggering fierce opposition (Economy and Levy 2014).

Book overview

These possible domestic and international consequences raise questions. Are they temporary phenomena caused by China's rapid and drastic macroeconomic and SOEs reforms, as well as the associated energy development and FDI strategies, or transformational changes that will be institutionalized? Does China's climate-energy policy – the outcome of addressing the climate-energy conundrum – add on the existing impacts or have bland new impacts?

This book aims to give answers to these questions, taking Asian-Pacific energy-exporting countries as cases. It begins by defining the five key concepts throughout this volume and develops a logical framework among them. Then the case of China is used to explore the climate-energy conundrum and the resultant climate-energy policy, illustrating possible domestic and international consequences to raise the research questions of this book. Both qualitative analyses with in-depth case studies on specific energy exporters, along with quantitative analysis, such as input-output analysis and applied computable general equilibrium analysis will be made in the following chapters.

The first part consists of the underlying causes for the rapid increase in carbon emissions in China, as well as policies and measures the Chinese government has implemented to address them. In Chapter 2, Kiyoshi Fujikawa, Zuoyi Ye, and Hikari Ban use an input-output analysis to calculate embodied CO_2 emissions with the global input-output table initiated by the European Union to see if the slow development of climate-energy policy can be justified. In Chapter 3, Akihisa Mori and Mika Takehara revisit the history of China's climate policy to explore how the Chinese government has decided the detailed policy measures of its climate-energy policy.

The second part analyzes the domestic impacts of China's climate-energy policy. Nobuhiro Horii in Chapter 4 explores the underlying factors behind the recent decline in coal consumption in China, examining if it is a temporary phenomenon. In Chapter 5, Mika Takehara revisits the gas import estimates by the International Energy Agency (2015) and China Energy Research Society (2016), both of which are based on the government targets for 2015, to analyze the amount required to achieve both CO_2 emission and air pollutants reduction targets in 2030. To see if carbon-energy pricing will be widely accepted, Kiyoshi Fujikawa, Zuoyi Ye and Hikari Ban in Chapter 6 analyze its distributional consequences in urban and rural areas. In Chapter 7, Hikari Ban and Kiyoshi Fujikawa employ the Gdyn-E model and a dynamic CGE model to analyze the impacts on the GDP and energy mix from its unilateral 2030 peak-out and the Paris Agreement scenarios.

The third part explores the international impacts of climate-energy policy from the perspective of the resource curse, ecological disruption and macroeconomic assessments. In Chapter 8, Akihisa Mori and Le Dong take six Asian-Pacific and Central Asian energy-exporting countries to examine whether they suffer from a China-induced Dutch disease, employing the trade specification coefficient (TSC) and revealed comparative advantage (RCA) as indicators. Hikari Ban and Kiyoshi Fujikawa employ the Gdyn-E model again in Chapter 9 to analyze impacts on the GDP and mix of energy of Asian energy-exporting countries to see if China's climate-energy policy causes carbon leakage under its 2030 peak-out and the Paris Agreement scenarios.

The next two chapters are in-depth national case studies. Akihisa Mori in Chapter 10 takes the case of Indonesia as coal and gas exporter to perform an analysis on resource curse in view of resource governance. With rapid industrialization and diversification of resource exports such as palm oil, Indonesia is evaluated as a resource-rich developing country that has escaped the resource curse (Gylfason 2001). Nonetheless, it has increased its reliance on resource exports during the coal boom. Referring to Luong and Weinthal (2010), Mori analyzes how China has influenced the ownership structure of the oil, gas and coal sectors. In Chapter 11, Lynn Thiesmeyer takes the case of the Myanmar states of Shan and Kachin to analyze the impact of China's investment in large-scale hydropower on livelihood from the perspective of political ecology.

Our analysis ends with a wrap-up of the findings in each chapter, a discussion of future challenges to move the energy sector in both China and Asian-Pacific energy-exporting countries toward a low CO_2 emissions pathway.

Notes

1 The IEA creates the sustainable development scenarios that can attain climate, air pollution and universal energy-access targets in response to the effectiveness of the Sustainable Development Goals (SDGs) of the 2030 Agenda for Sustainable Development, which requires states to attain these integrated, multi-policy objectives.
2 The death toll in China's coal mining in 2008 was 91,172, down 15 percent from 2007 (*China Daily*, January 17, 2009).

References

Aldy, J.E., Krupnick, A.J., Newell, R.G., Parry, I.W.H. and Pizer, W.A. (2010) Designing climate mitigation policy, *Journal of Economic Literature* 48(4): 903–34.

Andersen, M.S. and Ekins, P. (eds.) (2009) *Carbon-Energy Taxation: Lessons from Europe*, Oxford: Oxford University Press.

Asia Pacific Energy Research Centre (APERC) (2007) *A Quest for Energy Security in the 21st Century: Resources and Constraints*, Institute of Energy Economics, Japan.

Auty, R.M. (2006) Resource-driven models of the development of the political economy, in Auty, R.M. and de Soysa, I. (eds.) *Energy, Wealth and Governance in the Caucasus and Central Asia: Lessons Not Learnt*, Oxon: Routledge, 17–36.

Blobel, D., Gerdes, H., Pollitt, H., Barton, J., Drosdowski, T., Lutz, C., Wolter, M.I. and Ekins, P. (2011) Implications of ETR in Europe for household distribution, in Ekins, P. and Speck, S. (eds.) *Environmental Tax Reform: A Policy for Green Growth*, Oxford: Oxford University Press, 236–90.

Boocock, C.N. (2002) Environmental impacts of foreign direct investment in the mining sector in sub-Saharan Africa, in Organisation for Economic Co-operation and Development (ed.) *Foreign Direct Investment and the Environment: Lessons from the Mining Sector*, Paris: Organisation for Economic Co-operation and Development, 19–53.

Borregaard, N. and Dufey, A. (2002) Environmental effects of foreign versus domestic investment in the mining sector in Latin America, in Organisation for Economic Co-operation and Development (ed.) *Foreign Direct Investment and the Environment: Lessons From the Mining Sector*, Paris: Organisation for Economic Co-operation and Development, 55–79.

Brautigam, D. (2009) *The Dragon's Gift: The Real Story of China in Africa*, Oxford: Oxford University Press.

Brenner, M., Riddleb, M. and Boyce, J.K. (2007) A Chinese sky trust?: Distributional impacts of carbon charges and revenue recycling in China, *Energy Policy* 35: 1771–84.

Burgis, T. (2015) *The Looting Machine: Warlords, Tycoons, Smugglers and the Systematic Theft of Africa's Wealth*, New York: Public Affairs.

Cáceres, S.B. and Ear, S. (2013) *The Hungry Dragon: How China's Resource Quest Is Reshaping the World*, Oxon: Routledge.

Caselli, F. and Cunningham, T. (2009) Leader behaviour and the natural resource curse, *Oxford Economic Papers* 61(4): 628–50.

Chandarany, O., Chanhang, S. and Dalia, P. (2013) Impacts on China on poverty reduction in Cambodia, in Jalilian, H. (ed.) *Assessing China's Impact on Poverty in the Greater Mekong Subregion*, Singapore: Institute of Southeast Asian Studies, 297–384.

Chen, G. (2012) *China's Climate Policy*, Oxon: Routledge.

Cherp, A. and Jewell, J. (2014) The concept of energy security: Beyond the four As, *Energy Policy* 75: 415–21.

China Energy Research Society (ed.) (2016) *China Energy Outlook 2030*, Beijing: Economics and Management Press (in Chinese).

Cockett, R. (2015) *Blood, Dreams and Gold: The Changing Face of Burma*, New Haven: Yale University Press.

Copper, J.F. (2016) *China's Foreign Aid and Investment Diplomacy, Volume III: Strategy beyond Asian and Challenges to the United States and the International Order*, Hampshire: Palgrave Macmillan.

Di Meglio, J.-F. and Romano, G.C. (2016a) Conclusions, in Romano, G.C. and Di Meglio, J.-F. (eds.) *China's Energy Security: A Multidimensional Perspective*, Oxon: Routledge, 251–4.

Di Meglio, J.-F. and Romano, G.C. (2016b) Introduction: From 'shaping' to 'framing' China's energy security and the example of the oil policy, in Romano, G.C. and Di Meglio, J.-F. (eds.) *China's Energy Security: A Multidimensional Perspective*, Oxon: Routledge, 1–21.

Dupont, C. (2016) *Climate Policy Integration into EU Energy Policy: Progress and Prospects*, Oxon: Routledge.

Economy, E.C. and Levy, M. (2014) *By All Means Necessary: How China's Resource Quest Is Changing the World*, Oxford: Oxford University Press.

Ekins, P. and Speck, S. (eds.) (2011) *Environmental Tax Reform (ETR): A Policy for Green Growth*, Oxford: Oxford University Press.

Extractive Industries Transparency Initiative (EITI) (2017) *Fact Sheet as of November 2017*, https://eiti.org/sites/default/files/documents/eiti_factsheet_en_nov2017.pdf, accessed on February 18, 2018.

Fang, Y., Li, J. and Wang, M. (2012) Development policy for non-grid-connected wind power in China: An analysis based on institutional change, *Energy Policy* 45: 350–8.

Fouquet, R. (2016) Path dependence energy systems and economic development, *Nature Energy* 1(1–5), http://dx.doi.org/10.1038/nenergy.2016.98.

Geels, F.W. (2014) Regime resistance against low-carbon transitions: Introducing politics and power into the multi-level perspective, *Theory, Culture & Society* 31(5): 21–40.

Grumbine, R.E. (2010) *Where the Dragon Meets the Angry River: Nature and Power in the People's Republic of China*, Washington, DC: Island Press.

Grundmann, R., Scott, M. and Wang, J. (2013) Energy security in the news: North/south perspectives, *Environmental Politics* 22(4): 571–92.

Gunningham, N. (2002) Voluntary approaches to environmental protection: Lessons from the mining and forestry sectors, in Organisation for Economic Co-operation and Development (ed.) *Foreign Direct Investment and the Environment: Lessons from the Mining Sector*, Paris: Organisation for Economic Co-operation and Development, 157–94.

Gylfason, T. (2001) Natural resources, education, and economic development, *European Economic Review* 45: 847–59.

Hatch, M.T. (2003) Chinese politics, energy policy and the international climate change negotiations, in Harris, P.G. (ed.) *Global Warming and East Asia: The Domestic and International Politics of Climate Change*, London: Routledge, 43–65.

Henzler, M. (2002) Environmental impacts of foreign direct investment in the mining sector: The Russian Federation and Kazakhstan, in Organisation for Economic Co-operation and Development (ed.) *Foreign Direct Investment and the Environment: Lessons from the Mining Sector*, Paris: Organisation for Economic Co-operation and Development, 81–101.

Hervé-Mignucci, M. and Wang, X. (2015) Slowing the growth of coal power outside China: The role of Chinese finance, *A CPI Report*, Climate Policy Initiative.

Hillebrand, R. (2013) Climate protection, energy security, and Germany's policy of ecological modernization, *Environmental Politics* 22(4): 664–82.

Intergovernmental Panel on Climate Change (2007) *Climate Change 2007: Impacts, Adaptation, and Vulnerability*, www.ipcc.ch/report/ar4/wg2/, accessed on January 25, 2018.

Intergovernmental Panel on Climate Change (2014) *Climate Change 2014: Impacts, Adaptation, and Vulnerability*, www.ipcc.ch/report/ar5/wg2, accessed on January 25, 2018.

International Energy Agency (2015) *IEA World Energy Outlook 2015*, Paris: IEA.

International Energy Agency (2017) *IEA World Energy Outlook 2017*, Paris: IEA.

Isham, J., Woolcock, M. Pritchett, L. and Busby, G. (2005) The varieties of resource experience: Natural resource export structures and the political economy of economic growth, *World Bank Economic Review* 19(2): 141–74.

Kondo, S. (2002) Foreign direct investment and the environment: Lessons from the mining sector, in OECD (ed.) *Foreign Direct Investment and the Environment: Lessons from the Mining Sector*, Paris: OECD, 7–8.

Levy, D.L. and Newell, P. (2002) Business strategy and international environmental governance: Toward a neo-Gramscian synthesis, *Global Environmental Politics* 2(4): 84–101.

Lieberthal, K. and Oksenberg, M. (1988) *Policy Making in China: Leaders, Structures, and Process*, Princeton: Princeton University Press.

Lockwood, M. (2015) The politics of dynamics of green transformations: Feedback effects and institutional context, in Scoones, I., Leach, M. and Newell, P. (eds.) *The Politics of Green Transformation*, Oxon: Routledge, 86–101.

Luong, P.J and Weinthal, E. (2010) *Oil Is Not a Curse: Ownership Structure and Institutions in Soviet Successor States*, Cambridge: Cambridge University Press.

Lyu, X. (2015) From Manwan to Nuozhadu: The political ecology of hydropower on China's Lancang river, in Matthews, N. and Geheb, K. (eds.) *Hydropower Development in the Mekong Region: Political, Socio-economic and Environmental Perspectives*, Oxon: Routledge, 54–82.

Mazzucato, M. (2015) The green entrepreneurial state, in Scoones, I., Leach, M. and Newell, P. (eds.) *The Politics of Green Transformation*, Oxon: Routledge, 134–52.

McKinzey & Company (2009) *Pathways to a Low-Carbon Economy: Version 2 of the Global Greenhouse Gas Abatement Cost Curve.*, https://www.mckinsey.com/~/media/mckinsey/dotcom/client_service/sustainability/cost%20curve%20pdfs/pathways_lowcarbon_economy_version2.ashx, accessed on May 5, 2018.

Mori, A. (2017a) Sociotechnical and political economy perspectives in the Chinese energy transition, *Energy Research & Social Science* 35, http://dx.doi.org/10.1016/j.erss.2017.10.043.

Mori, A. (2017b) Temporal dynamics of infrasystem transition: The case of electricity system transition in Japan, *Technological Forecasting & Social Change*, http://dx.doi.org/10.1016/j.techfore.2017.05.003.

Mori, A. and Hayashi, T. (2012) Transboundary environmental pollution and cooperation between Japan and China: A historical review, in Ueta, K. (ed.) *CDM and Sustainable Development in China: Japanese Perspectives*, Hong Kong: Hong Kong University Press, 1–22.

Moyo, D. (2012) *Dead Aid: Why Aid Is Not Working and How There Is a Better Way for Africa*, London: Penguin Group.

Pupphavesa, W., Paitoonpong, S., Chakrisinont, M. and Sakaeo, S. (2013) Impacts on China on poverty reduction in Thailand, in Jalilian, H. (ed.) *Assessing China's Impact on Poverty in the Greater Mekong Subregion*, Singapore: Institute of Southeast Asian Studies, 235–96.

REN21 (2014) *Renewables 2014 Global Status Report*, www.ren21.net/Portals/0/documents/Resources/GSR/2014/GSR2014_full%20report_low%20res.pdf, accessed on November 3, 2014.

REN21 (2016) *Renewables 2016 Global Status Report*, www.ren21.net/wp-content/uploads/2016/06/GSR_2016_Full_Report.pdf, accessed on July 22, 2016.

Rock, M.T., Murphy, J.T., Rasiah, R., van Seters, P. and Managi, S. (2009) A hard slog, not a leap frog: Globalization and sustainability transitions in developing Asia, *Technological Forecasting & Social Change* 76: 241–54.

Ross, M.L. (1999) The political economy of the resource curse, *World Politics* 51(2): 297–322.

Schmidt, T.S., Matuo, T. and Michaelowa, A. (2017) Renewable energy policy as an enabler of fossil fuel subsidy reform? Applying a socio-technical perspective to the cases of South Africa and Tunisia, *Global Environmental Change* 45: 99–110, http://dx.doi.org/10.1016/j.gloenvcha.2017.05.004.

Serge, M. and Beuret, M. (2010) *China Safari: On the Trail of Beijing's Expansion in Africa*, New York : Nation Books.

Sharples, J.D. (2013) Russian approaches to energy security and climate change: Russian gas exports to the EU, *Environmental Politics* 22(4): 683–700.

Smith, A. and Raven, R. (2012) What is protective space? Reconsidering niches in transition to sustainability, *Research Policy* 41(6): 106–19.

Stirling, A. (2014) Transforming power: Social science and the politics of energy choices, *Energy Research & Social Science* 1: 83–95.

Szarka, J. (2013) From exception to norm – and back again? France, the nuclear revival, and the post-Fukushima landscape, *Environmental Politics* 22(4): 646–63.

Toke, D. (2013) Climate change and the nuclear securitisation of UK energy policy, *Environmental Politics* 22(4): 553–70.

Torvik, R. (2002) Natural resources, rent seeking and welfare, *Journal of Development Economics* 67(2): 455–70.

Tunsjø, Ø. (2013) *Security and Profit in China's Energy Policy: Hedging against Risk*, New York: Columbia University Press.

van der Ploeg, F. (2011) Natural resources: Curse or Blessing? *Journal of Economic Literature* 49(2): 366–420.

van der Ploeg, F. and Poelhekke, S. (2009). Volatility and the natural resource curse, *Oxford Economic Papers* 61(4): 727–60.

Venables, A.J. (2016) Using natural resources for development: Why has it proven so difficult? *Journal of Economic Perspectives* 30(1): 161–84.

Verbong, G.P.J. and Geels, F.W. (2010) Exploring sustainability transitions in the electricity sector with socio-technical pathways, *Technological Forecasting & Social Change* 77: 214–21.

Vezirgiannidou, S.-E. (2013) Climate and energy policy in the United States: The battle of ideas, *Environmental Politics* 22(4): 610–26.

Vieira, M.A. and Dalgaard, K.G. (2013) The energy-security – Climate-change nexus in Brazil, *Environmental Politics* 22(4): 610–26.

Wang, Z. (2012) *Never Forget National Humiliation: Historical Memory in Chinese Politics and Foreign Relations*, New York: Columbia University Press.

Wong, F. (2014) Update 2-China to again levy coal import tariffs after nearly a decade, *Reuters*, October 9, 2014, www.reuters.com/article/china-coal-idUSL3N0S41QP20141009, accessed on July 28, 2016.

Yao, L. and Chang, Y. (2015) Shaping China's energy security: The impact of domestic reforms, *Energy Policy* 77: 131–9.

Ye, Z., Watanabe, T., Shimoda, A. and Fujikawa, K. (2016) Distributional impacts of carbon tax in China on households by region and income group, in Fujikawa, K. (ed.) *Input-Output Analysis and Applied Computable General Equilibrium Model*, Kyoto: Horitsu Bunkasha, 53–61 (in Japanese).

Zarsky, L. (1999) Havens, hallos and spaghetti: Untangling the evidence about foreign direct investment and the environment, in Organisation for Economic Co-operation and Development (ed.) *Foreign Direct Investment and the Environment*, Paris: Organisation for Economic Co-operation and Development, 47–74.

Zarsky, L. (2002) Stuck in the mud? Nation states, globalization and the environment, in Gallagher, K.P. and Werksman, J. (eds.) *The Earthscan Reader on International Trade and Sustainable Development*, London: Earthscan, 19–44.

2 China's impacts on global sustainability

Recent change in the consumption-based resource depletion and CO_2 emissions

Kiyoshi Fujikawa, Zuoyi Ye, and Hikari Ban

Introduction

Global warming requires a global solution, and controlling emissions of greenhouse gases in developing countries is essential. Producers must use natural resources, including energy and raw materials, as intermediate inputs. If such inputs are domestic, the environmental load of the production occurs domestically. Under the influence of globalization, however, producers now routinely import intermediate inputs and produce goods in multiple countries. In such cases, production in one country induces production elsewhere, and the environmental loads occurring in such countries are related. This behavior generates the phenomena of embodied environmental loads (EEL) or "direct and indirect environmental loads" and brings international trade to the fore of global environmental concerns.

Energy consumption patterns reveal that some countries achieve high growth by exporting industrial products with large environmental loads (i.e., energy-intensive products), whereas others transfer production with high environmental loads to other countries. Doing so disguises their domestic environmental load (i.e., disguises domestic CO_2 emissions). Generally, the importing country (consuming country) transfers the environmental load occurring during the production process to the producing country to show a smaller environmental load. Views differ as to which environmental burdens of production occur directly or indirectly and which should be attributed to producing versus consuming countries. Confrontations between advanced and developing economies concerning measures against global warming are bitter. This study insists that for a solution, it is essential that disputing parties consider the mutual dependence of environmental loads occurring from trade.

Imura et al. (2005) and Na (2006) examine this issue in the Pacific Rim. Our study extends theirs by analyzing the latest data (2009) in a standard input-output (I-O) model. I-O analysis determines the amount of produced goods required to fulfill an industry's final demand for products. With final demand known, we can estimate the energy consumption and quantity of natural resources consumed directly and indirectly during each stage of production.

Data and model

Data

We used I-O tables and data for CO_2 emissions from the World Input-Output Database (WIOD) from EUROSTAT, the EU statistics office.[1]

Table 2.1 consolidates I-O tables for 40 countries (27 EU countries, four in the Americas, and nine in Asia and the Pacific). Other countries and regions are grouped as other countries/regions (ROW). ROW is not an exogenous sector but an endogenous sector in this database. In sum, there are 41 endogenous countries, which we aggregate as China (CHN), Japan (JPN), Korea (KOR), Taiwan (TWN), Indonesia (IDN), India (IND), the United States of America (USA), Russia (RUS), European Union (EU), and other countries/regions (ROW).

The WIOD's original industry classifications are shown in Table 2.2. In this chapter, we aggregate three commercial industries (originally numbered 19, 20, 21) into "commercial" and aggregate two service-related industries (34, 25) into "service." In doing so, we advance analysis by industrial classification in which the number of industries is two fewer than 32.

Besides the international I-O table, WIOD provides the following.

1   World Tables (1995–2009)

    International Supply and Use Tables (35 industries by 59 industries)
    World I-O Table (35 industries by 35 industries)
    Six Interregional I-O Tables (35 industries by 35 industries)

2   National Tables (1995–2011)

    National Supply and Use Table (35 industries by 59 products)
    National I-O Tables (35 industries by 35 industries)

Table 2.1 Target countries in the WIOD

Europe			America	Asia Pacific
Austria	Germany	Netherland	Canada	China
Belgium	Greece	Poland	USA	India
Bulgaria	Hungary	Portugal	Brazil	Japan
Cyprus	Ireland	Romania	Mexico	Korea
Czech Republic	Italy	Slovakia		Australia
Denmark	Latvia	Slovenia		Taiwan
Estonia	Lithuania	Spain		Turkey
Finland	Luxembourg	Sweden		Indonesia
France	Malta	UK		Russia

Source: WIOD (2013).

3   Social Economic Accounts (1995–2009)

Gross output and gross value added (at fixed prices and current basic prices)
Real fixed capital stock and nominal gross fixed capital formation
Wages and number of employees by skill and industry (three skill categories
and 35 industrial categories)

4   Environmental Accounts (1995–2009)

Gross energy use by sector and energy commodity
CO_2 emissions modeled by sector and energy commodity
Airborne emissions by sector and pollutant
Land, materials, and water use by type and sector

We aggregated data for "CO_2 emissions by sector and energy commodity" in
Environmental Accounts into 32 industries.

Table 2.2 Industry classification in WIOD

New industry	Original industry	Original industry description
1	01	Agriculture, Hunting, Forestry, Fishing
2	02	Mining and Quarrying
3	03	Food, Beverages, and Tobacco
4	04	Textiles and Textile Products
5	05	Leather, Leather, and Footwear
6	06	Wood and Products of Wood and Cork
7	07	Pulp, Paper, Printing, and Publishing
8	08	Coke, Refined Petroleum, and Nuclear Fuel
9	09	Chemicals and Chemical Products
10	10	Rubber and Plastics
11	11	Other Non-Metallic Minerals
12	12	Basic Metals and Fabricated Metals
13	13	Machinery, Nec
14	14	Electrical and Optical Equipment
15	15	Transport Equipment
16	16	Manufacturing, Nec; Recycling
17	17	Electricity, Gas, and Water Supply
18	18	Construction
19	19	Sale, Maintenance, and Repair of Motor Vehicles and Motorcycles; Retail Sale of Fuel
19	20	Wholesale Trade and Commission Trade, Except Motor Vehicles and Motorcycles
19	21	Retail Trade, Except Motor Vehicles and Motorcycles; Repair of Household Goods
20	22	Hotels and Restaurants
21	23	Inland Transport
22	24	Water Transport
23	25	Air Transport
24	26	Other Supporting and Auxiliary Transport Activities; Activities of Travel Agencies

New industry	Original industry	Original industry description
25	27	Post and Telecommunications
26	28	Financial Intermediation
27	29	Real Estate
28	30	Renting of Machinery & Equipments and Other Business Activities
29	31	Public Admin and Defense, Compulsory Social Security
30	32	Education
31	33	Health and Social Work
32	34	Other Community, Social, and Personal Services
32	35	Private Households with Employed Persons

Source: WIOD (2013).

Note: Nec means not else classified.

Model

The main contributor to global warming is CO_2 emissions, which are mostly associated with fuel combustion. The two classifications of CO_2 emissions are production-based (CO_2 emitted per country) and consumption-based (CO_2 emissions embodied in final demand).[2] Generally, production-based accounting is adopted in international negotiations such as the Kyoto Protocol and the Paris Agreement. Below we explain how to calculate production- and consumption-based energy use and CO_2 emissions.

In a one-country I-O model, the following supply-demand relation holds between final demand for domestic goods ($\mathbf{f}^d$) and domestic supply ($\mathbf{x}$).

$$\mathbf{x} = \mathbf{A}^d\mathbf{x} + \mathbf{f}^d. \tag{2.1}$$

Matrix $\mathbf{A}^d$ is the domestic input coefficient matrix. Each column shows the quantity of domestically produced intermediate inputs directly required to produce one unit of output. Solving Eq. (2.1) for domestic output ($\mathbf{x}$), the following equilibrium output determination equation is derived. Matrix B is an Leontief inverse matrix.

$$\mathbf{x} = (\mathbf{I} - \mathbf{A}^d)^{-1}\mathbf{f}^d - \mathbf{B}\mathbf{f}^d. \tag{2.2}$$

Assuming a vector "$\mathbf{a}$" is an input coefficient of such resources as energy, land, or water,[3] multiplying resource input coefficient "$\mathbf{a}$" and domestic output ($\mathbf{x}$), derives the direct environmental load ($\mathbf{El}_d$) in production-based criteria.

$$\mathbf{El}_d = \begin{bmatrix} \mathbf{a}_1 & 0 \\ 0 & \mathbf{a}_2 \end{bmatrix} \begin{bmatrix} \hat{\mathbf{x}}_1 & 0 \\ \hline 0 & \hat{\mathbf{x}}_2 \end{bmatrix}. \tag{2.3}$$

The direct and indirect environmental load ($\mathbf{El}_{did}$) in consumption of final goods is calculated as

$$\mathbf{El}_{did} = \mathbf{aB} \begin{bmatrix} f_1^d & & \\ & \ddots & \\ & & f_n^d \end{bmatrix}. \tag{2.4}$$

CO_2 emissions are proportional to calorie-based energy consumption. CO_2 emissions by industry can be calculated by multiplying the CO_2 emission coefficient and energy consumption obtained in Eqs. (2.3) or (2.4).

The model thus far addresses a one-country I-O table, but it can be extended for multi-country/region I-O tables. We illustrate using a bi-regional I-O table for simplicity. The following supply-demand relation holds in Regions 1 and 2.

$$\begin{bmatrix} x_1 \\ x_2 \end{bmatrix} = \begin{bmatrix} A_{11} & A_{12} \\ A_{21} & A_{22} \end{bmatrix} \begin{bmatrix} x_1 \\ x_2 \end{bmatrix} + \begin{bmatrix} f_{11}+f_{12} \\ f_{21}+f_{22} \end{bmatrix}. \tag{2.1'}$$

Suffixes 1 and 2 denote regions. A_{ij} is the input coefficient. If $i = j$, A_{ij} is an intra-country input coefficient; if $i \ne j$, A_{ij} is the coefficient for inputs in region i to produce goods in region j. Final demand is f_{ij}. $i = j$ indicates a country's own final demand; $i \ne j$, indicates final demand for region i by region j.

$$\begin{bmatrix} x_1 \\ x_2 \end{bmatrix} = \begin{bmatrix} I - \begin{bmatrix} A_{11} & A_{12} \\ A_{21} & A_{22} \end{bmatrix} \end{bmatrix}^{-1} \begin{bmatrix} f_{11}+f_{12} \\ f_{21}+f_{22} \end{bmatrix} = \begin{bmatrix} B_{11} & B_{12} \\ B_{21} & B_{22} \end{bmatrix} \begin{bmatrix} f_{11}+f_{12} \\ f_{21}+f_{22} \end{bmatrix}. \tag{2.2'}$$

Direct Environmental Load (EL_d) in production-based criteria is expressed as follows based on the multi-region I-O table.

$$EL_d = \begin{bmatrix} a_1 & 0 \\ 0 & a_2 \end{bmatrix} \begin{bmatrix} \hat{x}_1 & 0 \\ \hline 0 & \hat{x}_2 \end{bmatrix}. \tag{2.3'}$$

Direct and indirect environmental load (EL_{did}) of final goods consumed by country i is expressed as

$$EL_{did} = \begin{bmatrix} a_1 & 0 \\ 0 & a_2 \end{bmatrix} \begin{bmatrix} B_{11} & B_{12} \\ B_{21} & B_{22} \end{bmatrix} \begin{bmatrix} \hat{f}_{11} & \hat{f}_{12} \\ \hline \hat{f}_{21} & \hat{f}_{22} \end{bmatrix}. \tag{2.4'}$$

Estimated results

CO_2 emissions embodied in international trade (1995)

Using Eqs. (2.3') and (2.4'), we calculated the transfer of EEL through international trade in 1995 and 2009. These years mark the beginning and end of WIOD but coincidentally coincide with the base year (1995) and target year (around 2010) of the Kyoto Protocol. We see how CO_2 emissions changed during that span.

Table 2.3 shows CO_2 emissions embodied in international trade in 1995. Column headers represent countries/regions that generated final demand. Row headers are countries/regions where CO_2 emissions are induced by final demand in countries/regions indicated in columns.

Table 2.3 CO_2 emissions embodied in international trade in 1995 (million t-CO_2)

	CHN	JPN	KOR	TWN	IDN	IND	USA	RUS	EU	ROW	Total
CHN	**2,130**	103	19	9	7	6	159	6	138	146	2,723
JPN	7	**877**	7	6	3	1	31	1	21	70	1,024
KOR	8	23	**264**	2	4	1	22	1	15	33	372
TWN	7	15	1	**103**	1	0	20	0	11	19	178
IDN	2	13	2	1	**131**	1	7	0	7	9	173
IND	2	16	2	1	2	**607**	24	2	34	31	721
USA	11	55	16	11	4	3	**3,890**	3	103	247	4,342
RUS	13	26	9	6	3	6	38	**976**	258	78	1,412
EU	13	37	11	9	7	8	108	16	**2,910**	262	3,381
ROW	29	117	30	18	11	18	320	15	295	**3,766**	4,620
Total	2,221	1,282	362	166	172	652	4,619	1,020	3,792	4,660	18,947

Source: Authors' calculation from WIOD (2013).

The rightmost column of Table 2.3 shows total CO_2 emitted in the country (region) indicated in the row (production-based CO_2 emissions). The bottom row of the table shows total CO_2 emissions induced by the country (region) indicated under each column (consumption-based CO_2 emissions).

Countries/regions where the figure in the rightmost column exceeds that in the bottom row (e.g., China) are where production-based CO_2 emissions exceed consumption-based CO_2 emissions. In other words, they are net exporters of embodied carbons. In an opposite case like Japan, production-based CO_2 emissions are less than consumption-based CO_2 emissions. They are net importers of embodied carbons.[4]

Boldfaced diagonal numerals represent CO_2 emissions induced from final demand in a home country/region. Diagonal numerals are the maximum in each row and column. Linear numerals – e.g., 103 at the intersection of Japan's column and China's row – show that final demand in Japan induced 103 million t-CO_2 in China. In Table 2.3, three-digit numbers (relatively large values) are shadowed.

The USA was the largest CO_2 emitter in 1995, followed by the EU and China. China was an exporter of embodied CO_2, whereas the USA, EU, and Japan were importers of embodied CO_2 in 1995. Shadowed cells stand out in the row for China, indicating China was already subrogating CO_2 emissions of various countries/regions in 1995. The USA and EU had made other countries/regions subrogate CO_2 emissions. Shadowed cells stand out under columns for the USA and EU. Entries such as those for South Korea and Taiwan indicate exporters of embodied CO_2.

For insight into emissions structures, we decomposed sectoral production-based CO_2 emissions into final demand by country origin. Figure 2.1 shows China's CO_2 emissions by industry in 1995. The lighter (darker) portions of the bars enumerate CO_2 emissions induced by final demand in China (foreign countries). Electricity accounted for about 39% of total emissions, about 21% of those CO_2 emissions was induced by overseas demand. This finding implies that foreign countries diverted CO_2 emissions arising from their domestic demand onto China.

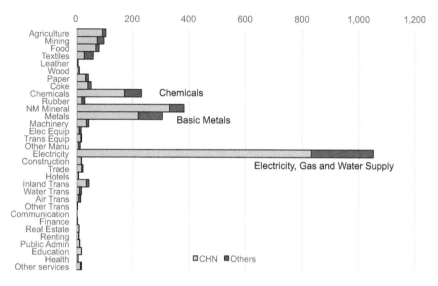

Figure 2.1 CO_2 emissions in China by industry in 1995 (million t-CO_2)
Source: Authors' calculation from WIOD (2013).

There are almost no CO_2 emissions in China's service sector. Figure 2.1 shows China was a manufacturing country in 1995.

Figure 2.2 shows CO_2 emissions by industry in Japan in 1995. Although the electricity industry in Japan also claims a commanding share, it was smaller than in China (23% of emissions). The explanation is Japan generates more of its electricity from efficient nuclear power. CO_2 emissions also were high for basic metals, non-metallic minerals, chemicals, and water transport. Japan's service sector, including transportation, generated more CO_2 emissions than China's.

Next we compare sectoral CO_2 emissions by country in 1995, focusing on CO_2-emitting electricity and basic metals (steel), in Figure 2.3. CO_2 emissions by China's electricity industry were below those in the USA and EU, as China's economic scale was modest by comparison. However, foreign demand induced more CO_2 emissions by China's electricity industry (21%) than in other countries.

Figure 2.4 shows CO_2 emissions in the basic metals industry by country/region in 1995. CO_2 emissions in China exceeded those in the USA and EU. This finding differs from findings for the electricity industry. Technological remodeling during the 1990s, the era of China's eighth and ninth five-year plans, accelerated investment in the steel industry, including introduction of continuous casting, construction of the electric furnace industry, and the tertiary construction of Baoshan. On the demand side, Deng Xiaoping's southern tour highlighted acceleration of China's Reform and Opening Up Policy. As construction of factories and infrastructure advanced, China became the world's largest steel producer.

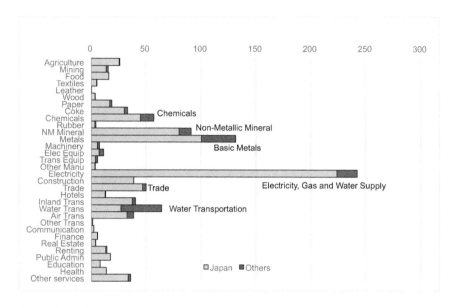

Figure 2.2 CO$_2$ emissions in Japan by industry in 1995 (million t-CO$_2$)
Source: Authors' calculation from WIOD (2013).

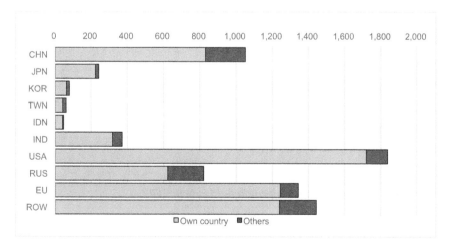

Figure 2.3 CO$_2$ emissions in electricity by country/region in 1995 (million t-CO$_2$)
Source: Authors' calculation from WIOD (2013).

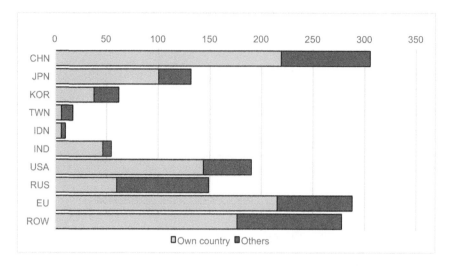

Figure 2.4 CO$_2$ emissions in basic metals by country/region in 1995 (million t-CO$_2$)
Source: Authors' calculation from WIOD (2013).

Table 2.4 World CO$_2$ trade in 2009 (million t-CO$_2$)

	CHN	JPN	KOR	TWN	IDN	IND	USA	RUS	EU	ROW	Total
CHN	**4,240**	146	56	18	26	60	419	43	429	777	6,214
JPN	38	**755**	9	5	4	2	28	3	26	85	954
KOR	44	13	**311**	2	4	4	27	4	31	93	533
TWN	30	23	2	**131**	2	2	27	1	27	45	290
IDN	10	11	4	1	**246**	2	11	1	13	31	331
IND	21	7	3	1	4	**1,267**	47	4	57	90	1,502
USA	44	24	9	5	3	8	**3,735**	4	101	255	4,188
RUS	42	16	7	3	3	6	45	**931**	189	170	1,410
EU	66	22	10	5	5	12	118	24	**3,542**	385	4,188
ROW	201	112	39	16	23	73	393	27	446	**4,958**	6,287
Total	4,736	1,130	449	187	318	1,436	4,851	1,040	4,860	6,888	25,896

Source: Authors' calculation from WIOD (2013).

CO$_2$ emissions embodied in international trade in 2009

This section discusses the structure of CO$_2$ emissions in 2009 and compares it with 1995. Table 2.4 shows CO$_2$ embodied in trade in 2009. China had become the world's largest CO$_2$ emitter, producing 25% of world CO$_2$ emissions. The directionality of CO$_2$ trade replicates that in 1995, when China was a net exporter of embodied CO$_2$ and the USA, EU, and Japan were net importers of embodied CO$_2$. Korea and Taiwan remained net exporters. China's net CO$_2$ exports were

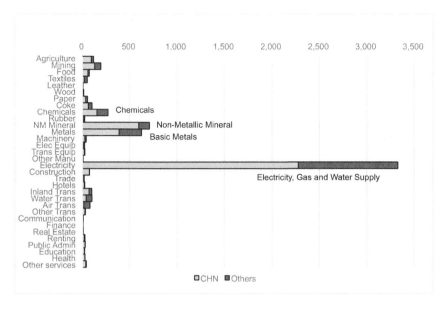

Figure 2.5 CO_2 emissions in China by industry in 2009 (million t-CO_2)
Source: Authors' calculation from WIOD (2013).

1,478 Mt-CO_2, larger than Japan's CO_2 emissions (954 Mt-CO_2) and comparable with India's 1,502 Mt-CO_2.

Next we examine CO_2 emissions by industry in China and Japan in 2009. Figure 2.5 shows CO_2 emissions by industry in China in 2009. China's electricity industry escalated to about 53% of total emissions in 2009. Foreign final demand induced about 32% of that industry's emissions. Both figures are daunting. CO_2 emissions by the service sector were limited, as in 1995.

Figure 2.6 illustrates CO_2 emissions by industry in Japan in 2009. The electricity industry share of domestic CO_2 emissions expanded to 34% from 1995. Considering that Japan's total emissions declined from 1,024 Mt-CO_2 in 1995 to 954 in 2009, energy required by the electricity industry apparently increased. From 1995 to 2009, CO_2 emissions declined from 312 to 111 in basic metals, the second-ranked emitter, and from 91 to 60 in non-metallic minerals the third-ranked. CO_2 emissions rose from 242 to 323 in the electricity industry. Energy demand by Japan's industries and households shifted to electric power. Beyond that point, reducing CO_2 emissions in the electricity industry became an issue.

Figure 2.7 shows production-based CO_2 emissions by the electricity industry. CO_2 emissions by China's electricity industry were extreme, exceeding emissions for that industry in the USA and EU. As mentioned, foreign demand induced one-third of CO_2 emissions in China's electricity industry, almost equal to the difference between China and the USA or EU.

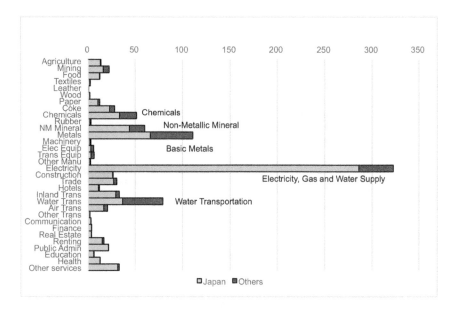

Figure 2.6 CO$_2$ emissions in Japan by industry in 2009 (million t-CO$_2$)
Source: Authors' calculation from WIOD (2013).

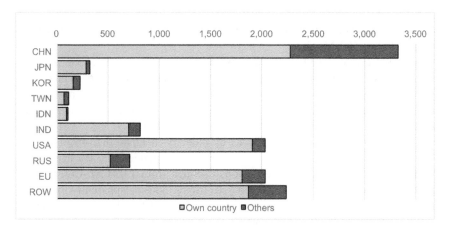

Figure 2.7 CO$_2$ emissions structure in the electricity industry in 2009 (million t-CO$_2$)
Source: Authors' calculation from WIOD (2013).

Figure 2.8 shows CO$_2$ emissions by the basic metals industry in 2009. Again, China's share is enormous. Foreign demand induced approximately 40% of China's basic metals CO$_2$ emissions. Since foreign demand induced 30% to 40% of CO$_2$ emissions by the electricity and basic metals industries, industrialized economies reduced their production-based CO$_2$ emissions by importing Chinese

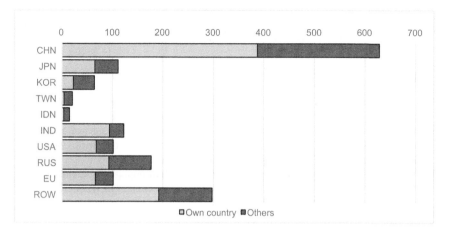

Figure 2.8 CO_2 emissions structure in the basic metals industry in 2009 (million t-CO_2)
Source: Authors' calculation from WIOD (2013).

goods. Expressed another way, China assumed the burden of CO_2 emissions for much of the industrialized world.

Conclusion

This study estimated embodied CO_2 emissions using the World International Input-Output Table of WIOD and investigated structural changes in world CO_2 emissions between 1995 and 2009. During the commitment period of the Kyoto Protocol, CO_2 emissions in Japan, the EU, and the USA fell slightly, but they increased in emerging industrialized economies, including China. Post-Kyoto cooperation among developing economies is indispensable for reducing global CO_2 emissions, but results show that industrialized countries subrogated their CO_2 emissions (or energy consumption) to developing economies such as China.

Industrialized economies blame emerging economies for pollution, yet trade shifted the burden of pollution onto those economies.

As Na (2006) points out, introducing a taxation based on consumption-based CO_2 emissions may incentivize energy conservation in developing economies. Since taxation would raise prices of exports that embody extensive CO_2 emissions, importing countries would favor goods with fewer embodied CO_2 emissions. As a result, exporting (developing) economies would upgrade efforts to conserve and develop renewable energy to retain competitiveness.

Notes

1 See the WIOD website <http://www.wiod.org/home> and Timmer et al. (2015) for the database.
2 Besides that, it is possible to consider energy extraction-based emissions. We omit it in this paper. See Davis et al. (2011) on the supply chain of CO_2 emissions.

3 Since we consider three kinds of fossil energies, there are three kinds of input coefficients for energies such as coal, petroleum, and natural gas.
4 See the OECD website <www.oecd.org/sti/ind/carbondioxideemissionsembodiedin internationaltrade.htm> for CO_2 emissions embodied in international trade.

References

Davis, S.J., Peters, G.P. and Calderia, K. (2011) The supply chain of CO_2 emissions, *Proceedings of the National Academy of Sciences* 108(45): 18554–9.

Imura, H., Nakamura, E. and Morisugi, M. (2005) International-dependence of environmental loads associate with trade among Japan, US and Asian countries, *Journals of the Japan Society of Civil Engineers* 790: 11–23 (in Japanese).

Na, S. (2006) Economic development of the East Asia and imputed CO2 emissions, in Na, S. (ed.) *Climate Change and International Cooperation: Efficiency, Equity and Sustainability*, Tokyo: Yuhikaku (in Japanese).

Timmer, M.P., Dietzenbacher, E., Los, B., Stehrer, R. and de Vries, G.J. (2015) An illustrated user guide to the World Input-Output database: The case of global automotive production, *Review of International Economics* 23(3): 575–605.

3 Revisiting China's climate policy

The climate-energy conundrum point of view

Akihisa Mori and Mika Takehara

Introduction

As stated in Chapter 1, in line with the macroeconomic and State of Enterprises (SOEs) reforms, China has shifted the notion of energy security from a stable domestic energy supply under the planned economy to an appropriate mix of energies and a way to access these energies under the socialist market economy. The Communist Party of China (CPC) and the state have perceived economic growth, poverty alleviation, and social stability as the foundation of their legitimacy and thus have placed these goals as their top priorities. They recognized that rapid economic growth was associated with increasing energy consumption and that an energy shortage had become the bottleneck of economic growth. The international hike in energy prices in the mid-2000s alerted the Chinese government that excessive dependence on fossil fuels would also become a bottleneck. But rapid expansion of production capacity increased inefficiency in energy production and consumption, and resulting serious air pollution. It also went through a massive increase in greenhouse-gas (GHG) emissions, making China as the world's largest GHG emitter.

In response, the United States threatened to impose a border carbon adjustment.

Chinese researchers, however, refuted this threat, claiming that most of the CO_2 emissions in China were accrued by industrial production for export, which permits the high level of consumption yet low level of CO_2 emission in developed countries (Chapter 2 in this volume). The Chinese government also refused to accept a legally binding GHG emissions reduction target, insisting on common but differentiated responsibilities.

Still, against mounting international pressure for urgent commitment, China gradually changed its hostile stance. Chinese researchers began to insist on China's contribution to a gradual commitment to GHG emission reductions, especially to an absolute emissions cap with technology transfers and financial support (see Zhang 2011). The Chinese government has outpaced the insistence of Chinese researchers' insistence, setting out the 40 to 45 percent reduction target for GHG emissions per GDP by 2020 prior to the 15th Conference of the Parties (COP) of the United Nations Framework Convention on Climate Change (UNFCCC) in 2009. It went further in the 2014 China-US Summit, submitting a pledge to reduce 60 to 65 percent of the 2005 level of GHG emissions per GDP by 2030 and to reach its CO_2 emission peak no later than 2030.

This poses a question as to what convinced the CPC and the state to change their minds and take a step toward a GHG emissions reduction. Climate change tends to be used, where compatible, in the context of entrenching energy interests, while no consistent association can be seen between climate change and energy security (Toke and Vezigiannidou 2013). The incentives for political elites to support the transformation of the energy system for GHG emissions reductions and for the state to intervene in this, vary dramatically and depend on the political-economic setting (Lockwood 2015).

Therefore, to answer this question, this chapter revisits the policy process the Chinese government has taken to reconcile CO_2 emission reductions with energy security, and the resultant policy and institutional outcomes.

A brief history of development

The first serious commitment to GHG emissions reductions was the release of China's National Climate Change Program in 2007, which outlined the objectives, basic principles, key areas of actions, policies and measures to address climate change for the period until 2010. The CPC supported the commitment by including the notion of a "conservation culture" in its political report, highlighting emissions and energy issues as new policy focuses (Chen 2012). Setting up the National Leading Group to Address Energy Savings, Emissions Cutting, and Climate Change – headed by Prime Minister Wen Jiabao, and assisted by the ex-NDRC commissioner and the ex-Foreign minister – the Chinese government has taken a top-down approach to implement a series of stringent policies, programs, and institutional changes toward low-carbon development (UNDP China 2012).

The National Leading Group led a discussion over a GHG emissions reduction target, resulting in a reduction of 40 to 45 percent per GDP in 2009. In accordance with this target, the 12th Five-Year Plan (FYP) (2011–15) set a mandatory target to reduce carbon intensity by 17 percent based on 2010 levels, coupled with a new target for energy intensity to be reduced by 16 percent by the end of this FYP period.

To achieve this target, the central government launched two pilot programs at the local level. One is the National Pilot Program on Low-Carbon Provinces and Cities in July 2010, under which five provinces and eight cities were selected as pilot communities. In 2012 the program's scale was expanded to cover 29 additional cities and provinces, including Beijing, Shanghai, Shijiazhuang in Hebei Province, and Hainan Province. Pilot cities and provinces are required to develop goals and principles, explore "low carbon green development models" and establish measuring and reporting systems for GHG emissions along with plans to curb these emissions (Nachmany et al. 2015:3).

The other program is a pilot carbon emission trading scheme (ETS). Five cities (Beijing, Chongqing, Shanghai, Shenzhen, and Tianjin) and two provinces

(Guangdong, Hubei) were selected as pilots and launched between 2013 and 2014. The scheme and coverage differ by city and province not only because of their different economic structures and access to energy sources, but also in order to better find an optimal way to reconcile the current intensity target with the total emission control assumed under the cap-and-trade emission trading scheme implemented in 2017.

In the 2014 China-US Summit, the Chinese government went further by pledging a 60–65 percent reduction by 2030 in comparison with the 2005 level of GHG emissions per GDP, reaching its CO_2 emission peak no later than 2030. Along with increasing the share of non-fossil fuels in primary energy consumption up to 20 percent, the Chinese government submitted this target as its intended nationally determined contributions (INDCs). Subsequently, the 13th FYP (2016–20) set a mandatory target to reduce carbon intensity by 18 percent of 2015 levels, coupled with a mandatory target of a 15 percent reduction in energy intensity.

Features

Centered on energy development strategy

The Chinese government has not implemented any detailed policy measures that directly affect CO_2 emission reductions. Measures have been centered on energy development strategies, and are implemented as such.

The long-standing concern about energy security and the framing of climate change as an issue of development (NDRC 2007a) prompted the Chinese government to put priority on new energy and energy efficiency to safeguard energy security, rather than policies that purely serve the purpose of reducing emissions at the cost of possibly putting a brake on economic growth. Faced with limitations and the rising costs of domestic energy production, the Chinese government changed its stance on energy security and regarded the additional development of oil and gas around the world as enhancing the energy security of China through increasing global energy security, thus justifying foreign investment and imports (Hayashi 2006).

This stance of China's top leaders determines the inter-agency system that designs climate change strategies. The National Development and Reform Commission (NDRC) and the Ministry of Foreign Affairs are authorized to take charge of making climate change strategies, not the State Environment Protection Administration or the Meteorological Administration, who would be more concerned about the impact on climate change. Just as the Ministry of Foreign Affairs plays a major role in international negotiations in view of protecting state sovereignty and enhancing China's international image, the NDRC plays a dominant role too. As the economic planning and energy regulation agency, the NDRC hopes to utilize climate change as a moral driving force to boost clean energy and other green industries (Chen 2012: 100). This makes China's climate change policy a part of its clean energy development strategy and focuses on mitigation rather than adaptation. It assumes that GHG emissions will be mitigated as fringe benefits of clean energy development. In this regard, the Chinese climate change policy can be renamed as climate-energy policy.

The National Climate Change Program 2007 highlights the development of renewable and nuclear energy, energy efficiency and conservation, a circular economy and emissions reduction as key areas for mitigation actions. This program was based on the Chinese government's perception that an increase in foreign reliance poses the risk of an external debt crisis resulting from the insufficient foreign reserves at that time. The Chinese government outlined its energy intensity target and revised the Energy Conservation Act to clearly appoint a responsible entity for energy conservation. It also initiated several complementary programs: namely, the Top 1000 Energy-Consuming Enterprises (Top-1000 program), the Ten Key Projects, and the Small Plant Closure and Phasing out of Outdated Capacity programs.

Top-down decision with local enforcement

The Chinese government takes the traditional implementation strategy of top-down decision-making and guidance, both in conjunction with decentralized enforcement – a strategy that resembles its economic strategy under the Reform and Open-door Policy. That is, China's leaders provide administrative and legal guidance but allocate far greater authority to provincial and local officials. Leaders in the central government utilize campaigns to implement large-scale initiatives, embrace the market as a force for change, and rely on private citizen initiatives and the international community to provide financial and intellectual capital (Economy 2004: 91). The responsibility of provincial government leaders are strengthened in the National Plan for Tackling Climate Change (2014–20), which mandated all provinces and municipalities to develop their own plans as well as establish a provincial Leading Group to Address Energy Savings, Emissions Cutting, and Climate Change.

Furthermore, the central government implemented more stringent regulations targeted specifically at coal power plants, consisting of: a prohibition on the construction and expansion of coal power plants in large and medium-size cities, a mandate for the installation of fuel-gas desulfurization (FGD) at new coal power plants, and the replacement of small and obsolete coal power plants with large and efficient ones. It also implemented a coal price reform to reduce coal demand and provide higher revenue for consolidated coal miners to invest in safety and health.

These top-down administrative measures, however, encountered an implementation deficit at the street level. Local industrial and coal power plants continued to operate and discharge severe emissions, while those of state enterprises did not run at full capacity even if they scrapped old plants and built large, efficient plants equipped with FGD (Horii 2006). This is not only because they could hardly afford renovation of their plants and install FGD, but also because local governments preferred the construction and purchase of power from locally owned coal power plants. The local environmental protection bureau (EPB) and judicial authorities imposed less stringent enforcement under the authority of their local governments due to funding and human resource management, as well as a lack of necessary monitoring and enforcement mechanisms, such as on-line continuous monitoring systems.

To tackle this implementation deficit, the central government has employed stick-and-carrot measures. As a stick, it has implemented the "down-by-one-vote system," under which the central CPC does not approve the promotion of local political leaders or presidents of state enterprises who are evaluated as having poor results in terms of energy efficiency and pollution reduction, even if they are evaluated as excellent in terms of local economic growth.

As a carrot, it has increased government financial support for massive deployment of clean energy and technologies. The central government made huge investments in developing natural gas fields in the western region of Sichuan and Xinjiang, as well as gas pipelines and electricity transmission lines to deliver energy from western to eastern regions. It has also increased investments in coal gas supply and district heating systems in the name of environmental protection investments (Figure 3.1) – capitalizing, for example – on its four trillion yuan stimulus package to massively and widely deploy solar heating into rural households amid the global financial crisis in 2008.

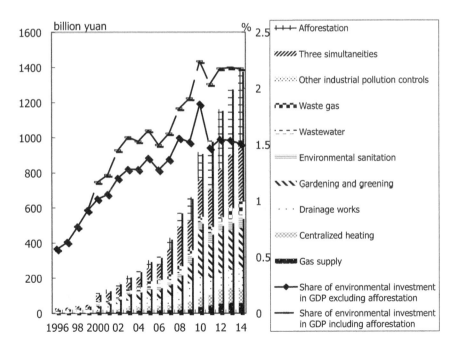

Figure 3.1 Environmental protection and afforestation investment in China 1996–2015

Sources: Author compilation based on China Statistical Press, *China Statistical Yearbook on Environment 2000 and 2015*, and *China Statistical Yearbook 2015*.

To consolidate the coal industry and to tackle air pollution and domestic acid rain, the government initiated forced closures of small and inefficient coal mining, boilers, and power plants in the late 1990s. This measure, however, deteriorated performance of heavy industries and infrastructure, which remained the backbone to economic development and caused frequent blackouts that were a bottleneck of economic growth in the early 2000s (Cheng 2013). This upset the government, which thus canceled forced closures and instead invested in state coal mining. At the same time, the government raised coal prices out of consideration for safety and environmental costs and scrapped the coal tariff in 2007 to allow coal imports. These measures boosted coal consumption for industrial use, resulting in an increase in coal production and imports (Figure 3.2). Despite the prohibition on operating license renewals for coal mines that did not satisfy the stringent safety and recycling standards – coupled with the raise in coal prices that enabled coal miners to take safety and recycling costs into account, the government failed to attain the SO_2 emission reduction target in the 11th FYP period (2006–10). The central government's 4 trillion yuan investment and monetary relaxation policy during the global financial crisis boosted its investments, owning for the failure to attain the energy intensity reduction target in the 11th FPY despite last-minute shutdown of operations in large industrial plants and restriction on electricity use across the country. Their investment in this period generated excess production capacity and caused severe and visible air pollution in many cities since 2011.

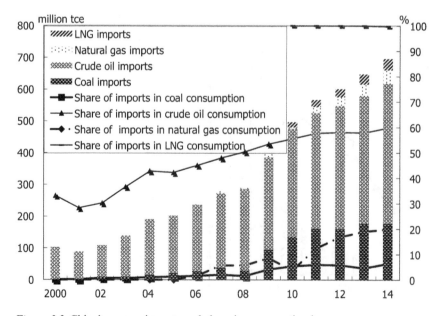

Figure 3.2 China's energy imports and share in consumption by source

Sources: Author compilation based on *China Energy Statistics Yearbook 2009; 2014 and 2015.*

Profit-driven

The third feature of China's climate policy is profit-driven. China's three main national oil companies (NOCs) of China National Petroleum Corporation (CNPC), the China Petroleum and Chemical Corporation (SINOPEC), and the China National Offshore Oil Corporation (CNOOC) became more autonomous and powerful after the SOEs reform and the decentralization (Zhang 2016). While they are motivated to expand oil and gas reserves and production, diversify the energy supply, become international state oil and gas companies, develop an integrated supply chain, capture technological know-how, and streamline their management capacities (IEA 2014), they have hesitated to acquire resources and technologies, especially in countries with authoritarian regimes or ministry control that disregards human rights (Halper 2010).

To mobilize these NOCs as implementing entities of the energy security strategy, the Chinese government has proactively pursued a strategic bilateral relation with key energy producers and resource-rich countries in Central Asia, Africa, and Latin America – especially countries whose leaders wanted to reduce the influence of the United States or where the United States had lost political interest after the Cold War. Chinese state oil and gas companies have exploited their long-standing ties with the CPC leadership to advance their corporate interests in foreign countries and make their projects commercially viable (Patey 2014).

In addition, the central government offers energy-backed loans and resource-financed infrastructure in concluding profit-sharing agreements, as well as long-term purchasing contracts on oil and natural gas to hedge energy exploitation and default risk (Tunsjø 2013). Capitalizing on over US\$ 1 trillion of foreign reserves,[1] the CDB and the Export-Import Bank of China (CEXIM) have provided loans for oversees upstream equity investments in oil and gas mining and in resource companies (Takehara 2009). These banks have employed a loan for oil or a resource for infrastructure arrangements that is securitized against the net present value of a future revenue stream from oil or resource extraction (Sanderson and Forsythe 2013; Halland et al. 2014). These loan arrangements are against the agreement among OECD member countries that restricts the use of loan arrangements as a competitive tool to secure deals (Cáceres and Ear 2013).

Profit motive is not limited to the oil and gas industry. Benchmark pricing, or de facto feed-in-tariff was implemented upon coal power in 2004, offshore wind in 2009, solar PV in 2011, and nuclear power in 2013 to incentivize competitive power producers to gain a larger profit (IESM 2014). Feed-in-tariff to solar power rescued Chinese manufacturers, which suffered financial distress by the anti-dumping measures imposed by the United States, by providing them with an opportunity to exploit domestic markets. This measure helped them enjoy scale effects and gain competitive edge in domestic and international markets. The high and unified benchmark price turned nuclear power to a profitable business, attracting coal power generators to join (Yang 2017).

In contrast, the Chinese government postponed policies and measures that would put additional burden on SOEs. A typical example would be policy calling for an upgrade of transport fuel quality, which is indispensable for improving air pollution caused by automobile combustion. Despite the urgent need, the fuel economy has been given special attention, putting a disproportional burden on automobile manufactures, most of which were established by foreign manufacturers or joint companies. It was not until Zhou Yong-Kang, the oil tycoon who for many years in charge of the Ministry of Land and Resources, was dismissed that the government enforced NOCs to improve the quality of transport fuel.

Fostering clean energy industries

The Chinese government reframed clean energies as new growth points so that climate policy should not restrict economic growth (Chen 2013). Faced with the trilemma between expansion of supply capacity, structurally heavy reliance on and inefficient use of coal, and air pollution (as depicted in Chapter 1), the government regarded the development and use of clean energy, including renewables and nuclear, as an inevitable choice for enhancing, diversifying, and conserving energy supply (Denjean and Cassisa 2016). As such, it initiated a national concession program for wind power in 2003, which guaranteed the purchase of power at winning price in competitive biddings for large projects over 25 years. Large power generators were mandated to supply renewable electricity at 3 percent by 2010 and at 8 percent by 2020. The government set out the target to increase nuclear energy production capacity fourfold by 2020 (NDRC 2007c).

In the process, the government takes several industrial policy measures, including: high local contents requirements in concessions; picking up winners through public biddings; financial supports; and carefully designed technology transfer policies for foreign manufacturers in China. As for wind turbines and their components, the government initially imposed a 50 percent local content requirement on project developers and raised the rate up to 70 percent in 2005 (Buen and Castro 2012). This prevented foreign developers from joining in the program, as many of them did not establish China-based manufacturing facilities in their partnership with Chinese-owned companies in order to protect their know-how or intellectual property rights from being leaked to their Chinese partners (Lewis 2007). In addition, the government coordinated with state-owned banks to offer large financial and investment incentives to state-owned or state-connected enterprises (Hochstetler and Kostka 2015). This enabled Chinese state-owned manufacturers to offer lower prices in the selection process, thus allowing them to win bids and take advantage of the scale of economics to lower the production cost. In contrast, foreign manufacturers were forced to play a minor role, sharing a small portion in the Chinese market (International Energy Agency 2015).

The clean development mechanism (CDM) provided additional financial support for the deployment of domestically manufactured wind power (Buen and Castro 2012). China hosted the highest number of CDM projects in the world, of which wind power shared 20 percent (Mori 2013). Although the mechanism was assumed to use foreign technology, China employed domestic technology once the CDM Board admitted unilateral CDM under which a host country organizes and implements a project and then sells the certified emissions reduction to developed countries and/or the international market.

Chinese state-owned wind turbine manufacturers successfully bypassed the export restriction clause in license agreements with foreign companies. They acquired the latest technologies, production licenses, and concessions from those in advanced countries to develop their production capacity (Horii 2014). However, to avoid fierce competitors in the world market, foreign companies required restrictive terms, restricting or prohibiting, for example, the export of the technology and offering licenses for only turbines below 1.5 MW capacity. To bypass this export restriction, Chinese SOEs acquired technology licenses from second-tier foreign manufacturers who had lost in the European market and had therefore been willing to sell licenses at a cheaper price (Mori 2015). They created join ventures with the world's top manufacturers and made direct investment in foreign power plants to acquire the latest technologies without any restriction, as well as to seek easier market penetration for national production (Denjean and Cassisa 2016).

This noteworthy performance led to an outline of new renewable energy development projects, which held priority as a means of rural electrification. Thus, the Renewable Energy Act was enacted in 2006 to describe the duties of the government, businesses, and other users, detailing mandatory grid connections, price management regulation, differentiated pricing, special funds, and tax relief. The Medium- and Long-Term Development Plan for Renewable Energy was followed by setting the target share of renewable energy as a percentage of total primary energy consumption, with targets rising from 10 percent by 2010 to 15 percent by 2020. These targets are succeeded in the 12th and 13th FPY by a national target to increase the share of non-fossil fuels in the primary energy supply to 11.4 percent and 15 percent, respectively (Table 3.1). Accordingly, the Renewable Energy 12th FYP outlined the targets for the share of renewable energy at 9.5 percent for primary energy consumption and at 20 percent for electricity generation.

In contrast, it was backing from local governments and financial support from the Chinese Development Bank (CDB) that fostered the Chinese solar photovoltaic (PV) module and cell manufacturers. While the government initiated the same national concession program with a public bidding for wind power, this only benefitted SOEs that had little market competitiveness. The government squeezed out private companies that had recruited skilled Chinese entrepreneurs from the Diaspora (de la Tour et al. 2011) and obtained backing from local governments to dominate the domestic market (Zhang 2011). The CDB rescued private manufactures, providing large amounts of subsidized loans to go out to foreign markets (Sanderson and Forsythe 2013). This enabled them to grow up rapidly and kick first-tier German and US manufacturers out of the world market, allowing them to dominate a lion's share.

As for nuclear power reactors, a foreign company retains the property right of Gen-II, the most common reactor in China. On the other hand, the official

Table 3.1 China's energy, CO_2 emission, and environmental performance

	9th FYP	10th FYP (2001–5)		11th FYP (2006–10)		12th FYP (2011–15)		13th FYP (2016–20)
	Actual	*Plan*	*Actual*	*Plan*	*Actual*	*Plan*	*Actual*	*Plan*
Carbon intensity	−26%	−	7%	−	−14%	−17%	−20%	−18%
Carbon emission[a]	9.8%		68.7%		45.0%		18.3%	
Energy Consumption (Gtce)	1.47	−	2.61	−	3.6	4.0	4.3	5.0
Coal Consumption (Gt)	1.36	−	2.43	−	3.49	−	3.96	< 4.1
Energy Intensity	−	−	−	−20%	−19.1%	−16%	−18.2%	−15%
Coal in primary energy consumption	68.5%	−	72.4%	−	69.2%	−	64%	58%
Natural gas in primary energy consumption	2.2%	−	2.4%	−	4.0%	8.0%	5.9%	10%
Non-fossil fuel in primary energy consumption (%)	−	−	−	−	8.3%	11.4%	12%	15%
Sulfur emission	−	−10%	27.8%	−10%	−14.3%	−8%	−18%	−15%
Nitrogen emission	−	−	−	−	−	−10%	−18.6%	−15%
Wind (GW)		−	1.056	8	31	100	145	210–250
Solar (GW)		−	0.07	0.07	0.86	21	43.5	110–150
Hydro (GW)	79	−	117	−	220	290	319	340
Nuclear (GW)			0.684		10.8	40	26	58
Coal (GW)					660	960	990	< 1100
Natural Gas (GW)					26.4	56		110

Sources: Author compilation based on NDRC (2007b, 2012), Ministry of Environmental Protection (2016), and World Nuclear Association (2016).

Note a: Olivier et al. (2016)

model for future home-built Gen-III reactor designs, the CAP 1400, will display Chinese intellectual property rights despite being based on a model created by the foreign company (Denjean and Cassisa 2016).

Integration of health concern

The Chinese government also adjusted its energy policy to address more seriously the worsening air pollution that spread out over many regions in China. Beginning in 2011, a thick cloud of smog spread not only from Beijing and Tianjin out to Hebei Province but also from the Yangtze River Delta to the Pearl River Delta and raised health concerns. By framing air pollution as an urgent health issue in compelling visual and intellectual terms, Chai Jing's 104-minute documentary *Under the Dome* (2015) opened doors to potential transformation in consumer behavior and government policy (Koehn 2016). Health concerns became so immense as to shake the legitimacy of the government (Ren and Shou 2013).

In response, the Chinese government identified the underlying causes as industrial coal combustion and exhaust from vehicles and outlined target for coal consumption to be below 65 percent of total energy consumption by 2017. It also issued the Action Plan on Prevention and Control of Air Pollution in 2013 to define countermeasures, including the forced closure and/or inhibition of new small-scale commercial boilers, industrial plants in heavy industry, and non-utility power generation plants. Moreover, the government restricted the use and long-distance transport of high sulfur and ash coal in major cities. The Energy Development Strategy Action Plan (2014–20) and the 2015–20 Action Plan on the Efficient Use of Coal set the cap for primary energy consumption at 4.8 billion tons of standard coal equivalent (tce), the cap for coal consumption at 4.2 billion tce, and the share of coal at 62 percent of primary energy consumption at 62 percent in 2020. It further revised the Air Pollution Control Act in 2015 to raise the maximum fine by a factor of 10 and mandated coal power to take countermeasures against nitrogen dioxide and mercury emissions, industrial plants to control emissions of volatile organic compounds, and automobile manufacturers to enhance fuel economy. These all resulted in more stringent targets in the Energy 13th FYP, which outlines more ambitious targets: the share of coal in total energy consumption to 58 percent – 4 percent below the Action Plan, and the generation capacity of wind and solar power rising to 210 to 250 GW and 110 to 150 GW, respectively (more than 10 GW higher than the Action Plan). The Chinese government announced an increase in natural gas power and ultra-super critical coal power in the 2016 congress to decrease the coal dependence to less than 50 percent. Moreover, it implemented coal consumption standards for power plants that require 10 GW of inefficient coal plants to close and a further 350 GW of capacity to improve their operational efficiency (Climate Nexus 2015).

The National Plan for Tackling Climate Change (2014–20) reflects this adjustment in energy policy. It expanded its scope of measures to include as key areas for mitigation: the elimination of backward steel production capacity, development of the service sector, control of construction and transport emissions, pilot demonstration projects, incentives, and restraint mechanisms. But it still views GHG emissions reduction as a co-benefit of energy policy, which prioritizes energy security and a reduction in health damage, instead of directly addressing the reduction of GHG emissions.

Achievements

The energy mix has changed during the 12th FYP period. China has increased energy imports up to 700 million tce, exceeding 16 percent of energy consumption (Figure 1.1). Oil and gas imports have been rapidly and massively increased since the Chinese government made a commitment to reducing GHG emissions intensity. Thus, the share of oil reached 60 percent in 2014, up from 50 percent in 2008. Natural gas imports jumped up and have been increasing since 2010, when China started to import liquefied natural gas (LNG) and pipeline gas (Figure 3.2). This brought CNPC more than 100 billion yuan of net profit and Sinopec and CNOOC more than 50 billion yuan between 2011 and 2013 (Abe 2016). The revision to the Natural Gas Use Policy in 2012 encourages the use of natural gas in automobiles, residential buildings, and combined heat and power (CHP) and, in accordance with the development of mainstream and branch pipelines, lifts the restriction on the use of natural gas for high energy-consuming industrial sectors, such as petrochemical, non-ferrous metal industries, and power plants. This promoted the rapid switch from coal to natural gas, raising the share of natural gas consumption during the 12th FYP period (Table 3.1).

Meanwhile, coal and lignite imports have increased since 2009 after import ban was lifted (Figure 3.2), and coal consumption was stimulated. It was not until 2014, when the import ban was revived, that both coal import and consumption fell (Figure 3.3). The successive decrease in coal consumption justifies the forced scrap of coal production capacity and reduction of production, and makes the target for lower coal dependency in the 13th FYP period seem realistic. Nonetheless, the government's abrupt and harsh measures brought about a hike in coal prices in 2016, forcing it to increase coal production to cool the price down.

In addition, Chinese wind turbine manufactures have enhanced their competitive edge, rapidly increasing their share of world production to 30 percent in

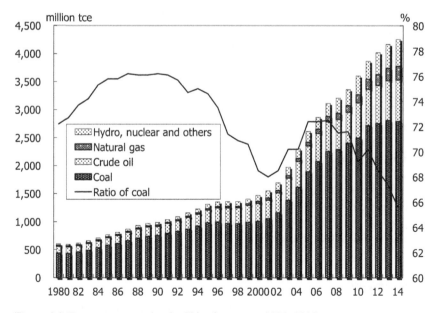

Figure 3.3 Energy consumption in China by source 1980–2014

Sources: Author compilation based on China Statistics Press, *China Energy Statistical Yearbook 2015*.

2015 (REN21 2016). Chinese solar PV cells and modules manufacturers dominate the world's production capacity and amounted to 60 percent between 2010 and 2014 (International Energy Agency 2015). In 2015, China surpassed Germany in having the world's largest capacity for both wind and solar power generation, with 199 GW of renewable power capacity (REN21 2016). This massive deployment of wind and solar power enabled the Chinese government to increase its share of non-fossil fuel to 12 percent of primary energy consumption in 2015 – higher than the targets in the 12th FYP. This achievement pushed the NDRC to set the target for non-fossil fuel share to 20 percent by 2020 in the Energy Development Strategy Action Plan (2014–20), in addition to ambitious wind and solar power installation capacity targets in the 13th Energy FYP (Table 3.1).

However, such change in energy mix has only made a minor contribution to the reduction of CO_2 emissions. In fact, it has even raised the emissions in some provinces, such as Heilongjiang (Xu et al. 2017), and in several industries, such as petroleum processing and coking (Jing et al. 2017a).

It is the energy intensity effect that has played a key role in mitigating CO_2 emissions (Xu et al. 2014). The effect becomes larger in the first half of the 12th FYP period (2011–13) than in the 11th FYP period (Jing et al. 2017b). However, it can hardly cancel out the economic expansion effect that dominantly drives emissions up in the 11th FYP period. This resulted in the smaller increase in CO_2 emissions and decrease in carbon intensity during the 12th FYP period (Table 3.1).

These observed achievements suggest that while China has shifted the energy mix from coal to gas and renewables by increasing energy imports and boosting renewable energy manufacturing, the shift has generated marginal effects on the reduction of CO_2 emissions until 2013.

Underlying factors behind sluggish achievements

To advance the shift in energy mix and reduce CO_2 emissions along with air pollution, the current energy-centered climate policy, or climate-energy policy and other related policies should be developed to transform the current energy supply infrastructure system towards one with low CO_2 emissions. Given China's high coal dependency, this implies a decrease in coal consumption and a switch to gas and renewable energy.

Such transformation, however, clashes with the interests of regime actors. The central government's measures to rationalize exploitation, transportation and consumption provoke conflicts with the interests of provinces in their coal industries, which expanded the grey coal markets that are not counted on the official statistics (Tu 2011). The government's commitment to limit coal production and decrease the share of coal is further damaging the industry, making 1.3 million workers redundant (Fukushima 2016). The rapid installation of renewable energy capacity also threatens the interests of provinces in their coal power. Local grids place higher priority on the connection with coal power, especially combined heat and power (CHP), to secure a stable supply of heating in winter. Moreover, the central government's insufficient compensation and slow payment of feed-in-tariffs for renewable energy discourages local grids from accepting these energies and investing in the transmission capacity for their connection. This led to the one-third of wind curtailment in the winter of 2010 (Davidson 2013). Despite the decrease in the curtailment rate between 2011 and 2013 (Fang, Li and Wang 2012), it rose to reach 39 percent in the northeast and 32 percent in northwest provinces in the winter of 2015 (World Nuclear Association 2016). Still, less than one-third of the installed wind power capacity was unconnected to the grid in 2015 (Li 2016).

To address renewable curtailment, the central government requires top solar-producing provinces to increase their transmission capacities (REN21 2016) and is developing ultra-high-voltage (UHV) transmission networks. However, the central government ignores interconnection among provincial grids, which enables renewable energy to be integrated into the system without impairing reliability and investing in costly and lengthy transmission lines (Mori 2018). In addition, the central government is suspending approval of new wind power construction and access to grid connections in the six top wind-producing provinces (China Daily 2017), and provinces with high coal dependency impose charges or production restrictions on renewable energy producers to protect their coal power (Yang 2017).

Switching from coal power and CHP to gas power can reduce renewable curtailment, as gas power enhances load-following capabilities (Li 2013). However, this clashes with the interests of NOCs and regional major suppliers. The government requires NOCs to sell imported gas under non-profitability conditions for fear of potential repercussions with residential consumers, most of who can hardly afford the international energy price (Romano et al. 2016). It also sets differentiated prices according to the type of consumer, requiring the cross-subsidization of residential consumers. In exchange, NOCs and local downstream suppliers are allowed a monopoly over supply. In addition, insufficient development of transportation and distribution infrastructure limits gas to major consumption areas in east coast cities. This all makes the domestic price for natural gas the world's highest for major consumers, such as industries and power, thus discourages them from switching to gas (Paltsev and Zhang 2015; Bloomberg News 2017). In order to accelerate this switch, gas price reforms are implemented that links the domestic price to international one and that allows third-party access to the pipeline network—, though gradually, as measures to encourage investments in domestic unconventional sources and to increase decentralized energy production. However, both NOCs and local suppliers effectively refused their participation to protect their control and monopoly (Liu et al. 2013).

In sum, China's energy supply system is so deeply embedded into local governments – which protect local coal mines and coal power, along with large state coal mines and NOCs – that the central government faces mounting difficulties to reconfigure it against their vested interests.

Reframing climate-energy policy

To ameliorate fierce conflicts of interests between coal, gas, and renewable energy suppliers, the Chinese government took three actions. First, it revived the coal tariff in 2014, which could protect local coal mines, together with restricting the use of high sulfur and ash coal in major cities and long-distance transport in the name of air pollution control (Wong 2014).

Second, it accelerated the development of hydropower. Since the publication of the Renewable Energy Mid- to Long-Term Plan, China has increased hydropower generation capacity by 165 GW to reach 320 GW in 2015. This includes not only small hydropower plants installed by capitalizing on the clean development mechanism (CDM), but also ones located in the upstream of the Mekong and Nu/Salween Rivers, which provoked significant local opposition in China and downstream countries (Brown and Xu 2010).

Third, the Chinese government reframed the climate-energy policy as part of its official slogan of "going global." It applies the "common fate and destination" model that it has employed in its South-South development cooperation for oil and gas contracts, state coal mines, coal and hydropower companies. Assuming a host country's decision on large infrastructure development projects, this model highlights establishing a joint venture company with the host country, international competitive bidding, mobilizing finance through combining export buyer credits and non-concessional loans without conditionality and questions on human rights, as well as service provisions by the company that won the bid (Lin and Wang 2017: 180–2). Services can include actual labor in the form of workers and intermediary goods when the project is implemented under an engineering, procurement, and construction (EPC) arrangement.

This reframing makes it easier for the central government to convince SOEs in these sectors as well as provinces that have concerns about shutdown of local small coal mines and plants, as SOEs can mobilize the redundant workers in foreign energy development projects. It can also enable the government to enhance mutual dependency between foreign countries, lowering the risk of energy insecurity.

Host countries, however, can suffer from this reframing. The "common fate and destination" model increases their dependency on China, not only as a main importer of their energy products, but also as a project developer and exporter of goods and services. As a result, China will gain higher economic and political power in host countries once joint venture companies set up by Chinese SOEs and influential local counterparts obtain concessions for large infrastructure projects. Chinese SOEs can then capitalize on this power to tame opposition against social and ecological damages caused by projects. Finally, this reframing will move the energy sectors of host countries toward a high CO_2 emission pathway and will intensify their institutional lock-in.

Conclusion

This chapter serves as a critical review of China's climate policy. It explores what changed China's initial hostile stance toward a proactive one. To answer this question, it revisits the policy process and outcomes that the Chinese government has taken to address the climate-energy conundrum, discussing the effectiveness of policy outcomes and the logical consequences of enhancing them.

The findings can be summarized as follows. First, China's climate policy has been centered on energy development strategies, framed as climate-energy policy. However, detailed policy measures have been adjusted to incorporate the vested interests of local governments and NOCs, reflecting the government's desire to create a new growth point, and to address the emerging heath concerns. This has made policy outcomes realistic.

Second, resultant climate-energy policies provoke conflicts of interest among provincial governments, NOCs, and distributed energy producers. This is the underlying cause that blocks changes in the energy mix from accelerating, thus impairing the structural effect for a reduction in CO_2 emissions.

Finally, these domestic conflicts of interest are too fierce for the government to find an easy solution. As the government feels increasing pressures from health concerns and assigns them higher priority in the climate-energy policy, it applies the "common fate and destination" model to accelerate "going global" in coal and hydropower industries in order to avoid the conflicts being intensified domestically. However, this can simply shift the conflicts of interest spatially in the international arena, which will be analyzed in depth in the Part III of this book.

Note

1 According to the World Bank's World DataBank, China's foreign reserve surpassed US$ 1 trillion in 2006 and reached US$ 3.9 trillion in 2014.

References

Abe, T. (2016) China's state oil companies lost momentum, *Nikkei Shinbun*, August 30, 2016 (in Japanese).

Bloomberg News (17 August 2017) *China's Blue Skies Target May Make for Winter Gas Crunch*, Retrieved from https://www.bloomberg.com/news/articles/2017-08-16/china-s-blue-skies-target-may-make-for-winter-gas-supply-crunch, accessed on December 14, 2017.

Brown, P.H. and Xu, Y. (2010) Hydropower development and resettlement policy in China's Nu river, *Journal of Contemporary China* 19: 777–97.

Buen, J. and Castro, P. (2012) How Brazil and China have financed industry development and energy security initiatives that support mitigation objectives, in Michaelowa, K. and Michaelowa, A. (eds.) *Carbon Markets or Climate Finance? Low Carbon and Adaptation Investment Choices for the Developing World*, Oxon: Routledge, 53–91.

Cáceres, S.B. and Ear, S. (2013) *The Hungry Dragon: How China's Resource Quest Is Reshaping the World*, Oxon: Routledge.

Chen, G. (2012) *China's Climate Policy*, Oxon: Routledge.

Chen, S. (2013) *Energy, Environment and Economic Transformation in China*, Oxon: Routledge.

Cheng, J.Y.S. (2013) A Chinese view of China's energy security, in Zhao, S. (ed.) *China's Search for Energy Security: Domestic Sources and International Implications*, Oxon: Routledge, 1–21.

China Daily (2017) New wind power projects banned in six regions due to wastage, February 23, 2017, www.chinadaily.com.cn/business/2017-02/23/content_28316786.htm, accessed on June 27, 2017.

Climate Nexus (2015) *China's Climate and Energy Policy: Leadership Efforts on the Road to a Low-Carbon Future*, http://climatenexus.org/learn/international-actions/chinas-climate-and-energy-policy, accessed on December 5, 2016.

Davidson, M. (2013) *Transforming China's Grid: Obstacles on the Path to a National Carbon Trading System*, www.theenergycollective.com/michael-davidson/259871/transforming-china-s-grid-integrating-wind-energy-it-blows-away, accessed on June 10, 2016.

de la Tour, A., Glachant, M. and Ménière, Y. (2011) Innovation and international technology transfer: The case of the Chinese photovoltaic industry, *Energy Policy* 39: 761–70.

Denjean, B. and Cassisa, C. (2016) Low-carbon energy in China's energy security strategy, in Romano, G.C. and Di Meglio, J.-F. (eds.) *China's Energy Security: A Multidimensional Perspective*, Oxon: Routledge, 69–100.

Economy, E.C. (2004) *The River Runs Black: The Environmental Challenge to China's Future*, Ithaca: Cornell University Press.

Fang, Y., Li, J. and Wang, M. (2012) Development policy for non-grid-connected wind power in China: An analysis based on institutional change, *Energy Policy* 45: 350–8.

Fukushima, K. (2016) *The Day China, the Red Empire Fall Down*, Tokyo: KK Bestsellers (in Japanese).

Halland, H., et al. (2014) *Resource Financed Infrastructure: A Discussion on a New Form of Infrastructure Financing*, Washington, DC: The World Bank.

Halper, S. (2010) *The Beijing Consensus: How China's Authoritarian Model Will Dominate the Twenty-First Century*, New York: Basic Books.

Hayashi, K. (2006) Conditions for high-performer in international oil and gas upstream industry: A CERA proposal for increasing international competitiveness of Japanese firms, *Oil and Gas Review* 40(3): 33–41 (in Japanese).

Hochstetler, K. and Kostka, G. (2015) Wind and solar power in Brazil and China: Interests, state–business relations, and policy outcomes, *Global Environmental Politics* 15(3): 74–94.

Horii, N. (2006) Challenges towards stabilization of energy balance, in Oonishi, Y. (ed.) *China: Challenges of Hu Jintao-Eleventh Five-year Long-term Plan and Sustainable Development*, Tokyo: Institute for Asian Economies, 105–35 (in Japanese).

Horii, N. (2014) The wind turbine industry: The role of policy and markets in the catch-up process, in Watanabe, M. (ed.) *The Disintegration of Production: Firm Strategy and Industrial Development in China*, Cheltenham: Edward Elgar, 127–48.

Institute of Economic System and Management, National Development and Reform Commission (IESM) (2014) *Strategy and Keys to Electricity Pricing Reform*, www.china-reform.org/?content_540.html (in Chinese), accessed on February 14, 2018.

International Energy Agency (2014) *Update on Overseas Investments by China's National Oil Companies: Achievement and Challenges Since 2011*, Paris: IEA.

International Energy Agency (2015) *Trends 2015 in Photovoltaic Applications: Survey Report of Selected IEA Countries Between 1992 and 2014*, www.iea-pvps.org/fileadmin/dam/public/report/national/IEA-PVPS_-_Trends_2015_-_MedRes.pdf, accessed on July 25, 2016.

Jing, J., Ye, B., Xie, D., Li, J., Miao, L. and Yang, P. (2017a) Sector decomposition of China's national economic carbon emissions and its policy implication for national ETS development, *Renewable and Sustainable Energy Reviews* 75: 855–67.

Jing, J., Ye, B., Xie, D. and Tang, J. (2017b) Provincial-level carbon emission drivers and emission reduction strategies in China: Combining multi-layer LMDI decomposition with hierarchical clustering, *Journal of Cleaner Production* 169: 178–90.

Koehn, P.H. (2016) *China Confronts Climate Change: A Bottom-up Perspective*, Oxon: Routledge.

Lewis, J.I. (2007) Technology acquisition and innovation in the developing world: Wind turbine development in China and India, *Studies in Comparative International Development* 42(3–4): 208–32.

Li, Y. (31 May 2016) Blowing in the wind, *China Dialogue*, www.chinadialogue.net/article/show/single/en/8965-Blowing-in-the-wind, accessed on June 26, 2017.

Li, Z. (2013) Natural gas use policy trends in China, *Institute of Energy Economics Japan*, https://eneken.ieej.or.jp/data/4878.pdf, accessed on September 18, 2016.

Lin, J.Y. and Wang, Y. (2017) *Going beyond Aid: Development Cooperation for Structural Transformation*, Cambridge: Cambridge University Press.

Liu, J., Wang, R., Sun, Y., Lin, Y. and Xiao, L. (2013) A barrier analysis for the development of distributed energy in China: A case study in Fujian province, *Energy Policy* 60: 262–71.

Lockwood, M. (2015) The political dynamics of green transformations: Feedback effects and institutional context, in Scoones, I., Leach, M. and Newell, P. (eds.) *The Politics of Green Transformations*, Oxon: Routledge, 86–101.

Ministry of Environmental Protection (2016) *Report on the State of the Environment in China 2015* (in Chinese).

Mori, A. (2013) Regional environmental regime in East Asia: Collapse or arrested development?, in Mori, A. (ed.) *Environmental Governance for Sustainable development: An East Asian Perspective*, Tokyo: United Nations University Press, 271–91.

Mori, A. (2015) Green growth and low carbon development in East Asia: Achievements and challenges, in Yoshida, F. and Mori, A. (eds.) *Green Growth and Low Carbon Development in East Asia*, Oxon: Routledge, 278–304.

Mori, A. (2018) Sociotechnical and political economy perspectives in the Chinese energy transition, *Energy Research & Social Science* 35: 29–36.

Nachmany, M., Fankhauser, S., Davidová, J., Kingsmill, N., Landesman, T., Roppongi, H., Schleifer, P., Setzer, J., Sharman, A., Singleton, C.S., Sundaresan, J. and Townshend, T. (2015) *Climate Change Legislation in China*, www.lse.ac.uk/GranthamInstitute/wp-content/uploads/2015/05/CHINA.pdf, accessed on September 25, 2016.

National Development and Reform Commission (NDRC) (2007a) *China's National Climate Change Programme*, http://www.china-un.org/eng/gyzg/t626117.htm, accessed on May 7, 2018.

National Development and Reform Commission (NDRC) (2007b) *Medium and Long-Term Development Plan for Renewable Energy in China,* http://www.martinot.info/China_RE_Plan_to_2020_Sep-2007.pdf, accessed on May 7, 2018.

National Development and Reform Commission (NDRC) (2007c) *Medium and Long-Term Development Plan for Nuclear Power in China 2005–2020*, www.etiea.cn/data/attachment/123(4).pdf, accessed on February 14, 2018.

National Development and Reform Commission (NDRC) (2012) *Energy Development Plan of the 12th Five Year Plan*, http://iepd.iipnetwork.org/policy/energy-development-plan-12th-five-year-plan, accessed on May 7, 2018.

Olivier, J.G.J., Janssens-Maenhout, G., Muntean, M. and Peters, J.A.H.W. (2016) *Trends in Global CO_2 and Total Greenhouse Gas Emissions: 2016 Report*, PBL Netherlands Environmental Assessment Agency, www.pbl.nl/en/publications/trends-in-global-co2-emissions-2016-report, accessed on February 14, 2018.

Paltsev, S. and Zhang, D. (2015) Natural gas pricing reform in China: Getting closer to a market system?, *Energy Policy* 86: 43–56.

Patey, L. (2014) *The New Kings of Crude: China, India and the Global Strategies for Oil in Sudan and South Sudan*, London: C. Hurst & Co. Ltd.

Ren, B. and Shou, H. (2013) Introduction: Dynamics, challenges and opportunities in making a green China, in Ren, B. and Shou, H. (eds.) *Chinese Environmental Governance: Dynamics, Challenges and Prospects in a Changing Society*, New York: Palgrave Macmillan, 1–18.

REN21 (2016) *Renewables 2016 Global Status Report*, www.ren21.net/wp-content/uploads/2016/06/GSR_2016_Full_Report.pdf, accessed on July 22, 2016.

Romano, G.C., Yin, N. and Zhang, X. (2016) Gas in China's energy security strategy, in Romano, G.C. and Di Meglio, J.-F. (eds.) *China's Energy Security: A Multidimensional Perspective*, Oxon: Routledge, 46–68.

Sanderson, H. and Forsythe, M. (2013) China's Superbank: *Debt, Oil and Influence: How China Development Bank Is Rewriting the Rules of Finance*, Singapore: John Wiley & Sons.

Takehara, M. (2009) From US dollar to resources: China's quest for oil after the global financial crisis, *Oil and Natural Gas Review (JOGMEC)* 43(6): 1–20 (in Japanese).

Toke, D. and Vezirgiannidou, S.E. (2013) The relationship between climate change and energy security: key issues and conclusions, *Environmental Politics* 22(4): 537–52.

Tu, J. (2011) Industrial organization of the Chinese coal industry, *Working Paper 103*, Program for Energy and Sustainable Development, Stanford University.

Tunsjø, Ø. (2013) *Security and Profit in China's Energy Policy: Hedging against Risk*, New York: Columbia University Press.

UNDP China (2012) *Climate Change and Development in China: 3 Decades of UNDP Support*, www.cn.undp.org/content/dam/china/docs/Publications/UNDP-CH-EE-Publications-Climate-Change-and-Development-in-China.pdf?download, accessed on September 25, 2016.

Wong, F. (2014) Update 2-China to again levy coal import tariffs after nearly a decade, *Reuters*, October 9, 2014, www.reuters.com/article/china-coal-idUSL3N0S41QP20141009, accessed on July 28, 2016.

World Nuclear Association (2016) *Nuclear Power in China*, www.world-nuclear.org/information-library/country-profiles/countries-a-f/china-nuclear-power.aspx, accessed on December 11, 2016.

Xu, S.C., Han, H.M., Zhang, W.W., Zhang, Q.Q., Long, R.Y. Chen, H. and He, Z.X. (2017) Analysis of regional contributions to the national carbon intensity in China in different five-year plan periods, *Journal of Cleaner Production* 145: 209–20.

Xu, S.C., He, Z.X. and Long, R.Y. (2014) Factors that influence carbon emissions due to energy consumption in China: Decomposition analysis using LMDI, *Applied Energy* 127: 182–93.

Yang, C.J. (2017) *Energy Policy in China*, Oxon: Routledge.

Zhang, C. (2016) *The Domestic Dynamics of China's Energy Diplomacy*, Singapore: World Scientific.

Zhang, Z.X. (2011) *Energy and Environmental Policy in China: Toward a Low-Carbon Economy*, Cheltenham: Edward Elgar.

Part II

Domestic impacts of China's climate-energy policy

4 Energy system reforms for the reduction of coal dependency

Nobuhiro Horii

Introduction

Prior to COP21, China released its own Intended National Determined Contributions (INDC) on June 2015, in which the Chinese government set targets for CO_2 emissions per unit of GDP to be reduced by 60–65%, and the ratio of non-fossil energy in primary energy to be increased to around 20%. As a result, coal consumption in China is assumed to pass a peak at around 2030. While China has reduced coal dependence in energy demand since 2008, it should obviously restrict coal consumption to achieve these targets.

This paper aims to investigate enabling factors and barriers toward a sustainable energy system in China, with special focus on the supply and demand of coal. The approach of this paper is based on an analysis of the coal industry. There are several studies that have taken the same approach, such as International Energy Agency (2009) and Yue (2010–2015). International Energy Agency (2009) is a comprehensive study on China's coal industry and its influence on environmental problems. However, it was published just around when the share of coal started to decline, and therefore lacks an analysis of this important phenomenon. On the other hand, Yue (2010–2015) summarized China's coal industry development for each year, providing a large amount of useful information, but not any focus from the view of economics on incentives of coal mines and users nor analysis regarding the influence of strengthening environmental regulations on coal demand.

The objective of this paper is to analyze the background of the reduced dependence on coal in China's energy mix after 2008, where coal's share in total primary energy dropped from 72.5% in 2007 to 62.3% in 2016. This paper considers two major factors influencing China's changing energy structure: the tightening of environmental regulations (first section) and the progress of the coal pricing reform (second section). Then, the outlook for a shift away from coal in the future is discussed, focused on important influencing factors, such as commitment to COP21 and the economic performance of coal compared to other energies (third section). Finally, the summary of this chapter is shown in the last section.

Progress of reduced dependence on coal in the 12th five-year period: policy initiative

It goes without saying that China is the world's largest energy-consuming country and also the largest greenhouse gas (GHG) emitter. It is also well known that China relies heavily on coal for its energy supply. In recent years, however, China's energy structure, in which coal was the main energy resource, has been undergoing significant changes.

In 2014, China's coal consumption showed negative growth (−0.6%) for the first time since 1987. This fall in coal consumption continued in the following two years: −2.0% in 2015 and −4.7% in 2016. As a result, the share of coal in total primary energy consumption, which was 72.5% in 2007, plummeted by more than 10 points in just eight years to 62.3% in 2016. Although the stagnated growth in overall energy demand is an important change, it is coal, the main energy source, which has played a crucial role in demand stagnation. This chapter focuses on China's ongoing rapid reduction in the share of coal in the energy structure along with its steep decline in coal dependence.

In fact, this is not the first time China has shifted the energy structure away from coal. As can be seen from Figure 4.1, the share of coal fell almost consistently before the 1980s, as the changeover to oil advanced with the discovery of several huge oil fields within China. Dependence on coal rose again from the 1980s because of the increase in energy demand arising from rapid economic growth. From the late 1990s, however, the share of coal fell again during the growth stagnation caused by the Asian economic crisis in addition to the impact of policy calling for the closure of small-sized coal mines. In the early 2000s, the dependence on coal rose once again in the tight energy supply and demand during the overheating of China's economy.

From the change in the share of coal in the past it is possible to discern a pattern where China's dependence on coal rises when economic growth accelerates. It is also necessary to bear in mind that the shift away from coal in the late 1990s was due to policy intervention at a time of sluggish demand. As it turned out, when energy demand grew rapidly due to the later overheating of the economy, coal production was increased to match a large part of the rise in energy demand. The shift away from coal in the late 1990s did not alter the existing energy structure, with coal as the main energy source; for as this shift could not have occurred without policy intervention, the share of coal quickly rose again.

In contrast, there is a shift away from coal that began in 2008: despite the continued robust economic growth up to at least 2012 (and the enduring growth in energy demand), the share of coal began to decline. Could China's energy structure be undergoing some kind of change? Let us analyze this point below.

The strengthening of environmental regulations in the 11th and 12th Five-Year Plans (hereafter 11th FYP and 12th FYP, which cover the periods from 2006 to 2010 and 2011 to 2016 respectively) can be identified as a background factor. As indicated in Table 4.1, targets for the reduction of the conventional air pollutant SO_2 were set at 10% in the 11th FYP and 8% in the 12th FYP, while for NOx emissions the target

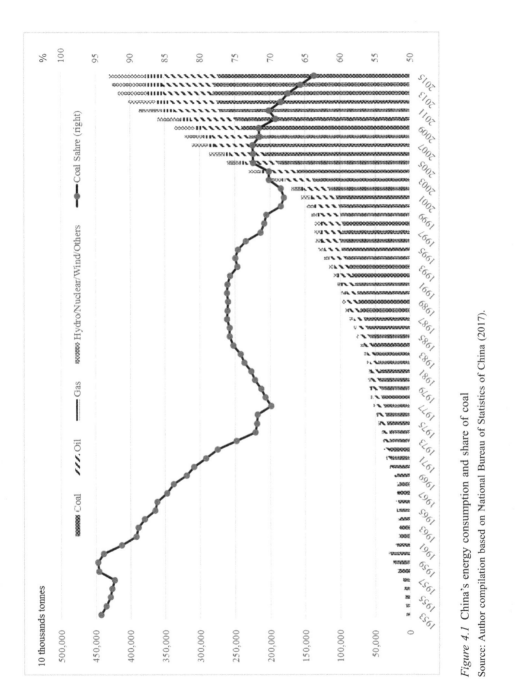

Figure 4.1 China's energy consumption and share of coal

Source: Author compilation based on National Bureau of Statistics of China (2017).

was set at a 10% reduction in the 12th FYP. In addition, the 12th FYP incorporated a target for the share of primary energy accounted for by non-fossil energy – including hydro, nuclear, wind, and photovoltaic power – to rise from 6.5% in 2005 to 11.4% in 2015. The target of a 17% reduction in the emissions of CO_2 per unit of GDP (CO_2 emissions per 10,000 yuan of GDP) was also proposed.

The environmental improvement targets for both the 11th and 12th FYPs served as a strong disincentive for the use of coal, which contains a high concentration of air pollutants along with a high CO_2 emission intensity. Additional targets for energy conservation (reduced energy consumption per unit of GDP) were set at 20% in the 11th FPY and 16% in the 12th FYP, with a target of suppressing total energy consumption in 2015 to four billion tons (standard coal equivalent). While the energy conservation target not only had an impact on coal but all energy sources, the greatest pressure for reduction was naturally placed on coal, the main energy source.

As shown in Table 4.1, with the exception of the target for reducing energy consumption per unit of GDP, the actual reduction achievements allowed all targets to be met. In particular, the actual results for SO_2 and NOx reduction during the 12th FYP were conspicuous by the fact that they far exceeded the targets. The fact that smog caused by PM2.5 became a political issue during the 12th FYP period contributed to the implementation of far stricter countermeasures than had originally been expected. SO_2 countermeasures did not stop at the conventional method of introducing flue-gas desulfurization equipment at power plants (the largest source of SO_2), but were also expanded to small-scale emitters, and flue-gas denitrification equipment was also introduced at almost all power plants to prevent emissions of NOx. This was indeed excellent progress in a mere five years.

In terms of low carbon development, the fact that the target of an 11.4% share of non-fossil energy was slightly exceeded at 12% and the target for the

Table 4.1 Targets and actual achievements in China's 11th FYP and 12th FYP

Targeted items	11th FYP		12th FYP		13th FYP
	Target (Compared to 2005)	Actual achievement	Target (Compared to 2010)	Actual achievement	Target (Compared to 2015)
Specific consumption of energy to GDP	20%↓	19.1%↓	16%↓	18.2%↓	15.0%↓
SO_2 emission	10%↓	14.3%↓	8%↓	18.0%↓	15.0%↓
Ratio of non-fossil energy consumption			11.4%	12.0%	15.0%
Specific emission of CO_2 to GDP			17%↓	20.0%↓	18.0%↓
NOx emission			10%↓	18.6%↓	15.0%↓

Source: Author compilation based on press release by NDRC.

reduced CO_2 emission per unit of GDP was exceeded by 3 points to achieve a 20% improvement is worthy of our attention. The introduction of hydro and wind power played an important role in raising the share of non-fossil energy. From 2005 to 2015, the installed capacity of hydropower facilities increased 201,950 MW, followed by wind power at 128,410 MW. Nuclear power was first introduced in the 1980s (far earlier than wind power) but its capacity was limited to 21,200 MW – lower than that of photovoltaic power, for which full-fledged introduction finally began in 2011, and which achieved a dramatic growth of 43,180 MW.

However, the growth in non-fossil fuel energy – especially wind power and photovoltaic power (both relatively expensive forms of power production) – was not due to market competitiveness, but rather the implementation of environmental policy. In this regard, it is necessary to consider if there has been any difference in the effectiveness of environmental policy between the 1990s and this more recent endeavor. In the past, there have often been times in China when policies had not been implemented according to their original intention; and it has been pointed out that this is due to the poor monitoring capability of the central government (this situation is described by the popular phrase, "The higher-ups have policies; the lower levels have countermeasures"). From the 11th and 12th FYPs, however, a system reform (the one-vote-down system) took place whereby an economic index and a new energy/environment index have been added to the achievement evaluation items of regional governments, with more importance being placed on an energy/environment index than an economic index. This system reform has enhanced effectiveness of China's energy/environment policy when compared with the past.

From the end of 2011, as this strengthening of environmental policy implementation was progressing, the occurrence of severe smog was reported in many areas (beginning with Beijing) and PM2.5 countermeasures surfaced as a political issue. The government was faced with strong public criticism; and with the State Council issuing an "Action Plan on Prevention and Control of Air Pollution" in September 2013, strong PM2.5 countermeasures were enforced, including limit on coal consumption especially in urban area; this included the ban on the small-scale coal-fired industrial boilers, the closure of production facilities by heavy industry companies, and a ban on the new installation of non-utility power generation facilities. In addition, in major cities such as Beijing, the use of high-sulfur and high-ash coals was limited, and a target for the reduction of total coal consumption was also introduced. Even before this time, limitations on the use of low-grade coal had been stipulated many times, but those efforts had been ineffective. In May 2013, however, new regulation (Temporary Administrative Measure on the Quality and Quantity of Commercial Coal) was introduced, stipulating that "long-distance transport will not be permitted for coal that does not meet the conditions of 25% or less ash content, 1% or less sulfur content, and a calorific value of above 19 MK/kg," and that "coal with an ash content of 25% or more must be used at local factories fitted with high-efficiency technology and environmental countermeasures." Low-grade coal was thus restricted from the transport side, thereby greatly reducing the quantity of coal flowing into the cities.

Finally, it is also important to note that the recent shift away from coal has proceeded through a change in China's energy mix itself, not simply through political pressure. More concretely, the relative economic performance of coal relative to other energy sources has changed, bringing about a structure where the shift away from coal is being promoted by market forces. To discuss this, we will next investigate the case of the electricity sector that accounts for the greatest consumption of coal.

Low carbon development in the electricity sector

Figure 4.2 shows an overall rising trend in the share of thermal generation in China's power generation facilities up to 2007 – the share reaching 77.7% in 2007, up from 69.7% in 1986. Thermal generation includes the use of coal, oil, and natural gas; but even in 2014 coal-fired thermal power accounted for the greater part of the whole thermal installed capacity at more than 90%. Nonetheless, the share of thermal generation fell rapidly after 2008, declining to 65.7% in 2015. Looking at the bar graph, it appears that the installed capacity of thermal generation itself is rising steadily. The fall in thermal generation share is instead due to accelerated growth in hydro, wind, nuclear, and photovoltaic power in recent years. It is only natural to assume that the relative share of thermal generation would decline.

However, looking at power generation output, one gets the impression that there is high risk attached to the situation thermal generation finds itself in. Thermal power output in 2015 was 4097trillion MWh (down 2.3% from the previous year), and in a similar fashion to coal consumption. Since thermal power output in 2007 had been 3226 trillion MWh, there had been average annual growth of 2.9% over eight years and installed capacity had also increased by 7.5%. Naturally, there was a large drop in facility utilization rate, which was 60.7% for thermal power generation facilities in 2007 and slumped to 49.4% in 2015. At the same time, the facility utilization rate for hydropower rose slightly from 40.3% in 2007 to 41.3% in 2015, and the nuclear power utilization rate in 2015 was 87.3% – an extremely high level even if simple comparisons are not possible due to operational characteristics of different facilities.

Thermal power generation, especially the construction of coal thermal power plants, requires massive investment; and since this results in the electricity sector having high fixed costs, from a business management perspective, it is advisable to maintain facility utilization rates as high as possible from the start of operation. Despite this, the reasons why thermal generation facility utilization rates are flagging include the fact that new electric power facilities (such as hydro, nuclear, wind, and photovoltaic power) have been given priority. These new electric power facilities have a higher proportion of fixed costs for power generation than for thermal power and variable costs (operational costs) that are lower than for thermal power. As a result, the facility utilization rate of thermal power has fallen dramatically by 11.3 points in eight years, and, naturally, profitability has deteriorated to a great extent.

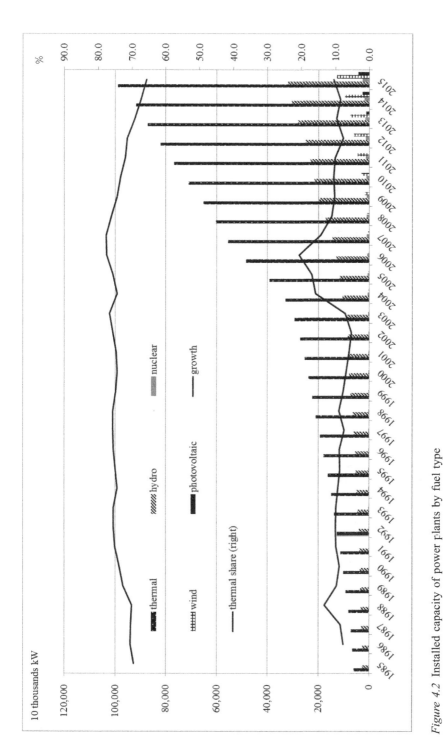

Figure 4.2 Installed capacity of power plants by fuel type

Sources: Author compilation based on China Electricity Council annual report, each year.

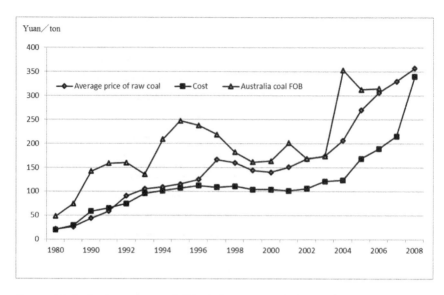

Figure 4.3 Coal price and cost of China's key state coal mines

Source: Author compilation based on China Coal Industry Association (2011).

The deterioration in the profitability of coal-fired thermal power is not due to the low level of the utilization rate alone. Rather, a more important factor is the sharp rise in the price of coal. As shown in Figure 4.3, the price of coal almost matched its production cost until 1996; but this is because the economic system at the time was based on the planned economy. The ideology of the planned economy was that capital was owned by all the people; and as the agents of the people, the state established state-owned companies to supply the people with goods and services. Due to this, it was not necessary to reflect profit (the return on capital) in prices, and the system allowed the government to set prices at a level that reflected supply costs. That the price of Chinese coal during this time was extremely cheap can be seen in comparison with the price of Australian coal shown in the figure. Australia has many of the world's most efficient coal mines; but in China, coal was being traded at a price well below that of Australian coal. What made this possible, as mentioned above, was that the price of Chinese coal did not reflect profits, labor costs were held at a low level, and the depreciation of capital was not fully accounted for.

However, by 1993, the planned economy system came to an end. Even so, in reality, coal[1] has still not yet fully adopted market mechanisms. Even though the "plan" no longer exists, the annual coal ordering meeting had taken its place. The coal ordering meeting brought together coal mines, key coal users from the power, steel, chemical, and construction (cement) sectors, and railways (the transport service provider) to conclude coal trading contracts and determine the transportation plan for the following year. The meetings were hosted by the National

Planning Commission (later renamed the National Development and Reform Commission) at the end of each year. Unlike the old system that allocated coal in accordance with the "plan," in the coal ordering meetings, coal mines and users negotiated and signed contracts. Price was negotiated by the parties within a certain range, following guiding prices set by the government.[2] As shown in Figure 4.3, from 1993 to 1996, the price nearly equaled the production cost.

After the abolition of the planned economy system in 1993 and up until the mid-2000s, the coal ordering meetings served as a substituted platform for the government to influence the coal pricing, and transaction volume in the coal ordering meeting then accounted for over 80% of the coal produced by major coal mines. However, increasing disputes associated with the coal trading system (dominated by coal ordering meetings) occurred, the most serious of which regarded the price of coal for power stations.

Taking into account social factors (safeguarding stable power supply to households, etc.), the price of coal for power plants was kept at a lower level compared to coal for non-power users – this discount widening since the beginning of the 21st century (as seen in Table 4.2). Particularly from 2003, demand for coal soared due to overheating of the economy; and the price gap between coal for power stations and coal for other users widened further until the price gap reached 35.5% in 2006.

Naturally, the coal mines were unhappy about giving power stations large discounts. Under the old system, so long as coal mines achieved the production target and supplied coal to designated users at designated prices, they would be compensated for the incurred losses and thus had little to complain about.

Table 4.2 Performance indicators of the coal industry and the price of coal

	Coal production (10,000 ton)	Investment (100 million Yuan)	Profit (100 million Yuan)	Price of steam coal used for non-power generation purposes (Yuan/Ton)	Price of coal for power plants (Yuan/Ton)	Discount (%)
1998	123,258			140	133	▲ 5.0
1999	104,363			140	121	▲ 13.6
2000	99,917	188		146	127	▲ 13.0
2001	110,559	218	11	151	122	▲ 18.8
2002	141,530	286	25	168	137	▲ 18.2
2003	172,787	414	35	174	141	▲ 18.8
2004	199,735	702	80	206	163	▲ 21.3
2005	215,132	1,144	148	270	213	▲ 21.3
2006	232,526	1,479	677	338	218	▲ 35.5
2007	252,341	1,805	950	331	246	▲ 25.7
2008	274,857	2,411	2,100	357	n.a.	n.a.

Sources: Author compilation based on China Coal Industry Association (2011) and various news reports.

However, since the late 1990s, there were no longer free grants for coal mines for capital investments, and coal mines had to resort to commercial bank loans to finance their needs. On top of this, subsidies to coal mines were no longer as generous as they used to be. There was simply no way that coal mines could willingly give generous discounts to power stations.

Because of this conflict of interest, the traded volume achieved through coal ordering meetings steadily declined. In fact, at its peak, 80% of coal from key state-owned coal mines was sold through coal ordering meetings. But this ratio plummeted. Particularly since 2004, it was reported in the news that coal mines and power plants failed to reach an agreement on pricing, and the parties included only the quantity in the contract and excluded price information (price was to be negotiated later). The disputes reached a peak in 2006, as only 20% of coal from key state-owned coal mines was sold through the annual coal ordering meeting; and no agreement was reached on pricing. Apparently, the price of coal for power plants (shown in Table 4.2) only served as a guideline on paper, and in reality few coal transactions were carried out by following the guiding price (shown in Figure 4.3). Although Table 4.2 shows that the price of coal for power plants in 2006 was nearly on the same level as the previous year, Figure 4.3 shows that the average selling price went up by wide margins, demonstrating that there were few transactions following the low political guiding price and that most transactions followed market prices.

The 2006 coal ordering meeting was the last such meeting hosted by the National Development and Reform Commission, and it was replaced in the following year by the National Key Coal Suppliers, Transporters, and Users Docking Conference hosted by China Coal Transportation and Sale Association. However, only quantities were negotiated during such conferences. Prices were to be confirmed upon monthly shipments in accordance with the reference price indicator (Qinhuangdao shipping price), and the guiding price (a product of government intervention) was repealed. In 2009, 651.68 million tons of coal was traded through the National Key Coal Suppliers, Transporters, and Users Docking Conference, accounting for only 20% of the overall transaction volume of coal in China in the same year. Of this, 389.22 million tons of coal was designated for power stations, much lower than the expected volume. Thus, the majority of coal had begun to be traded according to market forces.

In this way, with the market delivering a decisive "no" to government intervention in coal transactions, the functioning of the existing system ceased and a system reform towards allowing transactions to be governed by market forces was put in motion. At first, the government was reluctant to give up its stance of suppressing rapid price rises in the market through continued policy intervention. In order to rein in the surging price of coal, the Chinese government issued notices in June and August 2008, insisting to intervene in the price of coal to a certain extent by setting a cap on coal price hikes (in particular thermal coal) to within 8% year-on-year. However, coal mines, either by not selling or selling lower grade coal (lower calorific value), made it virtually impossible for the

Table 4.3 Electricity wholesale price to grid by type of power plant (2012)

| | Hydro | Coal-fired | Gas-fired | | Nuclear | Wind | | | Photovoltaic |
			Pipeline	LNG		Ground	Off-shore1	Off-shore2	
Selling price to grid (RMB/kWh)	0.27	0.46	0.57	0.72	0.45	0.54	0.62	0.74	1.00

Source: Author compilation based on press release by China Electricity Council.

government to keep coal prices artificially low through policy measures. Thanks to the market-oriented reforms conducted in all aspects of society, attempting to bind buyers and sellers together through mechanisms such as the coal order meeting would only result in ever-decreasing supplies.

Due to these developments, the price of coal began to rise sharply from the mid-2000s, continuing up to the autumn of 2012. Naturally, the generating cost of coal-fired thermal power rose due to increasing fuel costs; but the government maintained the system where it decided the electric power price and (apparently from social considerations) suppressed rises in price. As a result, a large number of power plants selling power below cost appeared, and 43% of power plants were said to be operating in the red in 2010. The worsening business conditions of power companies probably would hinder the stable supply of electric power; and in 2011 the government took decisive action to raise the wholesale price of power by the wide margin of 27% over the previous year's price of 0.36 yuan/kWh. Consequently, as indicated in Table 4.3, coal-fired thermal power was no longer an electric supply source that held a cost-competitive position in the energy mix.

It can be foreseen that coal-fired thermal power's deteriorating profitability will lead to a further loss of share in installed capacity for coal-fired thermal power. As seen in Figure 4.4, the value of investments in thermal power has declined sharply since 2006 – reaching its lowest point in 2012, when the price of coal peaked and was overtaken by hydropower for the first time. The rapid expansion of investments in nuclear power and other power supply sources (mostly wind power) has also forced down investments in coal-fired thermal power. Recalling that investment in coal-fired thermal power almost consistently maintained a share of about 80% for 30 years after China's Reform and Opening-up Policy, it can definitely be said that a huge structural transformation has occurred.

This section has analyzed factors other than policy encouraging the shift away from coal through the case of the electricity sector, which has the largest consumption of coal. It was pointed out that besides the tightening of environmental policy (analyzed in the first section) the deterioration of coal-fired thermal power's economic performance was a strong driving force propelling the shift away from coal. That economic performance played an important role in the shift away from coal can be demonstrated by Figures 4.4 and 4.5, where a slight return of

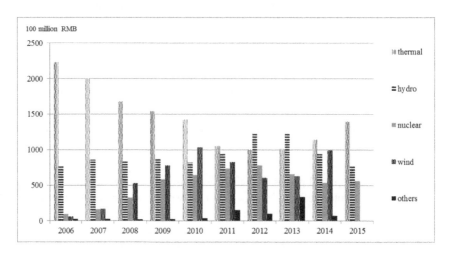

Figure 4.4 Investment for new power capacity by source
Sources: China Electricity Council annual report, each year.

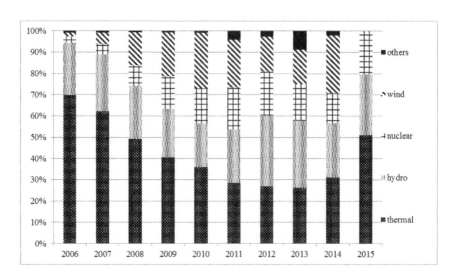

Figure 4.5 Share of investment for new power capacity by source
Sources: China Electricity Council annual report, each year.

investment towards thermal power can be seen after 2014. Environmental policy has also been tightening from 2013; but on the other hand, coal prices have fallen rapidly since the autumn of 2012, and the subsequent revival of economic performance is the reason for the return to coal-fired thermal power. The deterioration in the economic performance of coal was not a temporary phenomenon, because it was brought about by a reform of the system controlling the price and transactions of coal. The most important reform is the abandonment of the scheme for the government intervention in coal pricing, with the result that future coal prices will reflect the supply and demand balance for coal in the market. With the pressure holding down coal prices removed, the rapid rise in the price of coal according to supply and demand has already occurred and may occur again in the future.[3]

Political momentum towards a low carbon energy system at present and the future outlook

Let us now turn to the future outlook for the shift away from coal. It is worth noting, however, that there are a large number of uncertainties involved. In the changing economic conditions towards the "new normal," how far the economic growth rate will fall is a crucial factor influencing total energy demand (including coal). But this is extremely hard to predict. Moreover, how will the tightening of environmental restrictions move forward? Environmental regulations will undoubtedly tighten; but whether this will take the form of restrictions on the use of coal itself or simply as the encouragement of environmental countermeasures (where coal use continues under emissions-based regulations) is impossible to discern under present circumstances. This section will therefore attempt to suggest an outlook for the shift away from coal by organizing various factors the author believes should be especially highlighted.

Regardless of the trend in future economic growth rate, the development of the service sector will have an important impact on the growth of energy demand. There is a strong and widely held impression that since the Reform and Opening-up Policy economic growth in China has been driven forward by industrialization. But, as shown in Figure 4.6, the share of manufacturing industry (the secondary sector) has remained on the same level and, in recent years, has even shown signs of decline. In contrast, the share of service industries (the tertiary sector), despite occasionally dropping, has shown a rapidly rising trend – absorbing the fall in the share of agriculture (the primary sector). In 2012, the share of service industries finally overtook that of manufacturing industries to become the largest component of GDP. Even so, the share of the service industries was no more than 48%, indicating China's service economy to be still in the process of development when we recall that this share is 70 to 80% in developed countries. At present, China's economy is slowing down due to sluggish demand in the industrial sector for goods such as steel, coal, and cement; and considering that reductions in production capacity are being encouraged, it is highly unlikely that the speed of the shift towards the service economy will decline.

Despite the service sector accounting for almost half of GDP, its energy consumption share is a mere 16.7% (2015). Therefore, it is possible that the shift toward the service economy will curb increases in energy demand (which has been already brought about by the fall in the economic growth rate), placing downward pressure on the growth in energy consumption. Furthermore, energy consumption in almost the whole of the service sector relies not upon the direct

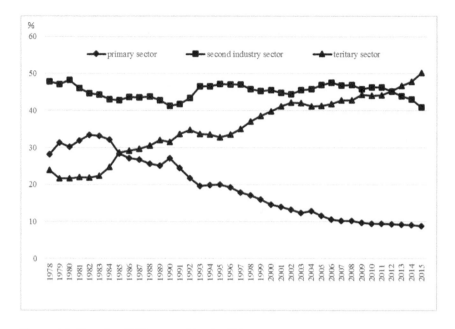

Figure 4.6 Changing GDP composition in China

Source: Author compilation based on National Bureau of Statistics of China (2017).

burning of coal but on electric power. Thus, as the shift toward a service economy proceeds, the demand for coal as fuel for coal-fired thermal power will see a rise in its share in the total demand for coal.[4]

How about the outlook for coal-fired thermal power? As we have discussed, investment in coal-fired thermal power has declined by a wide margin since 2007. Since the time required for constructing a coal-fired thermal power plant in China is about five years, the impact of the rapid decrease in investment will gradually become visible from 2016 onward; thereafter, an increase in the construction of new power plants will be limited for several years. In the current circumstances, however, the utilization rate of coal-fired thermal power plants is already declining. Thus, even if the introduction of new construction is delayed, the expanding operation of existing facilities will provide sufficient supply capacity. In addition, since coal prices began to decline again from the autumn of 2012, the economic performance of coal-fired thermal power has revived, resulting in a rebound of investments in coal-fired thermal power in 2014 and 2015. Concerned that a further drop in the coal-fired thermal power utilization rate might lead to a deterioration of profitability, the government has passed measures mandating a temporary suspension of power plant construction. The fact that investment in coal-fired thermal power is on the rise despite this situation, indicates that even if the utilization rate falls in a situation where the price of coal has sunk by a wide margin, coal-fired thermal power is assumed to be profitable because of the reduction of fuel costs. It can be said that the revival of coal-fired thermal power's economic performance and the increase in its installed capacity will offset the decline in coal demand.

On the other hand, in energy supply sources other than coal-fired thermal power (such as hydro, nuclear, wind, and photovoltaic power) cost reductions have also been occurring in recent years. As a result, coal-fired thermal power is no longer able to enjoy the overwhelmingly superior economic performance it once had. The government is also reacting to the low fuel costs brought about by the fall in coal prices with a reduction of the wholesale price of coal-fired power to the grid. The initial cost of capital investment is large for hydro, nuclear, wind, and photovoltaics, and their operational costs are far cheaper compared to coal-fired thermal power. That is, since fixed costs are high but marginal costs low, once they have been introduced there is an incentive to operate them at high utilization rates. Thus, as the shares of power supply sources other than existing coal-fired thermal power have presently expanded to levels far higher than before, it is highly likely that the utilization rate of coal-fired thermal power will be increasingly limited by the utilization of these other power supply sources.[5]

What, then, is the outlook for new power plant construction? The recovery in investments for coal-fired thermal power in 2014 and 2015 has been halted by policy for now; but what will become of this in the future?

One key is the trend in coal prices. The political campaign to reduce production capacity of the coal industry will have an important impact on prices. The government has put forward a target of shutting down coal mines with 500 million tons capacity and restructuring low-efficient coal mines to reduce capacity by a further 300 million tons by 2020. At the same time, by promoting merger and acquisitions (M&As) of small- and medium-sized coal mines by major firms, the government aims to consolidate the entire coal industry into company groups that have an annual scale of three million tons or more.

From 2015, when the price of coal dropped to as low of a level as in 2004, most of coal producing companies have fallen into the red. Since the closure of companies is not proceeding at a suitable pace and the supply of coal is not falling, there has been a serious impact on price from the decline in demand. The coal industry has seen a sharp expansion in capital investment in recent years (a total of 3.67 trillion yuan in the coal industry from 2006 to 2015). Therefore, even if coal companies are in the red, it is rational for them to continue to produce as long as the price exceeds the marginal cost because they can earn cash to repay the loan. It is because of the existence of a large number of such companies that the overall supply of coal is not falling. In response to this oversupply problem, which cannot be resolved by the market in a short period of time, it is expected that if supply cutbacks are begun by government intervention, the price of coal will bottom out and begin to rise again.[6] In this case, willingness for investment in coal-fired thermal power is likely to decrease.

One further key is the extent to which environmental regulations will be tightened. As political factors are influential, despite making the future hard to foresee, let us first examine the impact on coal use by environmental regulations already in place. We will firstly look at China's commitment to the Paris Agreement.

Regarding the Intended National Determined Contributions announced by China in June 2015 (prior to COP21), the Chinese government put forward targets of a 60 to 65% reduction in CO_2 emissions per unit of GDP by 2030 (compared with the baseline year of 2005) and increasing the share of non-fossil fuels in primary energy consumption to around 20%, leading to a peak in CO_2 emissions at around 2030.

China's setting of CO_2 emissions reduction targets by associating them with GDP has been frequently criticized in the past. The reason is that, in a situation where GDP is growing and the industrial structure, for example, shifts toward industries that use less energy, the index will improve even if the absolute value of emissions is not reduced. As mentioned above (Figure 4.4), though it is clear that the trend (from the 1980s onward) has been for service industries to increase their share within the Chinese economy, the manufacturing industry has seen slower growth triggered by wage rises in recent years and a simultaneous rapid expansion of investment in labor-saving technology. Great hopes are also pinned on the labor-absorbing feature of service industries; and industrial policy to promote service industries is likely to be strengthened in the future. Based on these points, it can be said that China will have promising conditions for achieving the reduction targets for CO_2 emissions per unit of GDP. In fact, as of 2014, the achievement status of the CO_2 emissions reduction targets per unit of GDP compared with 2005 showed a 33.8% improvement – an attainment of more than half the target in nine years with a sufficiently comfortable margin of 16 years remaining to complete the target. Considering that there is strong potential for progress in the transformation of the industrial structure, it seems we can take an optimistic view toward a rise in the share of tertiary industries.

At the same time, the share of non-fossil energy was 6.5% in 2005, and this had risen to 12.0% (up 5.5 points) in 2015. This is still 8 points short of the 2030 target; but based on the performance thus far the target may just about be achieved. There is likely to be a certain degree of difficulty attached to introducing an absolute supply volume of relatively expensive renewable energy sources. What we should surmise from the level of these targets is that there is a strong possibility that the rapid speed in the introduction of hydro, nuclear, wind, and photovoltaic power in the past ten years will continue into the future, though it is unlikely that this pace of introduction will increase.

In addition, it is also necessary to examine the outlook for a tightening of regulations for conventional air pollution countermeasures, especially PM2.5. At present, regulations have been introduced to restrict the use of coal through only a switch from coal to gas for consumer use and in small- to medium-sized industrial boilers in urban areas. No other regulations to restrict the use of coal have been introduced except for low-grade (such as high-sulfur) coals. However, in the winter of 2017, the replacement of coal-fired boilers by gas-fired ones was widely implemented in the provinces located in northern China. For example, in Hebei province (near from Beijing), 2.6 million households heating equipment and coal-fired boilers with 11,700 t/h capacity were replaced by gas-fired boilers, although only 1.8 million households and 4,500 t/h coal-fired boilers were scheduled in the original plan. The reason why 2.6 times boilers and 40% more households heating equipment were replaced lies in the political campaign started by Prime Minister Li's announcement of "Defensive War for Blue Sky" on March 2017. According to news reports, a notice requiring the replacement of coal-fired heating and boilers was suddenly sent to heating supply companies in many northern provinces around September. In spite of short notice, heat supply companies purchased gas-fired boilers at once to meet the deadline because they knew this as part of a political initiative. However, the result was a severe shortage of gas supply and gas (LNG) prices tripling only for two months. As a result, heating supply companies lost sales and users shivered in the cold. This is one example demonstrating that a strong policy neglecting market mechanisms often turns out unsustainable.

Except for the switch from coal to gas in winter 2017, formal environmental regulations mainly consist of emissions criteria. Of these, the adoption of "ultra-low emissions regulation" for coal-fired thermal power plants is having a great impact on coal use. Coal-fired thermal power is being required to make large improvements to comply with emissions regulations at a similar level as those imposed on gas-fired thermal power. The regulations are 10 mg/Nm^3 for soot dust (the current criterion being 30 mg/Nm^3), 35 mg/Nm^3 for SO_2 (the current criterion being 100 mg/Nm^3), and 50 mg/Nm^3 for NOx (the current criterion also being 100 mg/Nm^3). As such, the environmental countermeasures are near the same technological level as those of Japan, the highest level in the world.[7] The implementation rates in China for the installation of desulfurization and denitrification equipment have already reached 92.8% and 95.0% respectively at the end of 2015; but a gap has opened up between Japan and China due to the low level of the pollutant-stripping ratio of equipment in the latter country. As the tactic for adopting ultra-low emissions regulation is technological modification of environmental countermeasure equipment, the generating cost of coal-fired thermal power will naturally rise.

Technological development of equipment to meet the ultra-low emissions regulation has already been implemented in a number of power stations from 2015. For instance, one of the five largest power generating groups, the China Huaneng Group, had completed the remodeling of environmental countermeasure equipment at power plants equivalent to 22.3% of its total installed capacity by the end of 2015. In fact, these plants with new environmental countermeasure equipment have all realized emissions restrictions up to a level that exceeds the ultra-low emissions regulation.[8] Indeed, the domestic technology to meet these targets already exists in China. The problem, therefore, is how much the generating cost of coal-fired thermal power will rise as a result of these countermeasures. It has not been possible to obtain data for all power plants in China; but for power plants where studies have been conducted, the rise in generating cost has been kept down to around 5%. Owing to this ability to meet about the same level of environmental regulations as Japan with such a low degree of cost increase is the improvement of China's environmental technology. Furthermore, based on the supply chain for raw materials (which has become more sophisticated through competition and economies of scale), Chinese companies have cultivated the ability to cut costs during the process of industrialization. The tightening of environmental regulations that can be expected at present will not lead to great a suppression of coal-fired thermal power output; and it can be foreseen that the suppressive effect on overall coal demand will not be all that large.

The direction of important factors related to the outlook for a shift away from coal has been thus examined. Coal demand will be strongly influenced by the degree to which the economic growth rate declines; but it is expected to decline even more than the slowdown in economic growth would imply due to the progressing transformation towards a service economy. With this, there will be stronger downward pressure to reduce the direct use of coal by the industrial sector than other energy sources. At the same time, however, the targets indicated in the Paris Agreement will not impose a strong limit on coal use. Therefore, regarding coal-fired thermal power, which will be the main use for coal in the future due to shifts of economic engines toward the service sector, the adoption of the ultra-low emissions regulation will bring about countermeasures to combat conventional air pollution and CO_2 reduction. There are few factors inhibiting the expansion of coal-fired thermal power in spite of adverse wind to coal use on the whole.

However, since the China's commitment for the Paris Agreement also has targets related to the share of non-fossil fuel energy, electric supply sources other than coal-fired power are expected to advance at the pace of the last ten years. That is, the shift away from coal will go forward at a similar pace thus far. Moreover, whether the shift away from coal will accelerate or not will depend on growth in coal-fired thermal power; and an important factor influencing that growth is thought to be the economic performance of coal-fired thermal power. The trend in the price of coal thus holds the key; and if cuts in production capacity of the coal industry go ahead successfully, the continuously falling coal prices will bottom out and begin to rise once again (and in fact, on December 2016, coal prices turned and increased to double the level at the end of 2015). If that occurs, it will be a factor working toward the acceleration of the shift away from coal. If, on the other hand, coal prices fall even further due to a large fall in the economic growth rate and the advance of the service economy, there is also the strong possibility that the shift away from coal will decelerate.

Conclusion: the importance of market competition and economic incentives in low carbonization in China

This chapter has conducted an analysis of the rapidly advancing shift away from coal (low carbonization) by considering political factors such as environmental regulations and the economic factor of the economic performance of coal use. It is unmistakably true that the tightening of environmental regulations since the 11th FYP has provided tailwind for the shift away from coal. At the same time, the introduction of hydro, nuclear, wind, and photovoltaic power has progressed, leading to a decline in the facility utilization rate of coal-fired thermal power plants. Reform of the coal transaction and pricing system also removed factors suppressing coal prices, and the sharp rise in the price of coal brought about the loss of economic performance for coal use. As a result, the shift away from coal advanced. There is a tendency for political factors alone to receive attention in connection with China's shift away from coal; but it has become clear that changes in economic factors have had an important impact too.

The outlook for the future shift away from coal has been examined on the basis of these findings. There are factors that are difficult to forecast in the "new normal" economy, such as the fall in the economic growth rate and the tightening of environmental regulations. But as there is no certainty about strong restrictions being placed on the use of coal as a response to the Paris Agreement or as countermeasure against conventional air pollution, it is expected that the shift away from coal will progress at a similar pace to that of the past ten years in response to the targets for the share of non-fossil fuel energy set forth in the Paris Agreement. Moreover, while it is thought that the economic performance of coal will have an impact on whether or not the shift away from coal will accelerate, the price of coal – the key to the whole situation – is likely to be influenced by policy cutting the production capacity of the coal industry, and it will be necessary to pay due attention to developments in this area in the future.

Notes

1 Other forms of energy, such as oil and natural gas, are also the same, which are not the main topic of this chapter.
2 In this system, price under the "plan" was termed "mandatory price" in fact.
3 At present the price of coal is hovering at a low level, but this is quite natural when the price reflects the market supply and demand.
4 Other factors thought to have a significantly large impact on the demand for coal are coal liquification and gasification, as well as the demand for coal as a raw material in the chemical industry. This demand for coal by the chemical industry is thought to be one of the few growth areas for coal; but the margin available for growth depends on the levels of the international prices of crude oil and natural gas. In the present situation, where prices for crude oil and natural gas remain depressed, not only is the coal-chemical industry uncompetitive on a cost basis, future growth in demand cannot be considered to be all that large. On the other hand, rapid growth is possible if crude oil and natural gas prices begin to rise again.
5 Wind power and photovoltaic power have the problem of intermittent output, and power transmission and distribution companies are often reluctant to connect them to the utility grid. For example, regarding wind power in the past, grid connection was delayed in China and there was a time when 40% of power capacity was unused. However, this percentage later fell rapidly and is currently 15%. Thus, looking at the rapid introduction of wind and photovoltaic power in China, the delay in grid connection should perhaps be seen as an unavoidable circumstance brought about by the failure of connection work to keep pace with installation rather than as reluctance on the part of power transmission and distribution companies to connect them to the grid.
6 Depending on the region, mines in China are central to employment provision and tax revenues, and thus regional governments are obsessively devoted to prolonging the

life of "zombie companies" through means such as granting subsidies or continuing to finance them by putting pressure on local banks. It is therefore difficult to foresee whether mine closure measures will be successful or not; but it is thought that there is sufficient potential for success if additional policies (such as those implemented in Japan and the USA) are introduced, including unemployment countermeasures through public finance means already in place, a system of buyouts and dissolutions, or funding for restructuring zombie companies as small- and medium-sized enterprises for surplus facilities through public finance.

7   For example, in the case of Japan's Isogo Thermal Power Plant, the criteria are 5 mg/ Nm^3 for soot dust, 27 mg/Nm^3 for SO_2 and 25 mg/Nm^3 for NOx.

8   The specific content of the modification consists of the installation of wet type electrical dust eliminators prior to flue-gas stacks as a PM countermeasure, installation of a dual desulfurization process with refinement of the desulfurization reaction for desulfurization measures (in addition to management of the sulfur content of coal before entry into the furnace), and the refinement of low-NOx combustion technology using a combination of selective non-catalytic reduction (SNCR) and selective catalytic reduction (SCR).

References

China Coal Industry Association (2011) *Compiling Statistical Book on China Coal Industry 1949–2009*, Beijing: China Coal Industry Publishing House.

International Energy Agency (2009) *Cleaner Coal in China*, Paris: IEA-OECD.

National Bureau of Statistics of China (2017) *China Statistical Yearbook 2016*, Beijing: China Statistics Press.

Yue, F. (eds.) (2010) *Annual Report on Coal Industry in China*, Beijing: Social Sciences Academic Press (in Chinese).

Yue, F. (eds.) (2011) *Annual Report on Coal Industry in China*, Beijing: Social Sciences Academic Press (in Chinese).

Yue, F. (eds.) (2012) *Annual Report on Coal Industry in China*, Beijing: Social Sciences Academic Press (in Chinese).

Yue, F. (eds.) (2013) *Annual Report on Coal Industry in China*, Beijing: Social Sciences Academic Press (in Chinese).

Yue, F. (eds.) (2014) *Annual Report on Coal Industry in China*, Beijing: Social Sciences Academic Press (in Chinese).

Yue, F. (eds.) (2015) *Annual Report on Coal Industry in China*, Beijing: Social Sciences Academic Press (in Chinese).

5 To what extent must increasing natural gas imports contribute to pollution control and sustainable energy supply in China?

Mika Takehara

Introduction

Since the 11th Five-Year Plan (FYP) period (2006–10), the Chinese government has promoted the transformation of its energy production and utilization policy to achieve comprehensive, balanced, and sustainable development of its energy, economy, and environment. The government has promoted energy saving, efficiency improvement, emissions reduction, and energy diversification. The government has identified natural gas as an effective resource, along with nuclear and wind power, for achieving diversification of energy resources and reducing air pollution in China. The government has promoted the substitution of natural gas for coal and oil. Natural gas consumption has quadrupled in the past ten years, now accounting for 6% of primary energy consumption. The Chinese government has projected that the share of natural gas in primary energy consumption will reach between 8.3% and 10% by 2020.

Chinese and international research institutions, such as the Development Research Center of the State Council (DRC) and the International Energy Agency (IEA), expect that Chinese natural gas demand will increase over the medium to long term. They view the manufacturing industry, power generation, and heat supply as key drivers of demand growth. Currently, dependency on imports of natural gas has reached approximately 40%, and domestic gas production will be unable to satisfy the increase in demand.

This raises the question of how much China must increase gas imports to achieve its carbon reduction target and satisfy its energy demand until 2030. We hypothesize that the Chinese government and national oil companies have been continuing resource-related infrastructure investments, such as pipelines and liquefied natural gas (LNG) regasification terminals, and have been seeking gas purchase agreements in preparation to increase natural gas imports to almost four times of their current level by 2030. They assume that the volumes of imported gas achieved by 2030 can satisfy their air pollution reduction target and secure a stable supply of energy. To examine this hypothesis, we estimate Chinese natural gas supply and demand in 2030.

This paper is organized as follows. We review the current status of supply and demand of natural gas in the second section. In the third section, based on the medium- to long-term supply and demand scenarios of Chinese and international institutions such as the DRC, the China Energy Research Society (CERS), which is a subsidiary academic organization of the China Association for Science and Technology (CAST), and the IEA, we estimate Chinese natural gas demand in 2030, and find that domestic gas production will be unable to satisfy the demand growth. In the fourth section, we estimate how much natural gas China should import in 2030 to meet their environmental targets and satisfy the increase in demand.

Current status of supply and demand of natural gas

Supply and demand in 2015

The Chinese government expected that the share of natural gas in energy consumption would reach 7% by the end of the 12th FYP period in 2015. This was not a target with penalties but rather a forecast based on policy implementation. However, this expectation was incorrect and the actual figure of gas consumption was only 5.9% (excluding coal-based gas such as coalbed methane, coal mine methane, and coal-to-gas), according to *China Oil, Gas, and Petrochemicals* (Xinhua News Agency).

Besides consumption, the Chinese government's expectation of domestic supply was also incorrect. According to "A Work Scheme on Air Pollution Control in the Energy Sector" (NDRC/NEA/MEP) released in May 2014, the government expected natural gas supply would reach 145 billion cubic meter (bcm) by 2015, but the actual figure was only 129 bcm – about 16 bcm (11%) short of the government's expectation (Table 5.1).

The Chinese government has identified natural gas as an effective resource for diversifying energy resources and implementing environmental policies (e.g., reducing air pollution), and it promotes natural gas together with non-fossil energy such as nuclear and wind power. The government has promoted substitution of natural gas for coal and oil. According to the *China Energy Statistical Yearbook 2015*, natural gas consumption increased from 47 bcm in 2005 to 187 bcm in 2014, almost quadrupling during those ten years (Figure 5.1).

Table 5.1 Government forecasts and actual results of natural gas supply and demand in 2015

	2015		Attainment rate
	Actual	Government forecasts	
Share of natural gas in primary energy consumption	5.9%	7.0%	84%
Supply of natural gas	129 bcm	145 bcm	89% (below 16 bcm)
Import	57 bcm	80 bcm	71%
Demand	186 bcm	225 bcm	83% (below 39 bcm)

Sources: *China Oil, Gas, and Petrochemicals* (Xinhua News Agency), "A Work Scheme on Air Pollution Control in the Energy Sector" (NDRC/NEA/MEP 2014).

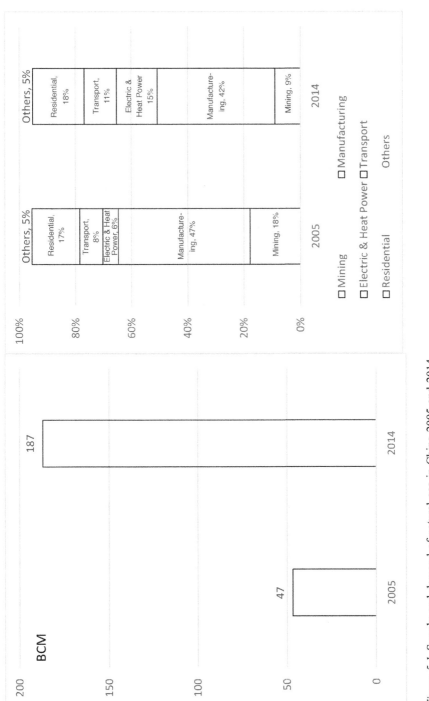

Figure 5.1 Supply and demand of natural gas in China 2005 and 2014

Source: Author compilation based on the *China Energy Statistical Yearbook 2015*.

Environmental policies have accelerated the use of natural gas, especially in the electric power and heating, transportation, and residential sectors. Substitution of natural gas boilers for coal-fired boilers for industrial and residential use has progressed, and natural gas vehicles have emerged in the public transportation sector. Also, conversion from coal to gas for home cooking has grown significantly.

However, natural gas consumption growth has been sluggish due to the economic slowdown in China since 2013. Manufacturing sector use accounts for almost 40% of gas consumption. In addition, regulated wholesale natural gas lost its price competitiveness versus other fuels. The price of crude oil dropped dramatically with the global price downturn since the second half of 2014.

Natural gas demand has sharply increased in the past ten years in China. China's domestic natural gas production cannot satisfy demand growth, so the country began to import LNG in 2006 and natural gas via pipelines in 2010. Dependency on imports of natural gas has reached nearly 30% in 2015. Due to the economic downturn and low prices of other fuels, growth in gas demand has been sluggish since 2013, with gas supply exceeding demand growth, leading to oversupply. In China, both LNG and pipeline purchase agreements contain take-or-pay clauses with long terms up to 20–25 years, and the amount delivered is gradually increasing.

Current status of natural gas imports (pipeline and LNG)

In 2015, natural gas imports increased by 3.4%, or 60 bcm year-on-year. The volume of gas imported via pipeline accounted for 56% of total gas imports, and imported LNG accounted for the rest. In 2015, imported pipeline gas volume were 33 bcm, up 7.2% (2 bcm) year-on-year. LNG import volumes were 27 bcm (19 million metric tons [MMt]), down 1.1% year-on-year. Net natural gas imports (excluding exports to Hong Kong) stood at 57 bcm, up 2.4% year-on-year in 2015, and gas imported via pipeline and imported LNG together accounted for 30% of consumption. Turkmenistan is the biggest supplier of gas to China, accounting for 46% of total imports in 2015. Australia is the biggest supplier of imported LNG to China, accounting for 12% of total LNG imports.

Pipeline gas imports

China imports natural gas from Turkmenistan, Uzbekistan, Kazakhstan, and Myanmar via four existing pipelines (Table 5.2). Three pipelines from Central Asia (Lines A to C) and Myanmar to China are in operation. China is also preparing for the construction of other pipelines from Central Asia (Line D) and Russia (Power of Siberia 1). The annual transmission capacity of the pipelines in operation has reached 72 bcm and is expected to reach 135 bcm once all pipelines under construction are completed.

Chinese policy banks, such as the China Development Bank and the Export-Import Bank of China, provided financing support to the above-mentioned

Table 5.2 Transmission capacity of major international natural gas pipelines to China

Route	Annual transmission capacity (bcm)	Current status
Turkmenistan-Uzbekistan-China (Line A to C)	30 to expand 55	Started operation in 2010
Turkmenistan-Kyrgyzstan-China (Line D)	30	Planned to start operation in 2022
Myanmar-China	12	Started operation in 2013
Russia-China eastern route (Power of Siberia 1)	38	Planned to start operation in 2019
Total	135	

Source: Author compilation.

gas-exporting countries for the pipelines and related infrastructure investment. It is often said that construction of an international pipeline will need at least ten years because of the difficulty of obtaining financing and coordinating related parties. Nonetheless, China was able to construct the pipelines and expand supply in a short time by providing financing support for pipeline construction and related gas field development. The Chinese approach seems not only to save the time but also to derive various benefits through acquisition of contracts, such as those for gas field development and provision of technical services.

China has been importing natural gas from Turkmenistan since January 2010, and imported 27 bcm in 2015. By volume, imports from Turkmenistan account for 46% of total gas imports and 76% of pipeline gas imports, making it China's biggest supplier of natural gas.

In July 2007, China National Petroleum Corporation (CNPC, China's largest national oil company) reached several agreements with the Turkmenistan State Agency for Management and Use of Hydrocarbon Resources and Turkmengaz, including one for the construction of a multinational natural gas pipeline (the "Central Asia Pipeline") from Turkmenistan to Horgos, Xinjiang Autonomous Region. This pipeline has a total length of 2,000 km and a designed annual transmission capacity of 30 bcm. CNPC signed an agreement to explore and develop gas fields on the right bank of the Amu Darya River, as well as a gas sales and purchase agreement. The two countries subsequently agreed to increase the sales and purchase volume to 65 bcm annually.

To construct the Central Asia Pipeline, China organized joint ventures with the Central Asian countries along the pipeline, and completed the pipeline in December 2009. China began to import natural gas from Turkmenistan in 2010 and from Uzbekistan in 2012. In 2015, China imported 1.5 bcm of natural gas from Uzbekistan. China signed a gas sales and purchase agreement with Uzbekistan for up to 10 bcm annually, but failed to reach that volume due to increased domestic demand in Uzbekistan and the sluggish export volume.

Though China began to import gas from Kazakhstan in 2013, it is not through the Central Asia Pipeline, unlike imports from Turkmenistan and Uzbekistan.

Guanghui Energy Co., Ltd. – a private company based in Xinjiang, China – has a contract area in which it can explore oil and gas fields in Kazakhstan. Guanghui constructed a short-distance pipeline from the contract area to the company's own natural gas liquefaction plant in Xinjiang. In 2015, Guanghui reduced imports due to China's oversupply of natural gas and the decreased competitiveness of LNG.

China signed a gas sale and purchase agreement with Myanmar and related companies in December 2008. China organized joint ventures with Myanmar, constructed a gas pipeline with a total length of 793 km from the Shwe gas field off the coast of Myanmar to Ruili, Yunnan Province, in southwest China. Imports via this pipeline began in 2013, and China imported 3.9 bcm from Myanmar in 2015.

LNG imports

The global LNG trade reached 245 MMt in 2015, with Asia being a main consumer of LNG, accounting for 72%, or 177 MMt. Japan is the largest LNG importer with a share of 35% (approximately 85 MMt). China accounts for 8% of imports overall and became the third largest LNG importer in the world after Japan and South Korea.

China mainly imports LNG from Southeast Asia and Oceania, especially Australia, Malaysia, Indonesia, and Papua New Guinea, under long-term sales and purchase agreements (over 20 years). Australia is China's largest LNG supplier and provides 28% of its LNG imports and 12% of its total gas imports. China's next-largest supplier is Qatar, which is the largest LNG supplier in the world. Chinese national oil companies signed several long-term LNG purchase agreements with Qatar.

In China, 14 LNG regasification terminals were in operation with a regasification capacity of 48.8 MMt/year (66 bcm/year) in 2015. Including regasification terminals under construction, China has 19 terminals with a regasification capacity of 60 MMt/year (81 bcm/year) (Table 5.3).

China's LNG imports have been steadily growing from 2006 to 2013, but have slowed since 2013 due to oversupply. The manufacturing sector accounts for 40% of gas consumption in China, but the country's economic slowdown directly hit demand in this sector. In addition, the wholesale prices of natural

Table 5.3 LNG regasification capacity in China, as of 2015

State	Number of plants	Capacity
In operation	14	48.8 MMt (66 bcm)
Under construction	5	11 MMt (15 bcm)
Total	19	59.8 MMt (81 bcm)

Source: Author compilation.

gas are regulated in China, and it lost price competitiveness due to the prices of other fuels, such as crude oil and coal, dropping substantially since the second half of 2014.

In spite of the downturn in demand, there is oversupply because sales and purchase agreements for both LNG and pipelines are mostly on a long-term (at least 25 years) take-or-pay basis. The import volume of LNG in 2015 showed a year-on-year decrease for the first time since 2006.

Forecast demand for natural gas by Chinese and international institutions

Despite the recent uncertainty in demand due to China's "new normal" and the slow pace of gas price reform, medium- to long-term growth of China's natural gas demand is expected by the Chinese government and international research institutions such as the DRC and IEA. According to their projections, gas demand growth will accelerate, especially in industry, power generation, and heat supply. They projected that China's gas production will be unable to satisfy its increased demand and that the country will need more imported gas.

IEA's outlook for natural gas supply and demand in China

The IEA projected that China will have a larger gas market than the European Union by the 2030s according to the World Energy Outlook 2015 IEA (2015) released in November 2015.

According to IEA (2015), China's natural gas demand will reach 315 bcm in 2020 and 483 bcm in 2030 (Figure 5.2). The size of the increase between 2020 and 2030 is expected to reach 168 bcm (an annual average growth rate of 4.4%, 17 bcm). Chinese gas demand in 2030 will be nearly 2.6 times that in 2015. The share of natural gas consumption in the energy mix will rise to 7.3% in 2020 and 9.7% in 2030. IEA (2015) considers that the substitution of natural gas for coal as fuel will progress, particularly in industry, power generation, and heat supply.

According to IEA (2015), China's natural gas supply will reach 172 bcm in 2020 and 260 bcm in 2030. In 2030, it will be double the 2015 levels. This projection seems to largely depend on unconventional gas production growth. Unconventional gas production will reach 88 bcm in 2030 (annual average growth rate of 4.2%, 9 bcm). This seems too ambitious. If all projections of the IEA (2015) become a reality, the gap between supply and demand will reach 143 bcm in 2020 and 223 bcm in 2030. Dependency on gas imports is expected to exceed 40% in 2030.

DRC's outlook for natural gas supply and demand in China

The share of natural gas supply in primary energy consumption is currently around 5.9%. The Chinese government expects this to increase to 10% by 2020 and at least 15% by 2030. "The Energy Development Strategy Action Plan"

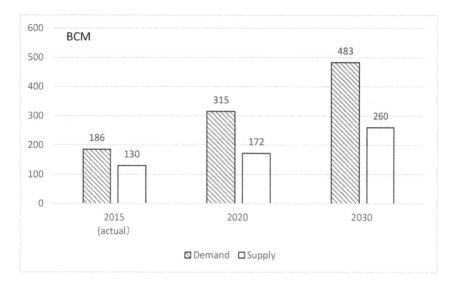

Figure 5.2 IEA's estimation of supply and demand of natural gas in China
Source: Author compilation based on IEA (2015).

released by the State Council in November 2014 set the 2020 energy consumption target at 4,800 million tons of coal equivalent (tce) (3,360 million tons of oil equivalent [toe]) and the percentage of primary energy accounted for by natural gas consumption at 10% (360 bcm) or higher. The Chinese government has revised its forecasts downward in light of the current economic slowdown and the oversupply of natural gas.

In May 2016, the DRC presented gas supply and demand outlooks at a conference in Beijing. According to the DRC, gas demand will reach 360 bcm by 2020. The breakdown of the demand outlook is 88 bcm (24%) for town gas, 40 bcm (11%) for transportation, 108 bcm (30%) for industry, 88 bcm (24%) for power generation and heat supply, and 36 bcm (10%) for chemicals.

According to the DRC, the gas supply capacity will reach 420 bcm in 2020, exceeding the demand outlook by 60 bcm. Domestic production capacity will reach 280 bcm (67%), broken down as follows: conventional gas will account for 210 bcm (50%) and unconventional gas (including shale gas) will account for 70 bcm (12%). Imported gas will reach 140 bcm (34%), with pipeline gas and LNG accounting for 70 bcm (17%), respectively.

CERS's outlook for natural gas demand in China

According to the *China Energy Outlook 2030* (China Energy Research Society 2016), a subsidiary academic organization of CAST, energy consumption will increase to 4,800 million tce (3,360 million toe) in March 2016 and 5,300 million tce (3,710 million toe) in 2030 (Figure 5.3).

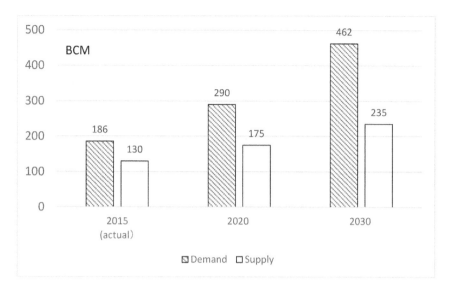

Figure 5.3 CERS's estimation of supply and demand of natural gas in China
Source: Author compilation based on China Energy Outlook 2030.

Demand for natural gas will reach 290 bcm in 2020 and 462 bcm in 2030. The size of the increase between 2020 and 2030 is projected to be 172 bcm (an annual average growth rate of 4.8%, 17 bcm). The share of natural gas in energy consumption will reach 6.1% in 2020 and 8.9% in 2030. Despite consumption in the industrial sector gradually declining, CERS projects that consumption will grow significantly, especially in the manufacturing industry. According to CERS, substitution of natural gas for fuel from coal will progress and the potential demand for power generation and heat supply seems to be high. Demand in the transportation sector is expected to increase along with the steady growth of LNG vehicles. CERS also points out that gas demand will have some uncertainties, such as gas price, the development of the pipeline network systems, and the structural adjustment of the economy, and industry in China appears to be the key driver of the demand growth.

Medium- to long-term outlook for natural gas imports

According to the IEA, natural gas demand will reach 315 bcm in 2020 and 483 bcm in 2030. Similarly, natural gas imports will reach 143 bcm in 2020 and 223 bcm in 2030. According to CERS, natural gas demand will reach 290 bcm in 2020 and 462 bcm in 2030. Similarly, natural gas imports will reach 155 bcm in 2020 and 265 bcm in 2030 (Figure 5.4).

In 2015, the actual gas demand reached 186 bcm and gas imports reached 57 bcm. According to the projections of the IEA and CERS, gas demand should

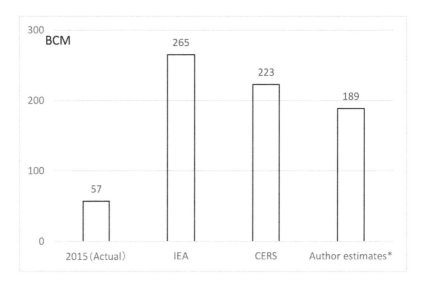

Figure 5.4 Estimations of natural gas imports to China

Sources: Author compilation based on IEA, CERS, and author estimates (based on the average annual growth gas imports growth in 2011–15).

increase by 21–26 bcm each year over the 13th FYP period. The annual average increase in gas demand over the 12th FYP period was only 17 bcm. If we adopt a more conservative assumption of future gas demand based on past five-year average growth rates, it will still reach 262 bcm in 2020. The demand outlooks of the IEA and CERS would be 28–53 bcm (annual average 5–10 bcm) higher in 2020 and 45–66 bcm (annual average 5–7 bcm) higher in 2030 than estimates made using the past five-year average of demand growth. Similarly, according to the scenarios of the IEA and CERS, gas imports should increase by 17–20 bcm each year over the next five years to reach 143–155 bcm in 2020. If we assume the past five-year average growth rates will continue, then gas imports will be 101 bcm in 2020. The outlooks for gas imports by the IEA and CERS would be 42–54 bcm (annual average 8–11 bcm) higher in 2020, and 34–76 bcm (annual average 3–8 bcm) higher in 2030 than estimates made using the past five-year average of demand growth.

Since 2013, China has faced with natural gas oversupply due to its economic slowdown, lower oil prices, and other factors. Given the current situation, these outlooks seem to reflect political expectations of the Chinese government and appear too optimistic. Nonetheless, under the more conservative assumption based on the past five-year average growth, gas imports will exceed 100 bcm in 2020, close to double the current level, and will reach at least 200 bcm in 2030, 3.5 times higher than the current level.

Import infrastructure development and securing
purchase agreements

China is promoting the development of gas import infrastructure to meet its future gas demand. China has currently developed import infrastructure such as pipelines, LNG regasification terminals, and natural gas storage facilities. Combined pipeline gas and LNG import capacities to reach 210 bcm annually when facilities under construction are included, with pipelines accounting for 60%, or 130 bcm, annually. Moreover, China has secured gas purchase agreements that will approach 200 bcm in 2020, and this is expected to satisfy the supply gap until at least 2020.

Natural gas demand may fluctuate due to various circumstances such as policy and economic conditions, gas price reform, and natural gas-related infrastructure development. The long-term gas demand is highly uncertain. However, imported natural gas should increase in the medium to long term, helping to achieve the objectives of reducing air pollution and securing a stable energy supply. The Chinese government and companies continue to secure more purchase agreements in preparation for such fluctuations and uncertainty.

Concluding remarks

Chinese and international institutions, such as the DRC, CERS, and IEA, assume that gas demand will increase in the medium to long term through the substitution of natural gas for coal and oil, especially in industry, power generation, and heat supply.

The outlooks for natural gas imports in 2030 by the IEA and CERS are 223 and 265 bcm, 3.5 and 4.6 times the current levels, respectively. However, natural gas demand has slowed and China currently has an oversupply of natural gas, mainly due to the country's economic slowdown and the oil price collapse since 2013. Even if we adopt a more conservative assumption of future gas demand based on the average growth rate during the 12th FYP period (2011–15), it will still reach 189 bcm in 2030, which is 3.5 times the current level. China will have to increase the volume of natural gas imported over the medium to long term to achieve its targets for reducing air pollution and securing a stable energy supply.

References

China Energy Research Society (2016) *China Energy Outlook 2030*. Economy & Management Publishing House, http://www.e-mp.com.cn/.
China's State Council (2013) *The 12th Five Year Energy Development Plan*, http://www.gov.cn/zwgk/2013-01/23/content_2318554.htm.
China's State Council (2014) *The Energy Development Strategy Action Plan*,
http://www.gov.cn/zhengce/content/2014-11/19/content_9222.htm.
IEA (2015) *IEA World Energy Outlook 2015*, Paris, https://www.iea.org/publications/freepublications/publication/IEA (2015).pdf.

6 Income distribution effects of a carbon tax in China

Kiyoshi Fujikawa, Zuoyi Ye, and Hikari Ban

Introduction

China has become the largest CO_2 emitting country in the world with rapid economic growth in recent years and a coal-dependent energy consumption structure. China's CO_2 emissions in 1990 were no more than 2.46 billion t-CO_2, but this increased rapidly to 7.03 billion t-CO_2 in 2008. In terms of world share, China's share in 1990 was only 11.0%, which was less than half of the US share of 21.9%. However, its share in 2008 reached as high as 21.9%, which was more than the US share of 17.0% (5.46 billion t-CO_2).[1]

The main reason for this increase in CO_2 emissions is an increase in the energy consumed by China's rapid economic growth; to make matters worse, most of China's energy consumption comes from coal whose CO_2 emissions is the highest among fossil fuels. Table 6.1 shows China's primary energy consumption by energy source. One can see that consumption has increased rapidly, especially after 2000. Coal consumption has increased the most among the three fossil fuels, coal, oil, and natural gas, and now coal accounts for more than 70 percent of the total primary energy consumption of China.

The UN Framework Convention on Climate Change (UNFCCC), the 21st Conference of the Parties (COP21), was held in November–December, 2015 in Paris where the framework on the target and quotas of CO_2 emissions reduction after 2020 was discussed. The Chinese government announced a 60% to 65% reduction of CO_2 intensity per GDP from 2005 levels and a peak-out of CO_2 emissions around 2030. It announced in March 2016 the 13th five-year plan, which includes the reduction of CO_2 emissions by 18% and of a decrease of CO_2 intensity per GDP during the plan period. Central and local governments put in place development plans named low-carbon economic strategy or low-carbon development strategy aimed at reducing the carbon footprint and began to enforce such laws as the "Energy Conservation Law," or "Environmental Protection Law."

One of the policies considered to reduce CO_2 emissions is the introduction of a carbon tax. Carbon tax was first introduced by Finland in 1990 before spreading to other European countries such as Norway, Sweden, Denmark, the Netherlands, Germany, Italy, Britain, France, and Switzerland as well as to Canada. The tax system varies greatly to meet the different conditions in the countries.[2] In October

Table 6.1 Primary energy consumption in China

	1980	1990	2000	2010	2014
Coal	313	528	665	1,789	2,012
Oil	89	119	221	428	504
Natural gas	12	13	21	89	154
Others	184	211	228	309	382
Total	598	871	1,135	2,615	3,052

Source: Authors' compilation based on the *EDMC Handbook of Energy & Economic Statistics in Japan* (Institute of Energy Economics 2017).

2012, Japan also introduced a carbon tax, with the tax rate on CO_2 determined as 289 JPY/t-CO_2, or approximately 3 USD/t-CO, for all fossil fuels; the tax revenue is used for CO_2 mitigation measures.

Introduction of a carbon tax will increase energy prices, and this increase will reduce fossil fuel consumption or give an impetus to carbon-free energy development, which will lead to a reduction of CO_2 emissions. This is the principle behind the market-based CO_2 mitigation measures. On the other hand, high energy prices will lead to a price increase of almost all goods and services. A carbon tax will, therefore, impose a burden on household consumption. This burden will not be the same for all income groups since the consumption basket of these groups differs. Previous studies, which focus on the burden imposed on Japanese households by the carbon tax, have confirmed that the incidence of the tax will hurt different groups differently.[3] In this study, we will estimate the impact of a carbon tax in China by income group.

Literature review

To repeat, a carbon tax is accompanied by an increase in fuel prices, and energy is an intermediate good with relatively low substitutability with other inputs in the short term. A carbon tax is, therefore, a negative factor in the price competitiveness of manufacturing, especially for energy-intensive goods. At the same time, energy also has low substitutability with other goods for households, and this means the burden of a carbon tax will vary by income strata or inhabited area. According to a report issued by the Research Institute for Fiscal Science (RIFS 2009), China was ready to introduce carbon tax around 2012–13 and proposed that the tax should start low (10 RMB/t-CO2, or approximately 1.5 USD/t-CO_2) and then be gradually raised to prevent a serious impact on the international competitiveness of Chinese manufacturing and on the living conditions of low-income households.

We now point to some studies that focus on the income distribution effects of a carbon tax where the prices of comedies are calculated by applying the price model of the input-output analysis.[4] Cornwell and Creedy (1996) discussed the price and revenue effect of a carbon tax based on the 1990 I-O table of Australia. They found that the carbon tax could be income regressive and aggravate the GINI index. Morgenstern et al. (2004) calculated the price effects of a carbon tax based on the 1992 I-O table of the USA. The principal conclusion is that within the manufacturing sector only a small number of industries would bear a disproportionate short-term burden of a carbon tax. Mathur and Morris (2014) calculated the price effects of a carbon tax based on the 2010 I-O table of the USA and estimated the carbon tax incidence across income classes and regions. They found that the carbon tax is regressive. Wier et al. (2005) found that the carbon tax is regressive in Denmark, in particular for the rural households based on the 1996 I-O table and Kerkhof et al. (2008) also found that the carbon tax is regressive in Netherlands based on the I-O table for the year 2000. On the other hand, Labandeira and Labeaga (1999) found that the carbon tax burden is not regressive but proportional across households in Spain based on the 1989 I-O table.

Fujikawa (2002) and Fujikawa and Watanabe (2004) investigated the Japanese case using input-output tables and household surveys. They found that a carbon tax is income regressive and its burden is heavy in the northern cold regions where energy demand is relatively high. Sugino et al. (2012) too investigated the impact of a carbon tax on Japanese households and arrived at similar results.

Sun and Ueta (2011) found an asymmetric impact on income distribution between urban and rural areas of a carbon tax in China, as of 2007. They concluded that the tax is regressive in urban areas but progressive in rural areas. Ye et al. (2016) confirmed this phenomenon. This paper will extend the result of Ye et al. (2016) and investigate the impact on income distribution of a carbon tax in China as of 2012 between urban and rural areas.

Model

Overview

The equilibrium price model of input-output analysis is applied to calculate the price change caused by the introduction of a carbon tax. We use 2012 input-output table (I-O table) with 139 sectors for China (National Bureau of Statistics of China 2015). In converting the I-O based prices into household expenditure based prices, we use the China 2012 Household Survey (National Bureau of Statistics of China 2013) for urban households and household expenditure in the China Statistical Yearbook (National Bureau of Statistics of China 2013) for rural ones, since the China Household Survey does not cover rural households.

In the China Household Survey, urban households are divided into eight groups by income, and consumption goods are classified into the following eight large categories: 1) Food, 2) Clothing and Footwear, 3) Housing, 4) Furniture and Household Articles, 5) Medical and Health expenses, 6) Communication and Transportation, 7) Education and Recreation, and 8) Others; these categories are further divided into more detailed sub-groups. On the other hand, in the *China Statistical Yearbook*, rural households are divided into five groups by income, and consumption goods are classified into the following seven large categories: 1) Food and Beverage, 2) Clothing and Footwear, 3) Housing, 4) Communication and Transportation, 5) Education and Recreation, 6) Medical and Health expenses, 7) Others, which are not divided further into sub-categories. The estimation of the burden on rural household burden is not entirely accurate (See Appendix 6.1).

Households' burden of a carbon tax is calculated in the following way:

1   Determination of the tax amount

    The tax amount by each type of fossil fuel is calculated based on the quantity of each type of fossil fuel consumed and its carbon content.

2   Estimation of rate of price increase by industry

    The tax amount is added to the value-added of the fossil fuel sector. The price increase caused by taxation is calculated by applying the equilibrium price model of I-O analysis.

3   Estimation of the increase in the consumption expenditure of households

    I-O based price increases are converted into those for commodities in household expenditure. The total increase in the consumption expenditure of households is then estimated.

Calculation of the carbon tax

As mentioned in the previous section, the carbon tax is imposed in the most upstream of production processes. More precisely, the calculated tax for each type of fossil fuel is added to the value-added of the corresponding energy sector. As to tax rate, we use a news report from the "National Energy Web."[5] According to this news report, the initial tax rate of carbon tax was 10 RMB/t-CO_2. The tax amount on each type of fossil fuel calculated is as shown in Table 6.2.

Table 6.2 Calculation of the carbon tax

	Energy consumption (million toe)	*Carbon coefficient (t-CO_2/toe)*	*Tax rate (RMB/t-CO_2)*	*Tax amount (million RMB)*
Coal	1,883.9	3.7620	10	70,873.2
Oil	464.2	2.8641	10	13,294.8
Natural Gas	120.5	2.0675	10	2,492.1

Source: Authors' compilation based on the *EDMC Handbook of Energy & Economic Statistics in Japan* (Institute of Energy Economics 2017).

Equilibrium price model

By the imposition of the carbon tax, the gross value-added increases and the ratio of it to gross production value rises. The equilibrium price model of I-O analysis is expressed as follows:

$$\mathbf{p}_1 = [\mathbf{v}_1 + \mathbf{p}_m \hat{\mathbf{M}} \mathbf{A}][\mathbf{I} - (\mathbf{I} - \hat{\mathbf{M}})\mathbf{A}]^{-1} \qquad (6.1)$$

$\mathbf{p}_1$ and $\mathbf{p}_m$, respectively, stand for a price vector of domestic goods and imported goods before taxation (row vectors). $\mathbf{v}_1$ stands for a vector of the value-added ratio (row vectors). $\mathbf{A}$ is an input coefficient matrix and $\hat{\mathbf{M}}$ is a diagonal matrix of the ratio of imported goods to total intermediate inputs. Therefore, $[\mathbf{v}_1 + \mathbf{p}_m \hat{\mathbf{M}} \mathbf{A}]$ stands for a vector of the ratio of total value-added for domestic products and leakage to imported goods before taxation, and $[\mathbf{I} - (\mathbf{I} - \hat{\mathbf{M}})\mathbf{A}]^{-1}$ is Leontief inverse matrix.

The price vector after taxation $\mathbf{p}_2$ can be expressed as follows with the value-added ratio vector $\mathbf{v}_2$ after taxation.

$$\mathbf{p}_2 = [\mathbf{v}_2 + \mathbf{p}_m \hat{\mathbf{M}} \mathbf{A}][\mathbf{I} - (\mathbf{I} - \hat{\mathbf{M}})\mathbf{A}]^{-1} \qquad (6.2)$$

The price increase caused by a carbon tax can be calculated as the difference between Equation (6.1) and Equation (6.2).

$$\mathbf{p}_2 - \mathbf{p}_1 = (\mathbf{v}_2 - \mathbf{v}_1)[\mathbf{I} - (\mathbf{I} - \hat{\mathbf{M}})\mathbf{A}]^{-1} \qquad (6.3)$$

Results

Price increase by sector

Table 6.3 shows the I-O table-based price increase calculated using Equation (6.3). As described above, the input-output table used for calculation is the 139-sector table in 2012. Table 6.3 shows the top 20 industries where the price increase is high. Naturally, the price increases are high in fossil fuel-related or fossil fuel-intensive industries. The price increase in the coal industry is the highest (3.81%), followed by coal products (1.60%), oil and natural gas (1.43%), electricity (1.01%), and gas (0.64%). Besides these industries, such energy-intensive industries as steel, chemicals, and pottery occupied a high ranking.

Increase in household expenditures by income group

We estimate price increases in consumer goods by converting the input-output table industries into household survey-based items. Furthermore, we estimate the increase in household expenditure, that is, the amount of burden, by multiplying the item-by-item expenditure on the original household survey by this

Table 6.3 Input-output table-based price change

Order	Industry number	Industry name	% change
01	006	Coal	3.81%
02	040	Coal products	1.60%
03	007	Oil and natural gas	1.43%
04	096	Electricity	1.01%
05	097	Gas	0.64%
06	041	Basic chemicals	0.54%
07	052	Cement and caustic lime	0.52%
08	039	Oil refinery	0.50%
09	054	Bricks and building material	0.49%
10	042	Fertilizer	0.46%
11	058	Other non-metal mineral products	0.45%
12	059	Steel	0.43%
13	060	Steel rolling	0.43%
14	053	Cement products	0.36%
15	049	Chemical fibers	0.35%
16	061	Ferroalloy	0.35%
17	045	Chemical materials	0.34%
18	055	Glass products	0.33%
19	046	Special chemical products and medicine	0.33%
20	057	Fire-resistant materials	0.30%

Source: Authors' compilation based on 2012 I-O table for China.

rate of price increase of consumer goods. This estimation is done by income group separately for urban and rural areas.

Regressive character in urban and progressive character in rural areas

Table 6.4 shows increased household expenses by income group in urban and rural areas, estimated using data from 2012 household survey. The percentage of carbon tax burden for urban residents is approximately 0.2%, which is not large. However, it has a regressive character in that poorer households bear a heavier tax burden. On the other hand, the percentage of carbon tax burden for rural residents is 0.25%, which is not large either but greater than for urban areas. Moreover, it has a progressive character, which is the opposite of the trend observed in urban areas.

The reason carbon tax is regressive in urban areas is because of the consumption of water, electricity, fuel, and heating. This expenditure in the lowest income group is 7.2% while that in the highest income group is 5.0%. Since these goods are necessities in the urban areas, the consumption share is higher in the low-income group. On the other hand, the reason a carbon tax is progressive in rural areas is because of consumption with respect to the categories "housing" and "communication and

Table 6.4 Tax burden of carbon tax by income group (2012)

		Annual consumption expenditure before tax	Annual consumption expenditure after tax	Increase in living cost	Increased rate of living costs
Urban	Lowest (10%)	7,241	7,256	15.2	0.210%
	Upper lowest (10%)	9,475	9,493	18.3	0.193%
	Lower middle (20%)	12,182	12,206	23.6	0.193%
	Middle (20%)	15,652	15,681	29.4	0.188%
	Upper middle (20%)	19,859	19,897	37.2	0.187%
	High (10%)	25,883	25,931	48.3	0.186%
	Highest (10%)	38,061	38,133	72.3	0.190%
Rural	Lowest (20%)	3,742	3,751	8.7	0.232%
	Lower middle (20%)	4,464	4,475	10.5	0.234%
	Middle (20%)	5,430	5,443	13.1	0.242%
	Upper middle (20%)	6,924	6,942	17.3	0.250%
	Highest (20%)	10,275	10,301	25.7	0.250%

Sources: Authors' compilation based on 2012 I-O table for China, *China Household Survey 2012*, and *China Statistical Yearbook 2013*.

transport." In the rural areas, consumer spending on "housing" and "communication and transport" increases rapidly with an increase in the income. It should be pointed out that heating and automobiles are categorized as luxury goods in rural China.

Higher burden in rural areas

Figure 6.1 visualizes the numbers presented in Table 6.4. The horizontal axis represents income and the vertical axis, the rate of increase in household expenses. Although the carbon tax is regressive in urban areas, the degree of regressiveness is not strong. The tax ratio is almost the same after the third group and the burden on the wealthiest households (the seventh group) is slightly higher than that for the sixth group.

The fact that the burden in rural areas is higher than that in urban areas is noteworthy. This is because energy use in rural area includes its use in agriculture for operating tractors and for heating greenhouses.

Comparison with 2007

Table 6.5 shows the results for 2007 and Figure 6.2 is a graphical representation of Table 6.5. The method of calculating the rate of increase in household expenses is the same as that used for 2012. The carbon tax rate is also the same at 10 RMB/t-CO_2 ton. One sees the same trend as in 2012. Thus, a carbon tax is regressive in urban areas while it is progressive in rural areas, and the tax burden in rural areas is heavier than in urban areas.

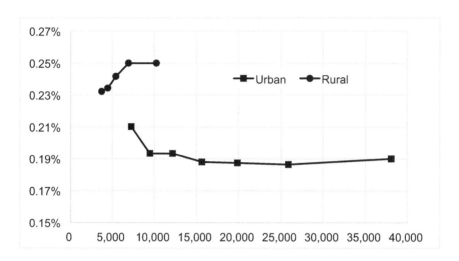

Figure 6.1 Household burden by income group (2012)

Sources: Authors' compilation based on 2012 I-O table for China, *China Household Survey 2012*, and *China Statistical Yearbook 2013*.

Table 6.5 Tax burden of carbon tax by income group (2007)

		Annual consumption expenditure before tax	Annual consumption expenditure after tax	Increase in living cost	Increased rate of living costs
Urban	Lowest	3,419	3,430	10.6	0.31%
	Middle lowest	4,000	4,012	12.0	0.30%
	Upper lowest	5,580	5,595	15.5	0.28%
	Lower middle	7,055	7,074	18.9	0.27%
	Middle	9,013	9,036	22.7	0.25%
	Upper middle	11,472	11,500	28.1	0.24%
	High	15,172	15,207	35.3	0.23%
	Highest	23,184	23,235	50.7	0.22%
Rural	Lowest	1,851	1,855	4.9	0.26%
	Lower middle	2,358	2,364	6.3	0.27%
	Middle	2,938	2,947	8.2	0.28%
	Upper middle	3,683	3,693	10.5	0.28%
	Highest	5,994	6,013	18.6	0.31%

Source: Authors' compilation based on Ye et al. (2016).

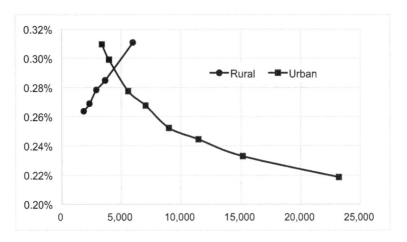

Figure 6.2 Household burden by income group (2007)
Source: Authors' compilation based on Ye et al. (2016).

However, there are also some changes from 2007 to 2012. First, in 2012, the burden declines overall compared to 2007. The highest rate of increase in household expenses in 2007 was 0.31% in both urban and rural areas, but in 2012 the highest rate in urban areas decreased to 0.21% and the highest rate in rural areas decreased to 0.25%. This decrease may be natural given the rise in prices during this period. Secondly, from 2007 to 2012, the regressiveness in urban areas and the progressiveness in rural areas seems to have weakened somewhat. We predicted that energy goods would become necessities in 2012 as income increased in rural areas, rendering a carbon tax regressive. However, there has been no major change, barring a slight weakening of the progressiveness of the tax.

Increase in household expenditures by region[6]

Figure 6.3 shows the estimated results of a carbon tax burden of households by province. The gray bar stands for urban areas and the white bar stands for rural areas respectively for each province. The national average of a carbon tax burden in the urban areas is 32 yuan and 0.190% to a household expense before the introduction of carbon tax. The top five provinces are Shanxi (0.236%), Hebei (0.235%), Jilin (0.230%), Heilongjiang (0.225%), and Shandong (0.211%). They are all located in the northern part of China. Heating-related expenses would be a reason of high carbon tax burden in these provinces.

The national average of a carbon tax burden in the rural areas is 37 yuan and 0.622% to a household expense before the introduction of carbon tax. The top five provinces are Jiangsu (0.841%), Shaanxi (0.738%), Beijing (0.724%), Jilin (0.714%), and Shanxi (0.700%). They are not necessarily cold provinces in China unlike in the case of urban areas. The share of "transportation expense" in rural

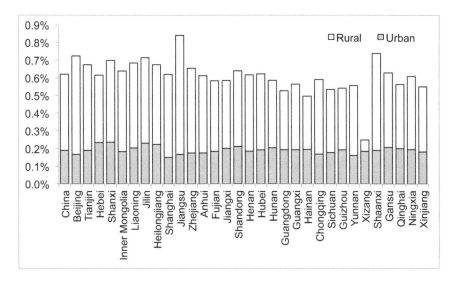

Figure 6.3 Household burden by region (2012)

Sources: Authors' compilation based on 2012 I-O table for China, *China Household Survey 2012*, and *China Statistical Yearbook 2013*.

areas is relatively high in the coastal provinces based on the data of the household survey and this includes the fuel expanse in the household survey. For instance, the share of "transportation expense" in Zhejiang is 14.1% and that in Beijing is 11.3%. It is possible that the rise of fuel expenses by a carbon tax influences the rise of the household expense though this cannot be said with certainty because the commodity division of the household survey in rural areas is rough as shown in Appendix 6.1.

Moreover, the carbon tax burden in rural areas is higher than that in the urban areas in all provinces when the carbon tax burden is compared between urban and rural areas. In the farm village area, it is thought that one possible factor for the high tax burden is that the fuel is used for driving the farm machinery and air-conditioning for greenhouses in addition to utility charges for daily life. On the other hand, it is thought that the fuel consumption is relatively controlled in the urban areas since use of public traffic in urban areas is more widespread than in rural areas.

Concluding remarks

We examine the impact of the introduction of a carbon tax in China, based on the assumption of 10 RMB/t-CO2, using I-O tables and household surveys, by estimating the burden of such a tax on households by income group in urban and rural areas. As to I-O-based price changes, relatively large price increases are observed in such industries as coal, coke, oil and natural gas, electricity, as well as steel, chemicals, and pottery.

Looking at rates of increases in household expenditure by income group, we find that the burden is 0.21% for the poorest households in urban areas while it is 0.19% for the wealthiest households, which implies that the tax burden for households is regressive in urban areas. In contrast, the burden is 0.23% for the poorest households in rural areas and 0.25% for the wealthiest households, which implies that it is progressive in rural areas. When comparing this result with the result for 2007, it seems that the regressiveness of a carbon tax in urban areas and its progressiveness in rural areas weakened somewhat.

From the viewpoint of the absolute value of household living costs, the household burden is marginal since the tax rate assumed in this study is very low. However, the burden is higher in rural areas than in urban areas and the characteristics of the burden by income group differ between urban and rural areas. Given these analytical results, it is expected that the introduction of a carbon tax will not be easy.

If the tax rate is the same in urban and rural areas, households in rural areas will have to bear a relatively high burden compared with urban households. If the tax is introduced only in urban areas, low-income households will have to bear a relatively higher burden compared with high-income households. The Chinese government would do well to carefully consider a carbon tax. As long as a carbon tax is progressive in rural areas, implementing it is not going to be easy.

Appendix 6.1

Commodity classification

Table 6A.1 Commodity classification for urban area

Major classification	Medium classification	Small classification
1. Food and beverage	(1) Cereals and Oils	1. Grain
		2. Starch and potato
		3. Dried beans and soy products
		4. Fats and oils
	(2) Meat, Poultry, Eggs, and Aquatic products	1. Meat
		2. Poultry
		3. Eggs
		4. Aquatic products
	(3) Vegetables	1. Fresh vegetables
		2. Dried vegetables
		3. Vegetable products
	(4) Condiments	1. Condiment
	(5) Sugar, Tobacco, and Beverages	1. Sugar
		2. Tobacco
		3. Liquor
		4. Beverages
	(6) Dried fruits and vegetables	1. Fresh fruit
		2. Fresh melons
		3. Other dried fresh fruits and products
	(7) Pastry, milk, and dairy products	1. Pastries
		2. Milk and dairy products
	(8) Other foods	1. Other foods
	(9) Catering	1. Food processing
		2. Outside foods
2. Clothes and Footwear	(1) Clothing	1. Clothing
	(2) Clothing material	1. Clothing material
	(3) Footwear	1. Footwear
	(4) Other clothing items	1. Other clothing items
	(5) Fashion designing	1. Fashion designing

(*Continued*)

Table 6A.1 (Continued)

Major classification	Medium classification	Small classification
3. Housing expenses	(1) Housing	1. Housing
	(2) Hydropower fuel and others	1. Hydropower fuel and others
	(3) Living services	1. Property management fees
		2. Maintenance service fee
		3. Others
4. Furniture and Housework Articles	(1) Durable consumer goods	1. Furniture
		2. Home equipment
	(2) Interior decoration	1. Interior decoration
	(3) Bed linings	1. Bed linings
	(4) Household daily groceries	1. Household daily groceries
	(5) Furniture material	1. Furniture material
	(6) Housekeeping services	1. Housekeeping
		2. Processing and maintenance service fees
5. Communication and Transportation	(1) Transportation	1. Home transport
		2. Vehicles for fuel and spare parts
		3. Expenditure on transport services
		4. Transportation fee s
	(2) Communication	1. Communication tools
		2. Communication services
6. Education and recreation expenses	(1) Cultural and entertainment supplies	1. Cultural and entertainment supplies
	(2) Cultural and recreational services	1. Cultural and recreational services
	(3) Education	1. Teaching materials
		2. Education costs
7. Medical and Health expenses	(1) Medical equipment	1. Medical equipment
	(2) Health care equipment	1. Health care equipment
	(3) Drug charges	1. Drug charges
	(4) Nourishing health care products	1. Nourishing health care products
	(5) Medical fees	1. Medical fees
	(6) Other	1. Other
8. Other expenses	(1) Other goods	1. Other goods
	(2) Other service	1. Other service

Source: *China Household Survey 2012.*

Table 6A.2 Consumption expenditure classification for rural areas

	Major classification
1.	Food and Beverage
2.	Clothing and Footwear
3.	Housing
4.	Communication and Transportation
5.	Education and Recreation
6.	Medical and Health expenses
7.	Other expenses

Source: Authors' compilation based on *China Statistical Yearbook 2013.*

Notes

1 The data source is the *EDMC Handbook of Energy & Economic Statistics in Japan* (Institute of Energy Economics 2017).
2 See the website of the ministry of environment <www.env.go.jp/policy/tax/about.html> for the carbon tax in other countries.
3 Fujikawa (2002) and Fujikawa and Watanabe (2004).
4 Callan et al. (2009) has a comprehensive literature survey on the income distribution effects of a carbon tax.
5 China's website that puts out energy-related news and data: <www.china5e.com/>.
6 We here also use the data from 2012 household data. The household expenses in rural areas of each province, however, are not consistent with those by income group in whole China rural areas. That is why the tax burden in rural areas is much higher than in urban areas.

References

Callan, T., Lyons, S., Scott, S., Richard, S.J. and Verde, S. (2009) The distributional implications of a carbon tax in Ireland, *Energy Policy* 37: 407–12.
Cornwell, A. and Creedy, J. (1996) Carbon taxation, prices and inequality in Australia, *Fiscal Studies* 17(3): 21–38.
Fujikawa, K. (2002) On burden of carbon tax by region and income group, *Business Journal of PAPAIOS, the Pan Pacific Association of Input-Output Studies* 10(4): 35–42 (in Japanese).
Fujikawa, K. and Watanabe, T. (2004) Burden of global warming countermeasure tax by income group and region, in Society for Environmental Economics and Policy Studies (ed.) *Environment Tax*, Tokyo: Toyo Keizai Inc, 93–106 (in Japanese).
Institute of Energy Economics, Japan (ed.) (2017) *EDMC Handbook of Energy & Economic Statistics in Japan*, Tokyo: Energy Conservation Center, Japan.
Kerkhof, A.C., Moll, H.C., Drissen, E. and Wilting, H.C. (2008) Taxation of multiple greenhouse gases and the effects on income distribution: A case study of the Netherlands, *Ecological Economics* 67(2): 318–26.
Labandeira, X. and Labeaga, J.M. (1999) Combining input-output analysis and micro-simulation to assess the effects of carbon taxation on Spanish households, *Fiscal Studies* 20(3): 305–20.
Mathur, A. and Morris, A.C. (2014) Distributional effects of a carbon tax in broader U.S. fiscal reform, *Energy Policy* 66: 326–34.
Morgenstern, R., Ho, M., Shih, J. and Zhang, X. (2004) The near term impacts of carbon mitigation policies on manufacturing industries, *Energy Policy* 32: 1825–41.
National Bureau of Statistics of China (2012) *China Household Survey 2012*, Beijing: China Statistics Publishing House (in Chinese).
National Bureau of Statistics of China (2013) *China Statistical Yearbook 2013*, Beijing: China Statistics Publishing House (in Chinese).
National Bureau of Statistics of China (2015) *2012 Input Output Tables for China*, Beijing: China Statistics Publishing House (in Chinese).
Research Institute for Fiscal Science (2009) *Research on Levying Carbon Tax*, Ministry of Finance (in Chinese) www.efchina.org/Reports-zh/reports-efchina-20090930-en
Sugino, M., Arimura, T. and Morita, M. (2012) The impact of a carbon tax on the industry and household: An input-output analysis, *Environmental Science, Society of Environmental Science* 25(2): 126–33 (in Japanese).

Sun, W. and Ueta, K. (2011) The distributional effects of a China carbon tax: A rural-urban assessment, *The Kyoto Economic Review* 80(2): 188–206.

Wier, M., Birr-Pedersen, K., Jacobsen, H.K. and Klok, J. (2005) Are CO_2 taxes regressive? Evidence from the Danish experience, *Ecological Economics* 52: 239–51.

Ye, Z., Watanabe, T., Shimoda, M. and Fujikawa, K. (2016) Burden of introducing China's carbon tax by region and income group, in Fujikawa, K. (ed.) *Input-Output Analysis and CGE Analysis on Chinese Economy*, Kyoto: Houritsu Bunka Sha, 53–61 (in Japanese).

7 Economic and carbon impacts of China's NDC and the Paris Agreement on China

Hikari Ban and Kiyoshi Fujikawa

Introduction

The Paris Agreement to limit global warming was adopted on December 12, 2015 and came into force on November 4, 2016. This agreement is based on the comprehensive national climate action plans known as Nationally Determined Contributions (NDCs) submitted by 153 countries and regions as of December 7, 2016. China is a signatory to the Paris Agreement and has a target to peak out its CO_2 emissions by 2030 at the latest.[1] As China is the largest CO_2 emitter in the world and plays an important role in the global supply chain, its carbon constraint may have large impacts not only on China's economy and CO_2 emissions but also on those of other countries.

From the viewpoint of energy production and consumption, China is a net energy importer as well as a major global energy producer. The global shares of China's coal, oil, and gas production are respectively 46.1%, 5.3%, and 3.1% in terms of tons of oil equivalent (toe), and the global shares of their imports are 18.0%, 11.7%, and 3.3% respectively (GTAP 9 Data Base). China imports oil mainly from the Middle East and Africa, while it imports coal and gas from its bordering countries.[2]

Both energy-exporting and -importing countries have signed up to the Paris Agreement. Therefore, more advanced and supportive international cooperation will be required for the success of this first global agreement on climate change. Studying the impacts of China's carbon restriction, both as energy producer and net importer, will provide useful insights on international cooperation.

In this chapter, we study how China's carbon policy will affect China's economy and CO_2 emissions. We focus on outputs, imports, and CO_2 emissions in China's energy sectors and show that their behavior is related to their carbon intensity, capital intensity, and substitutability between energy sources. In addition, we analyze how the impacts of China's carbon policy on China's economy and environment differ when the NDCs of major countries are simultaneously implemented.[3]

We use the GDyn-E model, which is a multisector, multiregion, recursive dynamic computable general equilibrium (CGE) model developed by Golub (2013). This allows us to analyze the impacts of intertemporal global climate policies. We apply the GDyn-E model to estimate the impacts of China's NDC scenario and the Paris Agreement scenario for the period from 2020 to 2030.

Energy substitution

We use the GDyn-E model that combines the GDyn model with the GTAP-E model. The GDyn model addresses capital accumulation and international capital movement, and distinguishes between asset location and ownership. The GTAP-E model is a multisector, multiregion static CGE model that is suitable for energy and environmental policy analysis. It links economic activity with energy and environment by introducing energy substitution.[4] The additional details of the GDyn-E model are provided in Appendix 7.2.

Here, we explain energy substitution in the production function in the GDyn-E model to understand the simulation results. The production function is an equation which describes the maximum output associated with given inputs. The elasticity of substitution measures the difficulty of substituting one input for another with output being held. The greater the value of elasticity is, the easier the substitution is.

Figure 7.1 shows that this function has a Leontief structure with zero elasticity of substitution at the top level and a constant elasticity of substitution

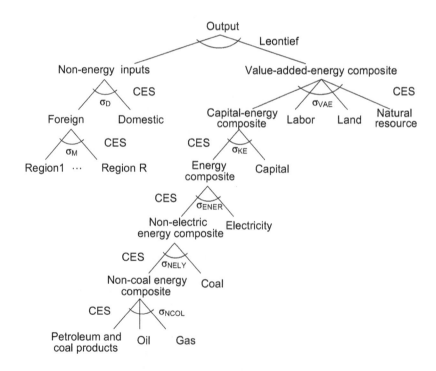

Figure 7.1 Production structure in the GDyn-E model

Source: Authors' modification based on Figures 16 and 17 in Burniaux and Truong (2002).

Note: For electricity, coal, gas, oil, and petroleum and coal products, a graphical description of substitutability between domestic and imported goods is omitted in the figure.

(CES) structure at the lower level. The Leontief structure implies that the inputs will be used in fixed proportion and the CES structure allows for constant substitutability between the inputs. The energy composite is combined with capital and incorporated into the value-added nest to consider energy-capital adjustment to a relative price change. The substitution elasticity within the capital-energy composite (σ_{KE}) is 0.5 for all industries and countries except coal, oil, gas, and petroleum and coal products ($\sigma_{KE} = 0$). The substitution elasticity within the value-added-energy composite (σ_{VAE}) differs between industries and regions.

Energy commodities are incorporated into the energy composite at three levels of nested substitution: 1) substitution between the non-electric energy composite and electricity, σ_{ENER}; 2) substitution between the non-coal energy composite and coal, σ_{NELY}; and 3) substitution between non-coal products, σ_{NCOL}. We use the following parameters: Coal, oil, gas, and petroleum and coal product industries: $\sigma_{ENER} = 0$, $\sigma_{NELY} = 0$, $\sigma_{NCOL} = 0$; electricity industry: $\sigma_{ENER} = 0$, $\sigma_{NELY} = 0.5$, $\sigma_{NCOL} = 1$; other industries: $\sigma_{ENER} = 0$, $\sigma_{NELY} = 0.5$, $\sigma_{NCOL} = 1$.

Baseline and scenarios

We use the GTAP 9 Data Base, which corresponds to the global economy of 2011 with 140 countries/regions and 57 industries. It contains regional I-O tables, macro data, bilateral trade data, and production data. In addition, energy volume data and CO_2 emission data are available. We aggregate these data into the following 23 regions and 28 sectors:

> 23 regions: Oceania, China, Japan, Korea, Taiwan, Indonesia, Malaysia, Singapore, Thailand, Vietnam, Other ASEAN, India, Other Asia, Canada, Mexico, Latin America, EU, Other Europe, Russia, Turkestan, the Middle East, North Africa, and sub-Saharan Africa;
> 28 sectors: Agriculture, Livestock, Forestry, Fishing, Coal mining, Crude oil, Gas and distribution, Petroleum and coal products, Electricity, Other mining, Processed food, Textiles and clothing, Paper and publishing, Chemical products, Nonmetallic minerals, Iron, Automobile and parts, Transportation equipment, Electronics equipment, Machine equipment, Other manufactures, Water, Construction, Trade, Water transport services, Air transport services, Other transport services, and Other services.[5]

Our simulation starts from the global economy in 2011 that is described by the GTAP 9 Data Base. We form our baseline using the GTAP 9 Data Base and Chappuis and Walmsley (2011). The estimated growth rates in GDP, population, skilled and unskilled labor are incorporated into the baseline scenario. Figure 7.2 shows China's baseline of GDP and CO_2 emission growth rates. In this study, China's GDP growth rate in 2030 is expected to be about 6%. China must restrict CO_2 emissions to achieve its NDC.

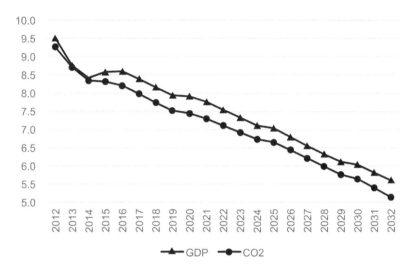

Figure 7.2 Baselines for GDP and CO_2 emission growth rates in China (annual rate %)

Source: Authors' simulations with the GDyn model, the GTAP 9 Data Base, and Chappuis and Walmsley (2011).

Table 7.1 China's CO_2 emission growth rates for the baseline and the C-NDC scenario (%)

	2020	2021	2022	2023	2024	2025	2026	2027	2028	2029	2030
Baseline	7.44	7.30	7.11	6.92	6.74	6.65	6.44	6.22	5.99	5.77	5.65
C-NDC	6.77	6.09	5.41	4.74	4.06	3.38	2.71	2.03	1.35	0.68	0

Sources: Authors' simulations with the GDyn model and the GTAP 9 Data Base.

We investigate the following two scenarios: China's NDC (C-NDC) scenario, in which China alone achieves its carbon peak-out target in 2030; and the Paris Agreement (PA) scenario, in which major countries including China achieve their NDCs.

In both scenarios, CO_2 emission growth rates of countries with restriction targets are exogenous variables and carbon prices are calculated to achieve their targets, which means that a carbon tax is imposed on all CO_2 emissions in countries with restriction targets. For China's NDC scenario, we set China's CO_2 emissions growth rate so that it approaches zero in 2030. The growth rate decreases by 0.68% every year. Table 7.1 shows China's CO_2 growth rates for the baseline scenario and China's NDC scenario.

For the Paris Agreement scenario, we set target CO_2 growth rates in the last column of Table 7.2. We deal only with countries that have unconditional carbon

Table 7.2 NDCs and corresponding targets for CO_2 growth rate

	NDCs (unconditional target)	Target CO_2 growth rates (%)*
Oceania	Australia: 26%–28% reduction by 2030 compared with 2005; New Zealand: 30% reduction by 2030 compared with 2005	−4.47
China	Peaking of CO_2 emissions around 2030	See Table 7.1
Japan	26% reduction by 2030 compared with 2013	−1.23
Korea	37% reduction by 2030 compared with business-as-usual (BAU)	−2.22
Taiwan	20% reduction by 2030 compared with 2005	−4.85
Indonesia	29% reduction by 2030 compared with BAU	1.93
Malaysia	35% reduction of emissions intensity (CO_2/GDP) by 2030 compared with 2005	2.45**
Singapore	36% reduction of emissions intensity (CO_2/GDP) by 2030 compared with 2005	−1.82**
Thailand	20% reduction by 2030 compared with BAU	2.39
Vietnam	8% reduction by 2030 compared with BAU	3.62
Canada	30% reduction by 2030 compared with 2005	−4.85
USA	26%–28% reduction by 2025 compared with 2005	−5.00
Mexico	25% reduction by 2030 compared with BAU	0.32
EU	40% reduction by 2030 compared with 1990	−4.85
Russia	25%–30% reduction by 2030 compared with 1990	−2.28

Source: Target CO_2 growth rates are authors' calculations based on the NDCs, IEA (2015), and the baseline.

Note
* In this study, Other ASEAN, India, Other Asia, Latin America, Other Europe, Turkestan, the Middle East, North Africa, and sub-Saharan Africa do not have targets.
** For Malaysia and Singapore, we convert emission intensity targets into CO_2 level targets using the baseline.

restrictions. First, we estimate the target CO_2 levels based on NDCs using CO_2 data from IEA (2015) and the baseline. Then, we calculate the target CO_2 growth rates by year required to achieve the target levels. For China, we use the target CO_2 growth rates given in Table 7.1.

Simulation results

Analysis of macro impacts

In this section, we discuss the macro impacts on China of the two scenarios. Table 7.3 shows the impact of China's NDC and the Paris Agreement scenarios on China's macro economy and CO_2 emissions in 2030. In China's NDC scenario,

Table 7.3 Macro impacts on China (differences from the baseline, 2030)

	GDP	EV*	Terms of trade	Domestic equity income**	Foreign equity income***	Carbon price of CO_2 ($/ton)		CO_2
	(%)	(Billion $)	(%)	(Billion $)	(Billion $)	Nominal	Real	(%)
C-NDC	−1.1	−138	−0.0	−192	55	3.2	3.3	−28.5
PA	0.3	−236	−0.4	−326	−39	3.6	3.8	−28.5

Sources: Authors' simulations with GDyn and the GTAP 9 Data Base.

Note
* EV is the total differences from the baseline of equivalent variation from 2020 to 2030.
** Income on equity paid to the regional household in China by domestic firms.
*** Income on equity paid to regional household in China by the global trust.

Table 7.4 Impact on production factors (differences from the baseline, 2030, %)

	Output		Price	
	C-NDC	PA	C-NDC	PA
Land	0	0	−2.4	2.5
Unskilled labor	0	0	−1.9	−1.1
Skilled labor	0	0	−1.9	−2.0
Capital	−1.7	1.9	−2.1	−4.6
Natural resources	0	0	−8.6	−1.9

Sources: Authors' simulations with GDyn and the GTAP 9 Data Base.

the impact on GDP will be less than baseline by 1.1%, but slightly positive in the Paris Agreement scenario. As we show later, under the Paris Agreement scenario, production is likely to increase in most sectors more than the baseline, so the impact on GDP will be slightly positive. However, the impact on equivalent variation (EV) is below the baseline in both scenarios.[6] CO_2 emissions are 28.5% below the baseline in either scenario, but the carbon price is higher in the Paris Agreement scenario.

Looking at the impact on production factors (Table 7.4), as they are exogenous variables, their differences from the baseline are all zero, other than capital. Capital stock is below the baseline in China's NDC scenario, but above in the Paris Agreement scenario. As the decline of the rate of return in China for the Paris Agreement scenario is relatively small compared with other carbon-constrained countries, it leads to an increase in investment and capital stock in China.[7] In China's NDC scenario, the negative impact on natural resource prices is particularly remarkable, whereas in the Paris Agreement scenario, the decline in the capital rental rate is notable. As described later, in China's NDC scenario, the output of coal and gas, which are natural resource-intensive goods, decreases considerably so that the natural resource price declines significantly. In the Paris Agreement scenario, demand for capital stock decreases due to the decline of worldwide demand, and then the capital rental price in China is lower than in China's NDC scenario.[8]

The difference of EV from the baseline is larger in the Paris Agreement scenario than in China's NDC scenario. By analyzing the reasons for this difference, we will understand more clearly how economic impacts differ under the Paris Agreement scenario. EV in the GDyn-E model is broken down into the following factors: allocative efficiency, terms of trade, price of investment relative to saving, nonaccumulable endowments, financial assets (ownership of capital endowments), technology changes, population, changes in preferences, and emissions trading.[9] When the total differences of EV from the baseline from 2020 to 2030 are expressed as a ratio (%) of the total EV of the baseline in the same periods, it is −1.2% in China's NDC scenario. Furthermore, when calculating the contributions, the main factors are technology change (−0.5%), resource allocation (−0.4%), and financial asset (−0.2%). In the Paris Agreement scenario, the overall difference is −2.1% and important contributions are financial assets (−1.6%), terms of trade (−0.2%), and price of investment relative to saving (−0.2%).

Although the rate of technological progress in China always has a positive value for the simulation period, the sign of the technology change effect can be negative if technological progress cannot be utilized fully due to output change caused by carbon constraints. In the Paris Agreement scenario, the negative contribution of technology change and allocation efficiency is relatively small. This is related to the results that output in most sectors increases from the baseline for the Paris Agreement scenario (Table 7.5).

The contribution of financial assets is negative in either scenario, but the Paris Agreement scenario has a greater negative contribution. Table 7.3 also shows that income from financial assets is less in the Paris Agreement scenario than in China's NDC scenario. The rate of return in China is 1.5% below the baseline in China's NDC scenario and 4.4% below the baseline in the Paris Agreement scenario.

In the Paris Agreement scenario, the terms of trade and price of investment relative to saving also work negatively. For terms of trade, in China's NDC scenario, both the export price index and the import price index fall by about 0.5% from the baseline, indicating little effect on the terms of trade. In the Paris Agreement scenario, the export price index drops by about −0.4%, whereas the import price index hardly decreases and the terms of trade deteriorate. For the price of investment relative to saving, when the investment goods price rises relative to the saving price (equity price), economic welfare increases, because more financial assets can be acquired with one unit of domestic investment goods. The investment goods price decreases relatively in either scenario, but

Table 7.5 Impacts on sectorial output in China (differences from the baseline, 2030, %)

	C-NDC	PA		C-NDC	PA
Agri	0.1	0.8	NMM	−4.0	1.9
Lvstc	−0.9	0.5	Iron	−2.6	0.6
Forest	−0.8	0.1	Auto	−2.9	1.5
Fish	−0.3	0.2	TrsEqu	−1.2	0.6
Coal	−30.6	−32.2	EleEqu	1.3	0.2
Oil	−0.5	−3.6	Machin	−1.4	−0.5
Gas	−84.7	−91.4	O_Mnf	−0.6	−0.3
P_C	−2.7	3.9	Water	−1.7	−1.0
Ely	−16.0	−16.0	Const	−5.4	2.2
Mining	−1.3	1.0	Trade	−1.0	0.3
Food	−0.2	0.3	W_Trs	−1.5	3.5
Text	0.3	0.0	A_Trs	−1.0	10.4
Paper	−0.9	0.7	O_Trs	−2.1	1.6
Chemical	−1.1	1.2	Service	−0.7	−0.1

Sources: Authors' simulations with GDyn and the GTAP 9 Data Base.

the Paris Agreement scenario has a larger negative impact because investment is larger and saving is smaller than in China's NDC scenario.

Analysis of sectorial impact

Table 7.5 shows the differences of output from the baseline by industry. In China, the peak-out itself has a negative impact on most industries. In particular, the decreases in output of gas, coal, and electricity are remarkably large. The carbon intensities (CO_2 emissions/production value, kg/\$) in these sectors are 13.38 for electricity, 2.96 for gas, and 1.08 for coal, which comprise the top three carbon intensities in China (GTAP Data Base Ver. 9). Moreover, China's carbon intensities are higher than those of other countries; for example, they are 4.45 for electricity, 0.39 for gas, and 0.10 for coal in Oceania; and respectively 8.29, 0.49, and 0.01 in Indonesia.

In the Paris Agreement scenario, output in most industries increases more than in China's NDC scenario. Moreover, output in most industries increases more from the baseline. Price changes in other countries with restriction targets are likely to have a positive impact on production in most sectors in China. In particular, an increase in capital and an increase in supply of global transportation services can be inferred as the reasons for output increases in the construction and transportation sectors, respectively.[10]

In contrast, production of coal, oil, and gas under the Paris Agreement scenario is smaller than under China's NDC scenario. In addition to the decrease in worldwide energy demand by the Paris Agreement, the relative rises in China's energy prices are related. For example, the percentage difference of supply prices from the baseline in the Paris Agreement scenario for coal is 1.8% in China, −5.3% in

Oceania, −4.4% in Indonesia; for oil it is −8.4% in China, −10.6% in the Middle East, and −11.1% in sub-Saharan Africa; and the percentage difference for gas is 6.9% in China, 0.6% in Turkestan, and 0.3% in Russia. The carbon intensity and capital intensity are likely to be related to the relative rises of China's energy prices. Because the carbon intensity of these sectors in China is higher than in other countries, China's energy sectors have to pay a large amount of carbon tax, even though the carbon price is relatively low. Because capital intensity in China is lower than in other countries, the benefit from lowering capital rental cost is relatively small.[11]

Table 7.6 shows the impacts of CO_2 emissions from China's energy and energy-intensive industries. More than 70% of total CO_2 reductions by industries from the baseline are made in the electricity sector, followed by nonmetallic minerals, coal, iron, and chemical products. Gas, coal, and electricity sectors show remarkable reduction rates from the baseline. This trend is the same as that of output shown in Table 7.5. When distinguishing between domestic and imported energy, we see that the reduction rates for domestic energy are larger than those for imported energy in all sectors, indicating that domestic energy is being replaced with imported energy. In China's NDC scenario, coal imports increase by 36.3% and gas imports increase by 29.2% from the baseline. In the Paris Agreement scenario, they increase by 50.2% and 39.6%, respectively.

Comparing the percentage differences of output from the baseline in Table 7.5 with those of CO_2 emissions in Table 7.6, we see that coal use will be replaced by other energy and capital use. As noted, the electricity sector accounts for

Table 7.6 Impacts of CO_2 emissions from China's energy and energy-intensive industries (2030)

	Reductions from the baseline (Mt)		Percentage reduction from the baseline (%)					
	CA	PA	C-NDC			PA		
			Domestic	Import	Total	Domestic	Import	Total
Coal	−397.3	−403.8	−64.1	−16.4	−62.3	−65.4	−8.8	−63.3
Oil	−20.2	−28.0	−24.9	10.5	−14.6	−32.9	10.3	−20.3
Gas	−66.6	−71.1	−88.6	−83.3	−86.8	−93.7	−90.5	−92.6
P_C	−25.5	−5.1	−9.8	8.4	−7.9	−3.7	16.3	−1.6
Ely	−5,353.3	−5,632.6	−36.8	40.5	−31.8	−39.5	52.7	−33.5
Chemical	−197.1	−171.5	−22.1	26.6	−18.7	−20.5	38.8	−16.2
NMM	−562.5	−508.1	−33.3	40.5	−29.6	−31.5	61.8	−26.7
Iron	−236.6	−190.3	−19.9	29.6	−17.4	−17.0	43.5	−14.0
O_Trs	−94.5	−25.2	−11.8	0.6	−10.2	−4.3	8.0	−2.7
W_Trs	−23.9	12.8	−6.0	−2.7	−5.7	2.8	4.8	3.0
A_Trs	−13.2	20.6	−6.2	−2.5	−5.5	7.9	11.2	8.5

Sources: Authors' simulations with GDyn and on the GTAP 9 Data Base.

Table 7.7 Differences from the baseline of energy and capital demand and purchase price of China's electricity sector (2030, %)

	Demand			Purchase price		
	Total	Domestic	Import	Total	Domestic	Import
China's NDC scenario						
Coal	−27.1	−36.7	43.0	64.2	72.0	31.6
Oil	−8.8	−8.9	−8.6	4.3	4.3	4.2
Gas	−14.4	−98.8	8.2	11.1	58.1	9.0
P_C	−7.0	−7.1	−6.3	2.2	2.3	1.9
Electricity	−23.8	−23.9	15.0	23.4	23.4	6.6
Capital	−6.7			−2.1		
The Paris Agreement scenario						
Coal	−28.1	−39.4	55.9	71.5	81.4	33.1
Oil	−4.5	−9.0	11.6	−2.9	−2.0	−5.8
Gas	−12.0	−99.4	11.5	5.3	60.8	3.3
P_C	−3.0	−2.9	−3.9	−4.5	−4.6	−4.1
Electricity	−24.2	−24.2	0.8	24.9	24.9	12.8
Capital	−4.9			−4.6		

Sources: Authors' simulations with GDyn and the GTAP 9 Data Base.

Note: Purchase price includes carbon tax.

most CO_2 emissions. Before interpreting the results, it is helpful to know that the share of coal in total energy in China's electricity sector is very high: 93% as measured by toe and 98.1% as measured by CO_2 emissions.

Table 7.7 shows the differences from the baseline of the energy and capital demand and purchase price of China's electricity sector. Because the substitution between electricity and non-electric composite is assumed to be zero in this study, the percentage difference from the baseline of electricity demand is the same as the percentage difference for energy composite demand. Therefore, when the percentage difference for each energy source is larger than the percentage difference for electricity, the share of the current energy source in the energy composite rises, and vice versa.

Because coal decreases more than non-coal products (oil, gas, petroleum and coal products), it can be said that coal is substituted in favor of non-coal products. In addition, the replacement of energy with capital is also observed. The replacement of coal for non-coal energy and capital is likely to progress further in the Paris Agreement scenario compared with China's NDC scenario. By country of origin, substitution of domestic goods for imported goods in gas and coal demand is notable, which is consistent with remarkable rises in the domestic purchase prices of coal and gas.

Sensitivity analysis

The previous section showed that carbon restriction causes a switch from coal to non-coal energy with lower carbon content. In this section, we investigate whether the impacts of carbon restriction depend on the extent of substitution between coal and non-coal energy in China. We set the value of elasticity of substitution between coal and non-coal composite (σ_{NELY} in Figure 7.1) for China's electricity sector from 0.1 to 1.0. Table 7.8 shows that As σ_{NELY} becomes larger, negative differences from the baseline GDP and EV in China become smaller, while negative differences from the baseline CO_2 emissions become larger.

Figure 7.3 shows plots of carbon prices corresponding to the elasticity of substitution between coal and non-coal composite. The horizontal axis of Figure 7.3

Table 7.8 Elasticity of substitution between coal and non-coal energy and macro impacts on China (2030)

σ_{NELY}	0.1	0.2	0.3	0.4	0.5	0.6	0.7	0.8	0.9	1.0
China's NDC scenario										
GDP	−1.2	−1.2	−1.2	−1.1	−1.1	−1.1	−1.1	−1.0	−1.0	−1.0
EV	−147	−144	−142	−140	−138	−137	−135	−134	−133	−132
CO_2	−28.1	−28.2	−28.3	−28.4	−28.5	−28.6	−28.7	−28.8	−28.9	−29.0
The Paris Agreement scenario										
GDP	0.1	0.2	0.2	0.3	0.3	0.4	0.4	0.4	0.5	0.5
EV	−250	−246	−242	−239	−236	−234	−231	−229	−227	−226
CO_2	−28.1	−28.2	−28.3	−28.4	−28.5	−28.6	−28.7	−28.8	−28.9	−29.0

Sources: Authors' simulations with GDyn and the GTAP 9 Data Base.

Note: For GDP and CO_2: percentage differences from the baseline in 2030 (%). For EV: total differences from the baseline of EV 2020–30 (billion $).

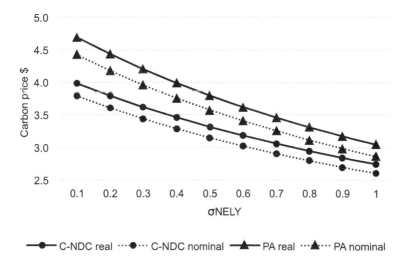

Figure 7.3 Elasticity of substitution between coal and non-coal composite and carbon prices in China (2030, US$)

Sources: Authors' calculations with GDyn and the GTAP 9 Data Base.

Table 7.9 Energy demand in China's electric power sector (differences from baseline, 2030, %)

σ_{NELY}	0.1	0.2	0.3	0.4	0.5	0.6	0.7	0.8	0.9	1.0
China's NDC scenario										
Coal	−27.3	−27.3	−27.2	−27.1	−27.1	−27.0	−27.0	−26.9	−26.9	−26.9
Oil	−23.8	−19.9	−16.1	−12.4	−8.8	−5.2	−1.8	1.6	5.0	8.2
Gas	−29.4	−25.5	−21.7	−18.1	−14.4	−10.9	−7.4	−4.0	−0.7	2.6
P_C	−22.3	−18.3	−14.5	−10.7	−7.0	−3.4	0.1	3.6	7.0	10.3
Ely	−26.6	−25.8	−25.1	−24.5	−23.8	−23.3	−22.7	−22.2	−21.7	−21.3
The Paris Agreement scenario										
Coal	−28.7	−28.5	−28.4	−28.3	−28.1	−28.0	−27.9	−27.9	−27.8	−27.7
Oil	−24.0	−19.0	−14.1	−9.3	−4.5	0.1	4.7	9.3	13.7	18.1
Gas	−30.9	−26.1	−21.4	−16.7	−12.0	−7.4	−2.9	1.6	6.0	10.4
P_C	−22.5	−17.6	−12.6	−7.8	−3.0	1.8	6.4	11.0	15.5	19.9
Ely	−27.9	−26.9	−25.9	−25.1	−24.2	−23.5	−22.8	−22.1	−21.4	−20.8

Sources: Authors' calculations with the GDyn model and the GTAP 9 Data Base.

is σ_{NELY} and the vertical axis is real and nominal carbon price ($). Figure 7.3 shows that the greater the elasticity is, the lower the carbon price is in either scenario. In addition, each carbon price in the Paris Agreement scenario is higher than in China's NDC scenario.

Table 7.9 shows the relationship between the intermediate energy demand of the electricity sector in China and the elasticity of substitution between coal and non-coal composite. Because coal has a lower percentage difference than electricity in all cases, the share becomes smaller than the baseline. In addition, as the elasticity increases, coal demand decreases relative to electricity demand; in other words, the higher the elasticity is, the smaller the share of coal is. Except for gas when elasticity is 0.1, because oil, gas, and petroleum and coal products have larger percentage differences than electricity, their shares become larger than the baseline. The larger the elasticity is, the greater the increases are in those energy demands relative to electricity demand. Therefore, the higher the elasticity is, the larger the share of non-coal energy is.

Concluding remarks

In this chapter, we analyzed the economic and carbon impacts on China caused by the carbon policy based on the NDCs of China and other major countries. The main conclusions from our simulation results are as follows.

First, as a result of China's carbon policy itself, China's GDP decreases 1.1% from the baseline in 2030. However, the impact on GDP is slightly positive in the Paris Agreement scenario due to an increase in investment in China. This is because decline in the rate of return is relatively smaller in China than in other countries under the implementation of the NDCs in major countries. This implies that China's NDC is not as ambitious as it looks when compared with those of other countries (Chapter 9 in this volume).

Second, when measuring the change of EV, the implementation of NDCs in major countries exacerbates China's economic welfare. Our factorial decomposition of EV suggests that the main cause of deterioration is a decrease in income from financial assets due to a decrease in worldwide rates of return. Although we have made strong assumptions about international capital movements, we can confirm globalization of investment causes this dynamic influence of carbon policy.

Third, China's output of coal, gas, and electricity decreases significantly given carbon restriction. On the other hand, China's imports of coal and gas increase. These results are likely to be related to the high degree of carbon intensity and low degree of capital intensity in China's energy sectors. In China's electricity sector, substitution of domestic energy for imported energy and substitution of coal for non-coal energy and capital will occur. Our sensitivity analysis has shown that the economic burden can be reduced if substitution between coal and non-coal energy is increased.

The policy implications from our research are as follows. Adverse impact on China's domestic production will be smaller when international society tackles carbon reduction than when China alone achieves its NDC. In order for the international society to cooperate with carbon reduction, China, the world's largest emitter of CO_2, needs to take the initiative and comply with its NDC. In other words, China's efforts to reduce the carbon will eventually be rewarded. In addition, the domestic policies of China and the cooperation of the international society which lead to decreasing carbon intensity, increasing capital intensity, and promoting energy substitution in China's energy sector are important. That is because they will play an important role in reducing the economic burden while encouraging carbon reduction.

Appendix 7.1

Table 7A.1 Regional aggregation

No	Code	Description	GTAP regions
1	OCE	Oceania	Australia; New Zealand; Rest of Oceania.
2	CHN	China	China; Hong Kong.
3	JPN	Japan	Japan.
4	KOR	Korea	Korea.
5	TWN	Taiwan	Taiwan.
6	IDN	Indonesia	Indonesia.
7	MYS	Malaysia	Malaysia.
8	SGP	Singapore	Singapore.
9	THA	Thailand	Thailand.
10	VNM	Vietnam	Vietnam.
11	O_ASEAN	Other ASEAN	Brunei Darussalam; Cambodia; Lao People's Democratic Republic; Philippines; Rest of Southeast Asia.
12	India	India	India.
13	O_Asia	Other Asia	Mongolia; Rest of East Asia; Bangladesh; Nepal; Pakistan; Sri Lanka; Rest of South Asia.
14	CAN	Canada	Canada.
15	US	United America	United States of America.
16	MEX	Mexico	Mexico.
17	Latin	Latin America	Rest of North America; Argentina; Bolivia; Brazil; Chile; Colombia; Ecuador; Paraguay; Peru; Uruguay; Venezuela; Rest of South America; Costa Rica; Guatemala; Honduras; Nicaragua; Panama; El Salvador; Rest of Central America; Dominican Republic; Jamaica; Puerto Rico; Trinidad and Tobago; Caribbean.
18	EU	European Union 28	Austria; Belgium; Cyprus; Czech Republic; Denmark; Estonia; Finland; France; Germany; Greece; Hungary; Ireland; Italy; Latvia; Lithuania; Luxembourg; Malta; Netherlands; Poland; Portugal; Slovakia; Slovenia; Spain; Sweden; United Kingdom; Bulgaria; Croatia; Romania.
19	O_Euro	Other Europe	Switzerland; Norway; Rest of EFTA; Albania; Belarus; Ukraine; Rest of Eastern Europe; Rest of Europe.

No	Code	Description	GTAP regions
20	Russia	Russia	Russian Federation.
21	Turkestan	Turkestan	Kazakhstan; Kyrgyzstan; Rest of Former Soviet Union.
22	MENA	Middle East and North Africa	Armenia; Azerbaijan; Georgia; Bahrain; Islamic Republic of Iran; Israel; Jordan; Kuwait; Oman; Qatar; Saudi Arabia; Turkey; United Arab Emirates; Rest of Western Asia; Egypt; Morocco; Tunisia; Rest of North Africa.
23	SSA	Sub-Saharan Africa	Benin; Burkina Faso; Cameroon; Cote d'Ivoire; Ghana; Guinea; Nigeria; Senegal; Togo; Rest of Western Africa; Central Africa; South Central Africa; Ethiopia; Kenya; Madagascar; Malawi; Mauritius; Mozambique; Rwanda; Tanzania; Uganda; Zambia; Zimbabwe; Rest of Eastern Africa; Botswana; Namibia; South Africa; Rest of South African Customs Union; Rest of the world.

Source: Authors' aggregation based on the GTAP 9 Data Base.

Table 7A.2 Sectoral aggregation

No	Code	Description	GTAP sectors
1	Agri	Agriculture	Paddy rice; Wheat; Cereal grains nec; Vegetables, fruit, nuts; Oil seeds; Sugar cane, sugar beet; Plant-based fibers; Crops nec.
2	Lvstc	Livestock	Cattle, sheep, goats, horses; Animal products nec; Raw milk; Wool, silk-worm cocoons.
3	Forest	Forestry	Forestry.
4	Fish	Fishing	Fishing.
5	Coal	Coal mining	Coal.
6	Oil	Crude Oil	Oil.
7	Gas	Natural gas and distribution	Gas; Gas manufacture, distribution.
8	P_C	Oil products	Petroleum, coal products.
9	Ely	Electricity	Electricity.
10	Mining	Other Mining	Minerals nec.
11	Food	Processed Food	Meat: cattle, sheep, goats, horse; Meat products nec; Vegetable oils and fats; Dairy products; Processed rice; Sugar; Food products nec; Beverages and tobacco products.
12	Text	Textiles and Clothing	Textiles; Wearing apparel.
13	Paper	Paper and publishing	Paper products, publishing.
14	Chemical	Chemical products	Chemical, rubber, plastic prods.

(Continued)

Table 7A.2 (Continued)

No	Code	Description	GTAP sectors
15	NMM	Nonmetallic minerals	Mineral products nec.
16	Iron	Iron	Ferrous metals.
17	Auto	Automobile and parts	Motor vehicles and parts.
18	TrsEqu	Transportation equipment	Transport equipment nec.
19	EleEqu	Electronics equipment	Electronic equipment.
20	Machin	Machin equipment	Machinery and equipment nec.
21	O_Mnf	Other manufacture	Leather products; Wood products; Metals nec; Metal products; Manufactures nec.
22	Water	Water	Water.
23	Const	Construction	Construction.
24	Trade	Trade	Trade.
25	W_Trs	Water transport service	Sea transport.
26	A_Trs	Air transport service	Air transport.
27	O_Trs	Other transport service	Transport nec.
28	Service	Other Services	Communication; Financial services nec; Insurance; Business services nec; Recreation and other services; Public Administration/Defense/Health/Education; Dwellings.

Source: Authors' aggregation based on the GTAP 9 Data Base.

Appendix 7.2
Framework of the GDyn-E model

The GDyn-E model consists of market equilibrium conditions and zero profit conditions basically. Economic entities in the GDyn-E model are firms, regional households, a global trust, and a global transportation sector. We begin by describing each role briefly.

Firms own only a physical asset (capital), rent land and natural resources, purchase labor from regional households, and produce goods using them. The representative regional household leases land and natural resources, provides its labor to firms, and purchases goods from firms. The regional household also possesses financial assets (equity), which are formed as indirect claims against physical assets. In this model, the regional household is defined as a combination of private household and government; it receives tax revenue and spends on public goods as well as private goods.

The global trust acts as a financial intermediary for all foreign investment. It issues equity, collects savings from each regional household, and purchases equities issued by each local firm. Therefore, the total financial assets of the regional household are composed of equity in local firms (as domestic asset) and in the global trust (as foreign asset). The global trust invests funds in local firms in each region according to the expected rate of return. International capital movements occur from regions with low expected rates of return to regions with high expected returns. Relatively rigid parameters are set for the allocation of domestic and foreign assets of regional households.

In addition to the global trust, another fictional global system is introduced into the model. A global transportation sector intermediates between the supply of and demand for international transport services. It purchases transport services from each region and supplies composite international transport services. The model assumes that the composite is used in fixed proportions with the volume of particular imports shipped via a particular route.

Notes

1 See UNFCCC (2016) for the NDCs. Although China's NDC includes also targets of CO_2 emissions per unit of GDP, the share of non-fossil fuels in primary energy consumption and forest stock volume, this chapter does not address those targets.
2 See Table 9.1 in Chapter 9 for details.
3 In Chapter 9, we analyze the global impacts of the same scenarios as in this chapter and, in particular, we deal with the impact on the bordering energy-exporting countries.
4 See Hertel (1997) for the standard GTAP model. See Truong (2007) and McDougall and Golub (2007) for the GTAP-E model. See Ianchovichina and Walmsley (2012) for the GDyn model. See Golub (2013) for the GDyn-E model.
5 See Table 7.A1 and 7.A2 in Appendix 7.1 for details.
6 EV is one of measures of economic welfare change. Briefly, EV is the income change at current prices that would be equivalent to the proposed change in the new equilibrium in terms of its impact on utility (Varian 1992: 161).
7 Percentage differences of rates of return from the baseline for China's NDC scenario are −1.5% in China, 0.3% in Oceania, and 0.4% in Indonesia; for the Paris Agreement scenario, they are −4.4% in China, −9.8% in Taiwan, −9.3% in Russia, −6.0% in the EU, −5.4% in the USA, −1.9% in India, and −1.0% in Latin America.
8 A decline in capital rental price leads to a lower rate of return. However, as the implementation of the INDs in major countries has a positive impact on China's production, the decline in capital rental price in China is relatively small, and the decline in profitability is relatively small as seen in note 7.
9 For EV decomposition, see Huff and Hertel (2000) and Walmsley et al. (2012).
10 For capital, see Table 7.4. Percentage differences from the baseline of supply of global transportation services as follows. In China's NDC scenario: 0.4% in water transportation, 0.4% in air transportation, and 1.2% in other transportation. In the Paris Agreement scenario, the respective percentage differences are 9.6%, 10.7%, and 6.1%.
11 Carbon intensity (kg/$): for oil: 0.19 in China, 0.03 in the Middle East, and 0.02 in sub-Saharan Africa. The share of capital rental cost to total cost (%): for coal: 11.8 in China, 21.4 in Oceania, and 55.3 in Indonesia; for oil: 24 in China, 53.8 in the Middle East, and 38.3 in sub-Saharan Africa; for gas: 2.7 in China, 18.7 in Turkestan, and 18.5 in Russia.

References

Burniaux, J.M. and Truong, T.P. (2002) GTAP-E: An energy-environmental version of the GTAP model, *GTAP Technical Paper 16*, West Lafayette, IN: Center for Global Trade Analysis, Purdue University.

Chappuis, T. and Walmsley, T.L. (2011) Projections for World CGE Model baseline, *GTAP Research Memorandum, 22*, West Lafayette, IN: Center for Global Trade Analysis, Purdue University.

Golub, A. (2013) Analysis of climate policies with GDyn-E, *GTAP Technical Paper 32*, West Lafayette, IN: Center for Global Trade Analysis, Purdue University.

Hertel, T.W. (1997) *Global Trade Analysis: Modeling and Applications*, Cambridge: Cambridge University Press.

Huff, K.M. and Hertel, T.W. 2000. Decomposing welfare changes in the GTAP Model, *GTAP Technical Paper 5*, West Lafayette, IN: Center for Global Trade Analysis, Purdue University.

Ianchovichina, E.I. and Walmsley, T.L. (2012) *Dynamic Modeling and Applications for Global Economic Analysis*, Cambridge: Cambridge University Press.

IEA (2015) *CO₂ Emissions from Fuel Combustion*, Paris: OECD Publishing.

McDougall, R. and Golub, A. (2007) GTAP-E: Revised energy-environmental version of the GTAP model, *GTAP Research Memorandum, 15*, West Lafayette, IN: Center for Global Trade Analysis, Purdue University.

Truong, T.P. (2007) GTAP-E: An energy-environmental version of the GTAP model with emission trading: User's guide, *GTAP Resource, 2509*, https://www.gtap.agecon.purdue. edu/resources/download/3552.pdf

UNFCCC (2016) *Intended Nationally Determined Contributions (INDCs)*, http://www4. unfccc.int/submissions/INDC/Submission%20Pages/submissions.aspx

Varian, H.R. (1992) *Microeconomic Analysis*, New York: W. W. Norton & Company.

Walmsley, T.L., McDougall, R.A. and Ianchovichina, E.I. (2012) Welfare analysis in the dynamic GTAP Model, in Ianchovichina, E.I. and Walmsley, T.L. (eds.) *Dynamic Modeling and Applications for Global Economic Analysis*, Cambridge: Cambridge University Press, 158–72.

Part III

International impacts of China-induced resource boom and climate-energy policy

8   Impact of the resource boom in the 2000s on Asian-Pacific energy-exporting countries

Akihisa Mori and Le Dong

Introduction

China is aggressively searching for resources to sustain its high-speed economic growth. While it contradicts the traditional view of energy security defined as ensuring a sufficient energy supply at an affordable price with little risk, it also changed its interpretation of this view: the additional development of oil and gas around the world enhances the energy security of China through increasing global energy security (Hayashi 2006).

This interpretation justifies a huge amount of fuel imports. China has rapidly increased its oil imports since 2003 when it suffered from frequent blackouts. It diversified its suppliers from the traditional Middle Eastern oil producers of Saudi Arabia, Oman, Russia, and Iraq (which came back to the oil market after its recovery) to the African and Asian autocratic countries of Angola, Venezuela, Kazakhstan, Iran, and Sudan, on which Western countries had imposed trade sanctions. It also increased imports of natural gas, not only from the traditional liquidated natural gas (LNG) exporters of Australia, Qatar, Malaysia, and Indonesia, but also from the autocratic countries of Turkmenistan, Myanmar, and Uzbekistan by developing gas pipelines.

It was not until 2009, after the global financial crisis, that China began massive coal imports. Its 4 trillion Chinese yuan fiscal stimulus, in line with its financial relaxation policy, stimulated local governments and state enterprises to invest in infrastructure and urban development to boost the demand for iron, steel, cement, and coal. However, a shortage of transport infrastructure along with a domestic coal price hike restricted a stable domestic supply (Horii 2014), driving China to seek imports from a variety of countries including Australia, Indonesia, Russia, Mongolia, and North Korea.

China's massive fuel imports gave an additional boost to the rise in global prices of most energy and metals commodities and for some agricultural commodities in real terms. These rose to their highest ever levels in the eight years after 2003 when the resource boom began. With only a brief interruption during the global financial crisis in 2008, this continued until 2014, when Chinese economic development began to show the influence of a new economic growth model (Garnaut et al. 2013).

Some research has explored the impact of the China-induced resources boom in the early 2000s on its trade partners. While the boom enabled most resource-exporting countries to enjoy high terms of trade, strong growth in investments in expanding exports of resource-intensive goods, and the ability to spend much of this increased income as it arrived, it caused export- and import-competing industries to experience slower growth or decline (Garnaut 2015). It reduced growth in the labor-intensive manufacturing sectors of Indonesia and Vietnam during between 2001 and 2004 due to their less diversified industrial structures (Coxhead 2007). It left Indonesia and Australia with domestic political cultures and institutions poorly structured to achieve productivity-raising reforms (Garnaut 2015). Other research focuses on the impacts in later periods, but with a different viewpoint. Massive exports of palm oil to China and India reduced jobs in skill-intensive industries and increased low skill-intensive industries, resulting the Dutch disease (Coxhead and Shrestha 2016). Chinese pipeline projects may not only pose social and environmental risks but also bring about few economic benefits and little employment to Myanmar (Zhao 2011). On the other hand, the China-led oil-for-infrastructure scheme can be viewed as providing several African countries with precious capital to develop infrastructure, which has been a bottleneck to economic growth (Brautigam 2009).

Among these effects, this chapter focuses on the Dutch disease to explore whether the global resource and China-induced booms generated it and increased vulnerability to resource price shocks in six Asian-Pacific energy-exporting countries with different characteristics, as well as what these countries have done to mitigate it. To examine whether these countries went through a pathway toward the Dutch disease, the chapter employs several macroeconomic indices to analyze changes in vulnerability.

The remainder of the chapter is organized as follows. The second section conducts a literature survey on the Dutch disease to draw out an analytical framework, which is then elaborated in the third section. The fourth section analyzes the macroeconomic impacts of the disease, while the fifth section examines change in vulnerability. Then, the sixth section discusses the factors behind these changes along with the different impacts upon the case study countries. The chapter concludes with the seventh section.

The recent resource booms and the Dutch disease

Recent resource booms can cause the resource curse prevalent in many resource-exporting countries. An increase in natural resource exports makes a country less competitive in non-booming tradeable sectors, especially labor-intensive manufacturing exports that bring increasing return to scale due to the delay in learning spillovers. This can frustrate growth through the Dutch disease phenomenon (Sachs and Warner 1997). This is induced by two factors. One is a shift of labor from non-booming tradeable sectors to booming sectors (the resource-moving effect), which can crowd-out entrepreneurial activity or innovation (Sachs and Warner 2001). The other is a higher level of spending for consumption of non-tradeable goods (the spending effect), which brings further appreciation of real exchange rate (van Wijinbergen 1984). Domestic investment and output rises and adds to the spending effect. This results in larger real appreciation and current account deficit and eventually increases external debt that must be paid back.

As long as the boom is permanent, high terms of trade make countries better off as they match the high productivity. Future generations can feel comfortable about redistributing income away from future to current generations to expand their spending.

However, if it is temporary, an increase in consumption by the spending effect brings about a current account deficit, which depreciates currency and cools down the domestic spending boom once the boom subsides (Corden 1984). This eventually results in a spending cut that brings about a fall in living standards, a growth collapse, and abrupt political change (Auty 2006).

The Dutch disease is likely to negatively affect institutions critical to economic growth. Countries whose major exports are point-source resources, e.g. coffee and cocoa, are likely to be hit harder, as these resources are far more susceptible to government capture (Isham et al. 2005). Higher concentration of export goods makes the economy more vulnerable to external shock, exerting a robust negative influence on those private investments contingent upon the positive impact of fossil fuel on investment (Bond and Malik 2009). Volatility in price and exports can swamp direct positive effect of resources on growth even though well-developed financial sectors can mitigate the impact of volatility (van der Ploeg and Poelhekke 2009). The disease also perpetuates surplus rural labor and amplifies income inequality and social tension, thus changing the survival function of political elites and discourages them to manage the rent properly or use it efficiently for wealth creation (Caselli and Cunningham 2009). Political elites do not always allow other sectors to grow for fear of an increase in the likelihood of challenges from outsiders. This unresponsiveness accelerates the concentration of single or a few export goods.

Effective stabilization policy has two elements. One is to the intention to minimize the temporary contraction of non-resource industries, which will have to be reversed after a resource boom. A large increase in exports from non-resource tradeable industries – such as manufacturing, services, and agriculture – has to be preceded by a large increase in investment in these sectors. If learning spillovers are generated in a non-tradeable sector and between tradeable and non-tradeable sectors, a resource boom can shift steady-state relative productivity in favor of the non-tradeable sector – thus resulting in real exchange rate depreciation (Torik 2001).

The other element is an avoidance of real expenditure that rises income so high in the boom that it requires being reduced later (Garnaut 2015). This needs substantially large budget surpluses, which should be derived from effective mineral rent taxation regimes. Extra savings generated from resource exports can be sterilized through investments in foreign financial assets during the boom and in domestic wealth creation or productivity-raising activities after the boom (Bresser-Pereira 2013). A "park fund" can be an effective institutional tool to reduce the spending effect by setting aside part of the resource revenue offshore.

While the floating exchange rate system serves to mitigate real expenditure and rising income, it does not completely prevent a real rising. A large real depreciation is required for a country that fails to avoid real appreciation during the resource boom. As real appreciation can occur through a rise in the nominal appreciation and/or inflation higher than in other countries, both nominal appreciation- and inflation-curbing measures are required. Nominal depreciation can be facilitated by a combination of tight fiscal policy and financial relaxation policy, which enable a lower interest rate without increasing inflation in a certain setting. A flexible economic structure with a flexible labor market, in addition to labor skills (Venables 2016), confronting measures against monopolies and protection of industries can prevent the passing through of the rising import costs (Garnaut 2013).

These theoretical arguments suggest that the Dutch disease should be analyzed first in view of its macroeconomic impacts, especially on real appreciation, export goods, and the productivity of non-resource tradeable industries.

Methodology

We follow the theoretical framework presented in Corden (1984) to analyze how the economy in Asian-Pacific energy and resource-exporting countries is "infected" with the Dutch disease. In this analysis, we employ macroeconomic indicators employed in Garnaut (2015).

We analyze the impact on vulnerability to external resource price shocks by employing the UNCTAD's export concentration index. It is defined as:

$$\text{EXCON} = \frac{\sqrt{\sum_{j-1}^{N}(Ej/E)^2} - \sqrt{1/N}}{1 - \sqrt{1/N}}$$

where exports are disaggregated into N products (97 two-digit HS product categories in the UNCTAD measure) and indexed by j, E is the total value of exports, and Ej is the value of exports of product j. This index has been normalized to lie from 0 to 1, so that higher values indicate a greater concentration of exports in a narrow range of products (Bond and Malik 2009).

To explore the impact of the China-induced resource boom on the index, we employ a trade specialization coefficient (TSC; METI 2013). TSC measures the trade specification of a good in a country against a trade partner. For country j, good k, and time period t, the TSC is defined as:

$$\text{TSC}_{jkt} = (X^j_{kt} - M^j_{kt})/(X^j_{kt} + M^j_{kt})$$

where X and M respectively denote export and import of good k from country j to a trade partner. By this definition, $\text{TSC}_{jkt} > 0$ means that the export of product k from country j in year t is greater than that from a trade partner: thus, country j relatively specializes in the production of good k relative to the trade partner.

For a given industry, relative export competiveness becomes stronger as TSC_{jkt} approaches 1 and weaker as it approaches -1. As such, the TSC can analyze the change in the relative industrial competiveness against China.

However, TSC is limited in illustrating the competitiveness of a domestic industry in the market other than that of a specific trade partner. To measure its competitiveness in the world market, we calculate the revealed comparative advantage (RCA; Balassa 1965). RCA measures the intensity of a country's exports of a good relative to the intensity of world exports of that good. For country j, good k, and time period t, the RCA is defined as:

$$RCA_{jkt} = (X^j_{kt}/X^j_{Kt})/(X^W_{kt}/X^W_{Kt})$$

where K denotes the sum of all exports from country j or the world (W). By this definition, $RCA_{jkt} > 1$ means that the share of product k in the exports of country j in year t is greater than its share in total world exports in the same year: thus, country j has a comparative advantage in the production of good k. RCA_{jkt} values less than 1 imply a comparative disadvantage (Coxhead 2007).

We choose six Asian-Pacific countries exporting energy and resources to China. Australia and Indonesia are chosen as exporters of both LNG and coal with relatively developed manufacturing and therefore, a diversified economic structure. They also adopt the floating exchange rate system with an inflation-targeting policy framework. Kazakhstan and Turkmenistan are chosen as countries that were previously a part of the Soviet Union and export a large amount of oil and gas through pipelines, whose sunk costs make it difficult to diversify their export destinations. Despite the difference in detailed arrangement, both countries employ the US dollar as an exchange rate anchor.[1] Finally, Myanmar and Mongolia are chosen as countries with a large economic dependence on China for historical and geographical reasons. Though Mongolia takes the floating exchange rate system (with multiple exchange rates) and Myanmar the dual exchange system, central banks in both countries intervene in the foreign currency market to maintain a steady exchange rate.

The trade data used in this chapter is drawn from the IMF's Direction of Trade Statistics and United Nations ComTrade Database, which list annual imports and exports at the two-digit, four-digit, and six-digit Harmonized System (HS) levels. The macroeconomic data is drawn from the World Bank's World Development Indicators Data Bank and is complemented by the ADB's Key Indictors. All data is taken from 2000 to the present in order to highlight the changes before and after the boom. Data availability restricts thorough analysis in Myanmar and Turkmenistan.

Macroeconomic impacts of the resource booms

The resource booms influenced all six countries first through an increase in export value. Export value became three to ten times higher between 2011 and 2014 than in 2000, with the interruption in the global financial crisis of 2008 to 2009. The increase in export value varies by countries. Indonesia and Australia confined the rise to three to four times, while Mongolia, Myanmar, Kazakhstan, and Turkmenistan

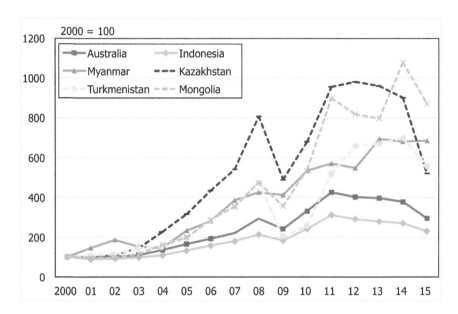

Figure 8.1 Export value index in the six countries
Source: Author compilation based on World Bank (2017).

enjoyed the hike by six to eleven times (Figure 8.1). The difference in the rise among Indonesia, Australia, and Mongolia can be explained by resource exports: while these three countries are major coal exporters to China, Australia and Mongolia also export ores and precious metals, which are much larger than coal exports.

The rise in export value prompted development in the resource sector, which helped expansion of consumption and generated the spending effect. The content of spending in the boom varied by country: whereas Australia and Mongolia enjoyed steadily higher growth in final consumption than in GDP, Kazakhstan and Indonesia saw a relatively higher growth in gross fixed capital formation (Figures 8.2a, 2b, 2c, 2d).

The expansion and composition of spending were largely affected by rent revenue and foreign investment. Turkmenistan, Kazakhstan, and Mongolia obtained a significant amount of resource rent during the boom (Figure 8.3), which prompted their governments to expand final consumption. Meanwhile, they also obtained a large inflow of foreign direct investment (Figure 8.4), most of which was directed for oil and gas deployment and pipeline development. In contrast, Australia, Indonesia, and Myanmar have obtained a relatively lower amount of resource rent – around 10 percent of GDP. Nonetheless, the governments in these countries also spent the higher revenue as it arrived, bringing about a fiscal deficit (Figure 8.5). In addition, they have rarely invested in foreign financial assets more than their inflow as a way of sterilizing the spending expansion (Figure 8.6). Most of the increased income was accrued in the private sector – including foreign companies – which spent most of it in consumption and investment.

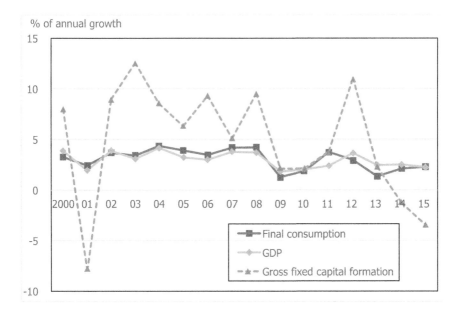

Figure 8.2a Annual growth of final consumption, GDP, and gross fixed capital formation in Australia

Source: Author compilation based on World Bank (2017).

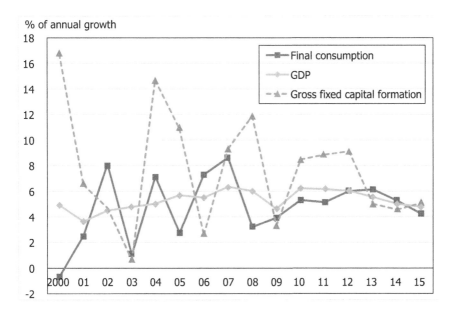

Figure 8.2b Annual growth of final consumption, GDP, and gross fixed capital formation in Indonesia

Source: Author compilation based on World Bank (2017).

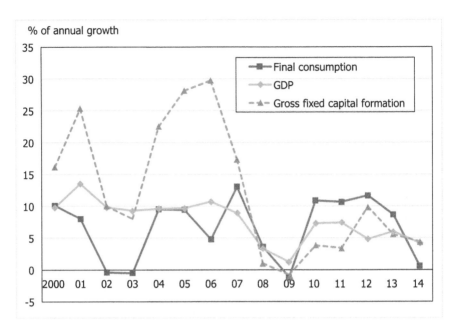

Figure 8.2c Annual growth of final consumption, GDP, and gross fixed capital formation in Kazakhstan

Source: Author compilation based on World Bank (2017).

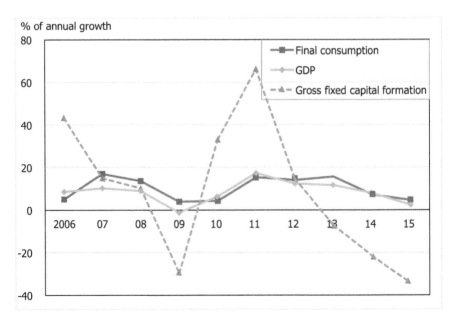

Figure 8.2d Annual growth of final consumption, GDP, and gross fixed capital formation in Mongolia

Source: Author compilation based on World Bank (2017).

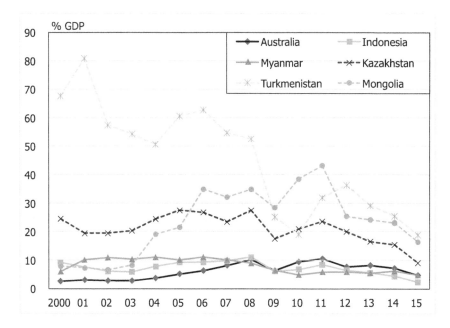

Figure 8.3 Total rent revenue from natural resources
Source: Author compilation based on World Bank (2017).

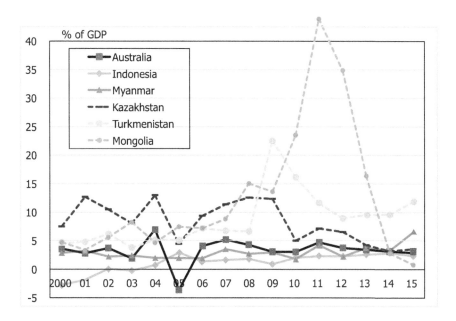

Figure 8.4 Net inflow of foreign direct investment in the six countries
Source: Author compilation based on World Bank (2017).

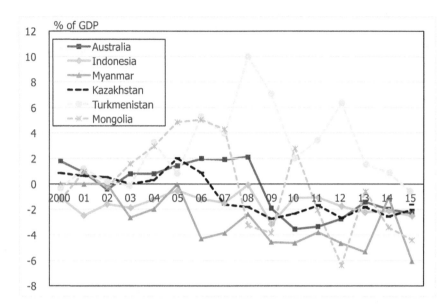

Figure 8.5 Fiscal balance in the six countries

Source: Author compilation based on Asian Development Bank (2017) and IMF (2016).

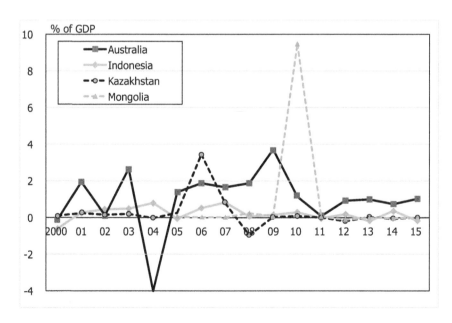

Figure 8.6 Net inflow of foreign portfolio investment in Australia, Indonesia, Kazakhstan, and Mongolia

Source: Author compilation based on World Bank (2017).

Expansion of spending has spurred a large appreciation of the real exchange rate in all six countries regardless of the composition (Figure 8.7). That is, this occurred despite the floating exchange rate system in Australia and Indonesia and the significant reductions in the external debt stock in Turkmenistan and Indonesia (Figure 8.8). Except that of Turkmenistan, the real rate was even higher

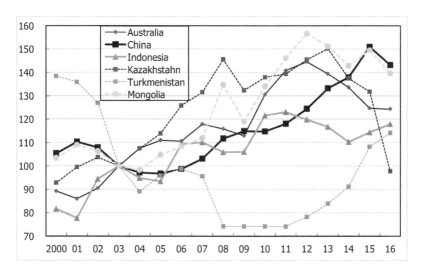

Figure 8.7 Real effective exchange rate in the six countries

Source: Author compilation based on http://bruegel.org/publications/datasets/real-effective-exchange-rates-for-178-countries-a-new-database/.

Note: 2003=100.

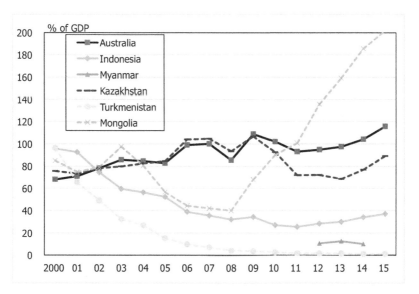

Figure 8.8 Foreign debt stock in GDP in the six countries

Source: Author compilation based on World Bank (2017).

for most years than in China, which has increased the productivity and competitiveness of manufactured goods.[2]

Real appreciation discouraged investment and production in tradeable goods and services in agricultural and industrial sectors. Their export shares fell markedly until 2011 (Figure 8.9), which increased current deficits (Figure 8.10). The

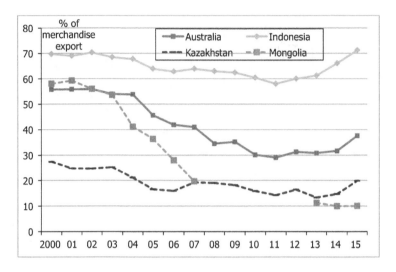

Figure 8.9 Share of agriculture and manufacturing products in the merchandise export
Source: Author compilation based on World Bank (2017).

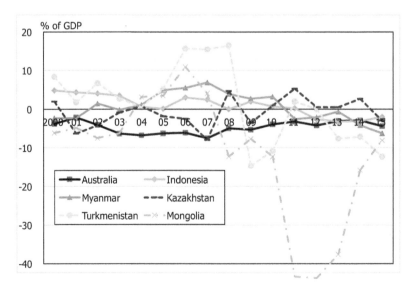

Figure 8.10 Current account in GDP in the six countries
Source: Author compilation based on World Bank (2017).

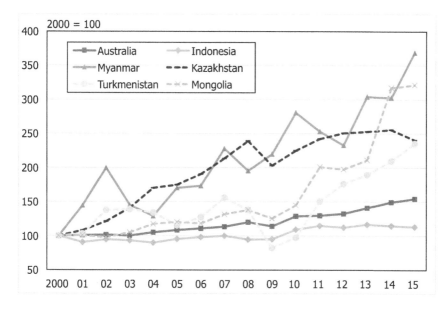

Figure 8.11 Export volume index in the six countries
Source: Author compilation based on World Bank (2017).

external debt stock leapt up and encouraged uninhibited expansion in Australia, while increasing foreign borrowing in Mongolia – first to finance investment and then consumption (Figure 8.8).

In response, Mongolia and to a less extent Australia increased their export volumes in 2012 (Figure 8.11) in order to compensate the decrease in export earnings. In contrast, until 2013, export volume does not seem to have a close relation with export value in Kazakhstan and Turkmenistan. This is resulted from the switch in their major export destination from Russia to China (Figure 8.12), enabling them to earn oil and gas revenues in long-term supply contracts regardless of fluctuations in the market prices. Nonetheless, China's economic downturn significantly reduced the 2015 trade surplus in both countries (Figure 8.13).

These macroeconomic indicators support the diagnosis of Australia, Indonesia, Kazakhstan, and Mongolia as all being infected by the Dutch disease. The seriousness of the infection varies, however. Mongolia is severely affected for a short period of time, whereas Indonesia is relatively less affected. Australia and Kazakhstan enjoyed the higher resource prices for so long a time – almost a decade – that they mistook the boom as not temporary but permanent. This accelerated real appreciation in both countries, by which Kazakhstan was more severely affected.

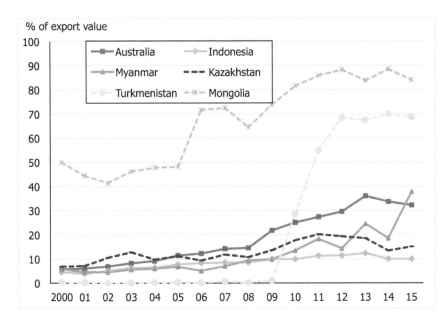

Figure 8.12 Export dependence on China

Sources: Author compilation based on IMF (2007, 2016, 2017).

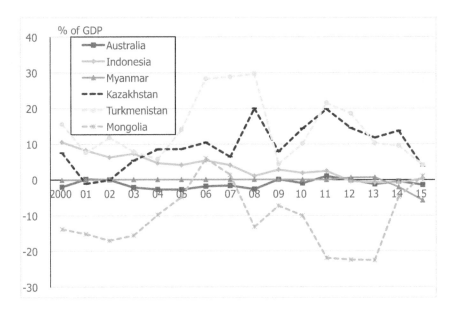

Figure 8.13 Merchandise trade balance in the six countries

Source: Author compiled based on World Bank (2017).

Export competitiveness and concentration

Trade dependence on China

The China-induced energy boom has increased export dependence on China in all six countries. In Mongolia and Turkmenistan, China accounts for more than 90 percent and 70 percent of their export destinations respectively (Figure 8.14). In Australia and Myanmar, trade dependence increased by 20 percent during the boom.

Higher export dependence on China has, in turn, increased volatility of the economy and economic growth in these countries. Turkmenistan and Mongolia regained high economic growth during 2010 and 2013 due to a steady growth of natural gas and coal exports to China (Figure 8.2a, 2b, 2c, 2d). Mongolia, on the other hand, has been hit severely by China's downturn in economic growth and restriction on coal imports and thus suffers from a declining growth rate. Kazakhstan's growth rate has also become highly affected by the oil price and China's oil demand.

Export specification

All six countries saw a rise in export concentration during the global resource and China-induced booms (Table 8.1). In Kazakhstan and Turkmenistan, the share of mineral fuels jumped up in the 1998 Russian financial crisis and further increased

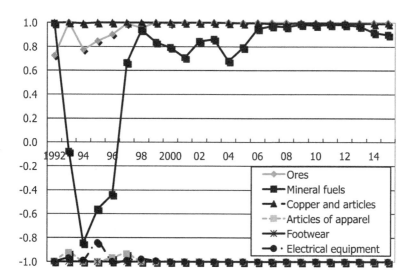

Figure 8.14 TSC of perpetuated specification subsectors in Kazakhstan
Source: Author calculation based on UN ComTrade database.

Table 8.1 Specification of export structure in the six countries

Australia

1996		2001		2004		2009		2014	
Mineral fuels	0.17	Mineral fuels	0.21	Mineral fuels	0.20	Mineral fuels	0.30	Ores	0.31
Pearls, precious stones	0.08	Ores	0.08	Ores	0.10	Ores	0.20	Mineral fuels	0.27
Ores	0.07	Meat	0.05	Meat	0.05	Pearls, precious stones	0.08	Pearls, precious stones	0.06
Cereals	0.07	Pearls, precious stones	0.05	Pearls, precious stones	0.05	Meat	0.03	Meat	0.04
Machinery	0.06	Cereals	0.05	Cereals	0.05	Cereals	0.03	Cereals	0.03
Sum	0.45		0.44		0.46		0.64		0.70
UNCTAD's export concentration index	0.16		0.18		0.19		0.31		0.35

Mongolia

1996		2001		2004		2009		2014	
Ores	0.52	Ores	0.34	Ores	0.36	N.A.	N.A.	Ores	0.56
Wool	0.18	Apparel	0.23	Gold	0.27	N.A.	N.A.	Mineral fuels	0.26
Fluorine minerals	0.05	Wool	0.15	Apparel	0.16	N.A.	N.A.	Gold	0.07
Apparel	0.06	Leather	0.13	Wool	0.06	N.A.	N.A.	Wool	0.05
Leather	0.05	Fluorine minerals	0.05	Mineral fuels	0.03	N.A.	N.A.	Fluorine minerals	0.01
Sum	0.87		0.89		0.88	N.A.			0.95
UNCTAD's export concentration index	0.51		0.37		0.41	N.A.			0.58

Myanmar

1992		2001		2004		2010		2014	
Wood	0.33	N.A.	N.A.	N.A.	N.A.	Mineral fuels	0.39	N.A.	N.A.
Vegetables	0.24	N.A.	N.A.	N.A.	N.A.	Pearls, precious stones	0.25	N.A.	N.A.
Cereals	0.10	N.A.	N.A.	N.A.	N.A.	Vegetables	0.12	N.A.	N.A.
Fish	0.08	N.A.	N.A.	N.A.	N.A.	Wood	0.08	N.A.	N.A.
Seed, fruit	0.07	N.A.	N.A.	N.A.	N.A.	Apparel	0.04	N.A.	N.A.
Sum	0.81						0.87		
UNCTAD's export concentration index	0.37		N.A.		N.A.		0.42		N.A.

Kazakhstan

1996		2001		2004		2009		2014	
Mineral fuels	0.33	Mineral fuels	0.56	Mineral fuels	0.64	Mineral fuels	0.70	Mineral fuels	0.76
Iron and steel	0.15	Iron and steel	0.12	Iron and steel	0.11	Iron and steel	0.07	Iron and steel	0.04
Copper	0.10	Copper	0.08	Copper	0.06	Precious metal	0.05	Precious metal	0.04
Cereals	0.07	Cereals	0.04	Ores	0.04	Ores	0.04	Ores	0.03
Precious metal	0.07	Precious metal	0.03	Precious metal	0.03	Copper	0.04	Copper	0.02
Sum	0.72		0.84		0.88		0.89		0.90
UNCTAD's export concentration index	0.33		0.54		0.62		0.67		0.74

Turkmenistan

1997		2001		2004		2009		2014	
Mineral fuels	0.77	Mineral fuels	0.97	Mineral fuels	0.96	Mineral fuels	0.80	Mineral fuels	0.97
Cotton	0.16	Cotton	0.01	Cotton	0.02	Cotton	0.02	Cement and Salt	0.01
Cement and Salt	0.01	Fabrics	0.00	Textile	0.00	Plastics	0.01	Plastics	0.00
Leather	0.01	Wool	0.00	Carpets	0.00	Vegetable	0.01	Cotton	0.00
Fabric	0.01	Apparel	0.00	Apparel	0.00	Apparel	0.01	Textile	0.00
Sum	0.95		0.99		0.99		0.85		0.99
UNCTAD's export concentration index	0.76		0.95		0.96		0.79		0.94

Source: Author compilation based on UN ComTrade.

Note: Export of Turkmenistan is the sum of its export to China, EU, Ukraine, Russia, and Kazakhstan, which accounts for 98 percent in 2001, 2004, 2009, and 2015.

during the resource boom in the 2000s, crowding out other exports. While export concentration in Turkmenistan declined between 2008 and 2009 from Russia's gas import ban, it returned once the country started exporting gas to China. As a result, the UNCTAD's export concentration index reached 0.74 and 0.94 in Kazakhstan and Turkmenistan respectively at the end of the China-induced boom.

Behind the larger export concentration is a change in the trade structure with China as well as in export competitiveness. Kazakhstan and Turkmenistan went through a major change in the specialization of mineral fuels in their trade with China. While they depended on oil products and electricity from China in the

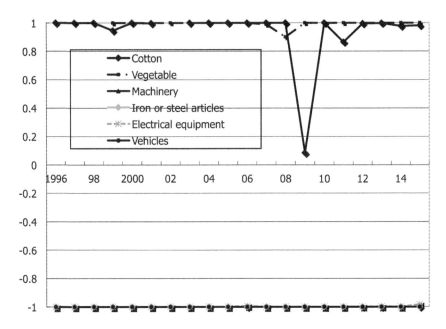

Figure 8.15 TSC of perpetuated specification subsectors in Turkmenistan
Source: Author calculation based on UN ComTrade database.

1990s, Kazakhstan and Turkmenistan had a surge in crude oil exports to China in 1997 and in 2010 respectively. The real appreciation accompanying the boom made both exports and imports specialization stronger. Both countries can only export goods that are strongly specialized in copper, iron, steel, and precious metals in Kazakhstan (Figure 8.14), and cotton and vegetables in Turkmenistan (Figure 8.15). Despite the decline, these products still retain a comparative advantage in the world market (Figure 8.16, 8.17).

Australia and Mongolia also experienced a significant rise in export concentration in mineral fuels *and ores* during the global resource and China-induced booms. In 2014, these two goods account for 58 percent and 82 percent of the total export in Australia and Mongolia, respectively. Accordingly, the UNCTAD's export concentration index increased to 0.58 in Mongolia. Though the index measures smaller in Australia, it is 20 points higher in 2014 than in 2001, which indicates ongoing export concentration.

As in Kazakhstan and Turkmenistan, both countries had not specialized in exports of mineral fuels in the trade with China, though they had for ores, wool, and copper before the boom. Australia imported petroleum products, whereas Mongolia depended on oil products and electricity from China. Real appreciation also strengthened specialization and only wool survives as an export good besides fuels ores and copper (Figure 8.18, 8.19), while aluminum, precious metals, machine and electric equipment in Australia, and apparel articles, iron, and steel in Mongolia

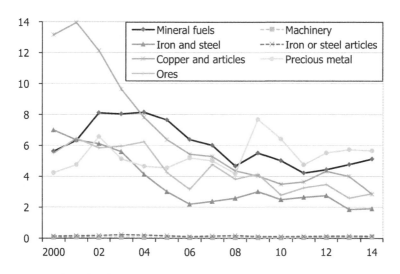

Figure 8.16 RCA of major traded goods in Kazakhstan

Source: Author calculation based on UN ComTrade database.

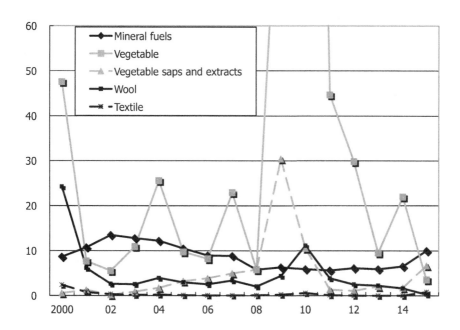

Figure 8.17 RCA of top five export goods in Turkmenistan

Source: Author calculation based on UN ComTrade database.

Note: Export of Turkmenistan is the sum of its export to China, EU, Ukraine, Russia, and Kazakhstan, which accounts for 98 percent in 2001, 2004, 2009, and 2015.

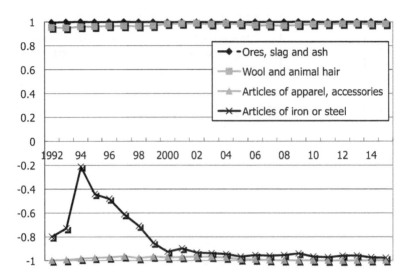

Figure 8.18 TSC of perpetuated specification subsectors in Australia
Source: Author calculation based on UN ComTrade database.

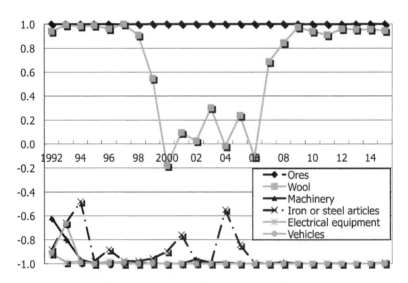

Figure 8.19 TSC of perpetuated specification subsectors in Mongolia
Source: Author calculation based on UN ComTrade database.

fell in import specialization (Figure 8.20, 8.21). Nonetheless, in addition to the above fuels and resources, Australia retains competitiveness in precious metals, precious stones as well as meat in the world market (Figure 8.22). This prevents export concentration from rising too much compared with Mongolia, which, besides mineral fuels and ores, retains competitiveness only in precious stones (Figure 8.23).

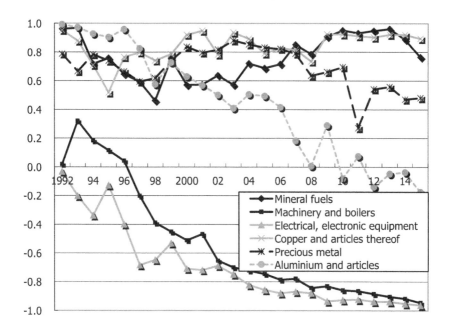

Figure 8.20 TSC in changing specialization sectors in Australia
Source: Author calculation based on UN ComTrade database.

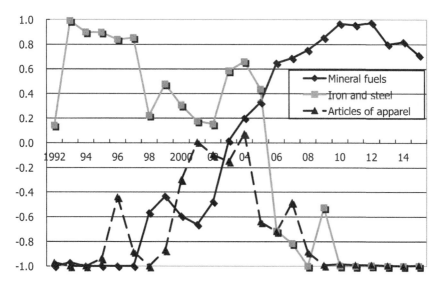

Figure 8.21 TSC in changing specialization sectors in Mongolia
Source: Author calculation based on UN ComTrade database.

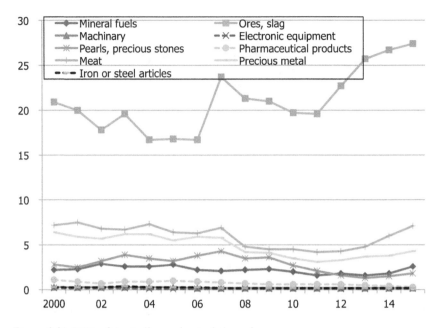

Figure 8.22 RCA of Australian major traded goods

Source: Author calculation based on UN ComTrade database.

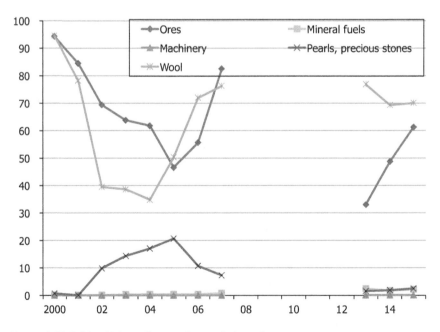

Figure 8.23 RCA of Mongolian top five traded goods

Source: Author compilation based on UN ComTrade database.

In its trade with China, Myanmar also changed its specialization in mineral fuel from import to export once it started exporting natural gas. This did not, however, affect specialization in other tradeable goods. In the 1990s, major exportable goods – such as precious metals, wood, and ores – had already been specialized in exports and major importable goods – such as manufacturing of iron and steel articles – as imports (Figure 8.24). Data availability inhibits us from concluding that the China-induced resource boom is associated with export concentration.

In contrast, the concentration index rises only slightly in Indonesia notwith-standing a significant increase in the share of vegetable oil in total export. This implies the Indonesian economy keeps relatively higher adaptive capacity to resource price shock despite a loss of manufacturing competitiveness against China.

Indonesia had not specialized in the exports of mineral fuels in its trade with China because of the latter's export surge in petroleum products. In fact, it did not completely specialize in fuel exports even during the China-induced boom. This creates a sharp difference in the extent of real appreciation and change in trade specialization from the other five countries. It did go through specialization in the imports of major exportable manufacturing goods – such as machines, electrical equipment, and chemicals – which used to be a main driving force for industrialization. But the speed of specialization is much slower than in other countries (Figure 8.25). This enables these products to keep comparative advan-tage in the world market despite decline in the exports (Figure 8.26).

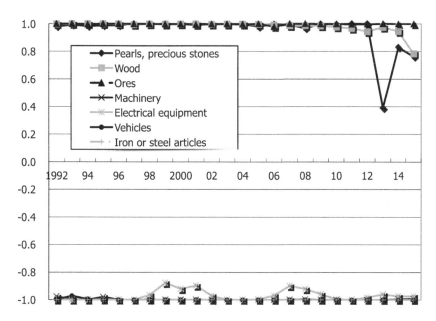

Figure 8.24 TSC of perpetuated specification subsectors in Myanmar

Source: Author calculation based on UN ComTrade database.

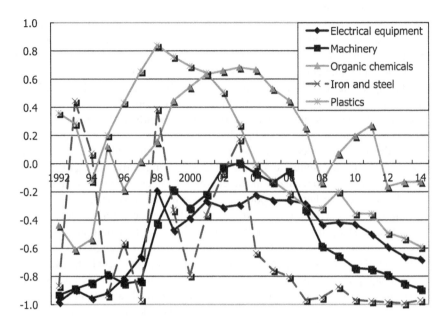

Figure 8.25 TSC in changing specialization sectors in Indonesia
Source: Author calculation based on UN ComTrade database.

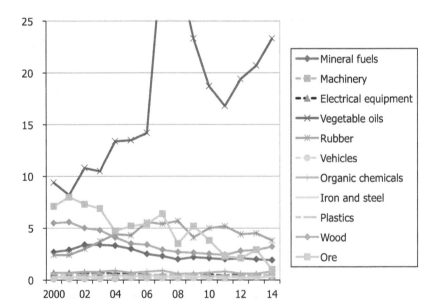

Figure 8.26 RCA of Indonesian major traded goods
Source: Author calculation based on UN ComTrade database.

These findings suggest that except Indonesia, the global resource and the China-induced booms raised their vulnerability of the case study countries to resource price shocks by *accelerating* specialization in the exports of resource-based commodities and the imports of manufacturing sectors, which either had been undergoing specialization prior to these booms, or had completed specialization through massive imports of these products from China. In addition, though the China-induced boom has changed the industrial structure and competitiveness of Indonesia, it has not severely affected Indonesia's adaptive capacity to resource price shocks so far.

Discussion

Vulnerability to resource price shock becomes apparent when a resource boom subsides. Declining export value after 2013 is associated with decelerating investment, lower GDP growth, and to a lesser extent consumption in Australia, Indonesia, Kazakhstan, and Mongolia (Figures 8.2a, 2b, 2c, 2d). Fiscal balance has deteriorated, turning into deficit even in Turkmenistan, which gains significant resource rent from pipeline gas exports to China (Figure 8.5). Real appreciation and accelerated export specialization have lowered competitiveness in most exportable agricultural and manufacturing goods. This leads to a decline in the share of agriculture and manufacturing in merchandise exports, with the regain between 2014 and 2015 owing to an increase of export volume (Figure 8.9). While a few resource-based products such as wool, cotton, and vegetable oil remain competitive, most of them generate low added-value and small learning spillover.

Indonesia retains several labor-intensive manufacturing products that are competitive in the world market. This results from the relatively low real appreciation, smaller natural resource endowment per capita, being less complementary with Chinese import specifications – except coal – (Garnaut 2015), and using resource rent to invest in agricultural development for self-sufficiency in paddy rice (Bature 2013), and tight fiscal controls. Sufficient domestic rice production helps stabilize food price, preventing labor costs from becoming too high for the manufacturing sector to be competitive (like in Africa). Structural adjustment imposed by the IMF and the World Bank in the 1980s and the requirement for fuel subsidy reform by IMF during the Asian financial crisis in 1997 onwards, all made the Indonesian government strengthen its fiscal discipline (Mori 1997), and thus restrict the spending effect. This enabled the country to escape from "hollowing-out" of manufacturing: a decline of domestic value addition in total output (Banga 2014; Figure 8.27).

Nonetheless, the China-induced resource boom has weakened resilience to resource price shocks in all six countries, including Indonesia. Growth of agricultural and manufacturing export is no longer powerful enough to balance the decline in real purchasing power of resource exports in Australia, Indonesia, Kazakhstan, and Mongolia (Figure 8.28a, 28b, 28c, 28d). An increase in RCA in vegetable oil and rubber (Figure 8.26) does not help reduce the vulnerability in Indonesia either, as these products are also hit by the decline in global price.

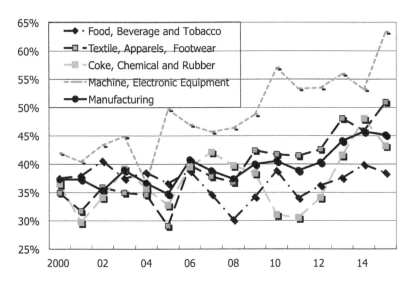

Figure 8.27 Manufacturing value added in the output value in Indonesia

Sources: Author compiled based on *Statistik Indonesia*, each year.

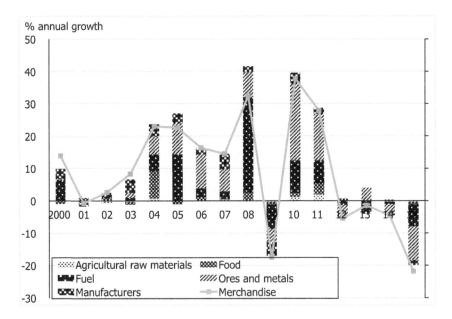

Figure 8.28a Composition of annual export growth in Australia

Source: Author calculation based on World Bank (2017).

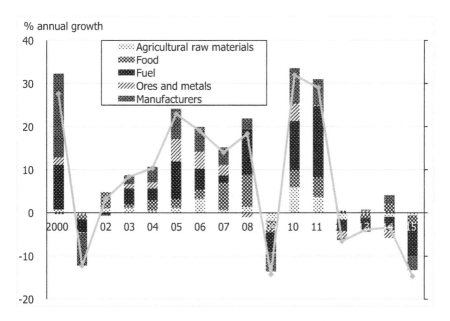

Figure 8.28b Composition of annual export growth in Indonesia
Source: Author calculation based on World Bank (2017).

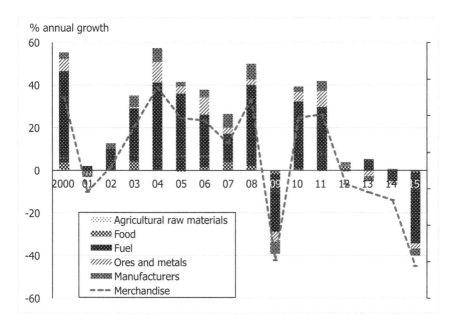

Figure 8.28c Composition of annual export growth in Kazakhstan
Source: Author calculation based on World Bank (2017).

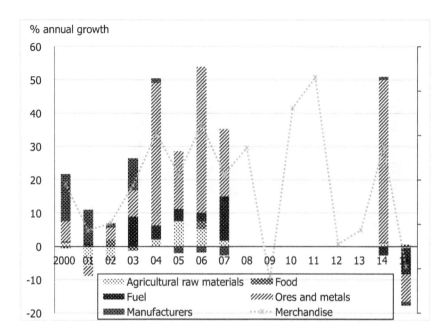

Figure 8.28d Composition of annual export growth in Mongolia
Source: Author calculation based on World Bank (2017).

Mongolia even lost half of its foreign reserves and suffers from economic stag-nation and inflation brought about by nominal currency depreciation.

Energy-exporting countries are primarily responsible for real appreciation. They regarded the resource boom as permanent and have made few systematic attempts to retain the large amount of resource revenue for use after the boom. The resource-to-cash program in Mongolia, which directly allocated windfall resource revenues to specific priority programs, simply expanded government spending – generating higher inflation and increasing its foreign debt stock (Yeung and Howes 2015). Kazakhstan allocated most of its gains directly to supporters through a fuel subsidy (Luong and Weinthal 2010). While Indonesia did allocate part of its increased revenue for *cutting* fuel subsidies, it spent most of this revenue as soon as it arrived, which generated a fiscal deficit. Australia and Indonesia continue ad valorem royalties without changing into a profit-based royalty system that is more economically efficient under private ownership. This short-sightedness made them slow down efforts to increase productivity and competitiveness in both resource and non-resource export sectors during the boom.

Despite inducing the resource boom, China has done little to help these countries escape from the Dutch disease and rescue them from economic distress. What the Chinese government has done so far is settle a bilateral currency swap agreement with Mongolia in 2011 at the size of CNY 15 billion yuan (US$2.18 billion) with an extension every three years. Still, this is implemented as part of an internalization strategy of its currency, not for compensating adverse impacts. This makes Mongolia rush to the IMF, World Bank, and Asian development Bank to ask for help in repaying the external debt it has accumulated in financing its boosted investments and consumption (Figure 8.8). The Chinese government neither provides financial assistance nor allows cancelation of loan repayments.

This stance also has implications for Turkmenistan and Kazakhstan, which developed gas pipelines with loans from the China Development Bank and the Export-Import Bank of China. Both countries are repaying these loans by selling natural gas to China at a lower price than the international price referenced to at the time of contract. Moreover, they must continue selling it at a low price beyond the contract period or at a much lower price if China reduces gas imports (unless the contract has the take-or-pay clause). This will make the adverse impacts of the Dutch disease worse, leading to the economic ruin and political turmoil happening already in Venezuela, where the government uses oil revenue in an unsustainable way, subsidizing the consumption by citizens in exchange for being able to regulate every aspect of their daily lives (Gallegos 2016). Here too, the Chinese government offered no financial rescue to Venezuela despite the huge amount of loan provision under its debt-for-oil contract.

The Chinese government also encourages its companies to make direct investments in energy-exporting countries to help them enhance productivity-raising activities. But this poses a risk of adverse impacts on livelihood and ecology, while creating pollution havens by increasing carbon emissions in host countries (Chapters 10 and 11 in this book).

Conclusions

This chapter aims to explore whether the global resource and China-induced booms caused the Dutch disease in six Asian-Pacific energy-exporting countries, along with what these countries have done to escape from it. It draws three conclusions.

First, macroeconomic indicators show that all six countries have been infected by the Dutch disease, but to varied degrees. While Mongolia was hit hardest with significant fluctuation of currency, trade and current accounts, and GDP in these booms, Indonesia was much less affected. Australia and Kazakhstan, on the other hand, enjoyed higher resource prices for so long a time that they left real appreciation unaddressed, leading to more severe impacts.

Second, besides Indonesia, all other case study countries have increased vulnerability to external resource price shocks during these booms as these booms *accelerated* specialization and export concentration that had already been ongoing beforehand. Although the China-induced resource boom weakened the industrial competitiveness and resulted in change of industrial structure in Indonesia, it has not seriously harmed the country's adaptive capacity to resource price shocks so far.

Finally, China has provided little supports for these countries to avoid the Dutch disease or counteract its adverse impacts despite inducing one of the responsible resource booms.

Notes

1 Kazakhstan adopts the soft peg (stabilized arrangement) and Turkmenistan takes the fixed exchange system.
2 Turkmenistan also suffered from real appreciation after its independence as it increased oil and gas imports to former Soviet Union countries. Russia's resurge as a major oil- and gas-exporting country has deprived Turkmenistan of international competitiveness as Turkmenistan's exports relied completely on pipelines that transported oil and gas to Russia. This brought about significant real depreciation in the mid-2000s. The rate recovered when Turkmenistan started gas exports to China, and goes well beyond the level of 2003.

References

Asian Development Bank (2017) *Key Indicators for Asia and the Pacific 2016*, Manila: Asian Development Bank.

Auty, R.M. (2006) Resource-driven models of the development of the political economy, in Auty, R.M. and de Soysa, I. (eds.) *Energy, Wealth and Governance in the Caucasus and Central Asia: Lessons Not Learnt*, Oxon: Routledge, 17–36.

Balassa, B. (1965) Trade liberalization and 'revealed' comparative advantage, *Manchester School* 33: 99–123.

Banga, R. (2014) Trade facilitation and 'hollowing-out' of Indian manufacturing, *Economic and Political Weekly* 49(40): 57–63.

Bature, B.N. (2013) The Dutch disease and the diversification of an economy: Some case studies, *IOSR Journal of Humanities and Social Science* 15(5): 6–14.

Bond, S.R. and Malik, A. (2009) Natural resources, export structure, and investment, *Oxford Economic Papers* 61: 675–702.

Brautigam, D. (2009) *The Dragon's Gift: The Real Story of China in Africa*, Oxford: Oxford University Press.

Bresser-Pereira, L.C. (2013) The value of the exchange rate and the Dutch disease, *Brazilian Journal of Political Economy* 33: 371–87.

Caselli, F. and Cunningham, T. (2009) Leader behaviour and the natural resource curse, *Oxford Economic Papers* 61: 628–50.

Corden, W.M. (1984) Booming sector and Dutch disease economics: Survey and consolidation, *Oxford Economic Papers* 36(3): 359–80.

Coxhead, I. (2007) A new resource curse? Impacts of China's boom on comparative advantage and resource dependence in Southeast Asia, *World Development* 35(7): 1099–119.

Coxhead, I. and Shrestha, R. (2016) Could a resource export boom reduce workers' earnings? The labour-market channel in Indonesia, *Bulletin of Indonesian Economic Studies* 52(2): 185–208.

Gallegos, R. (2016) *Crude Nation: How Oil Riches Ruined Venezuela*, Nebraska: Potomac Books.

Garnaut, R. (2013) *Dog Days: Australia after the Boom*, Melbourne: Black Inc.

Garnaut, R. (2015) Indonesia's resources boom in international perspective: Policy dilemmas and options for continued strong growth, *Bulletin of Indonesian Economic Studies* 51(2): 189–212.

Garnaut, R., Fang, C. and Song, L. (eds.) (2013) *China: A New Model for Growth and Development*, Canberra: ANU E Press.

Hayashi, K. (2006) Conditions for high-performer in international oil and gas upstream industry: A CERA proposal for increasing international competitiveness of Japanese firms, *Oil and Gas Review* 40(3): 33–41 (in Japanese).

Horii, N. (2014) Energy: Pricing reforms and the end of low energy price, in Watanabe, M. (ed.) *The Disintegration of Production: Firm Strategy and Industrial Development in China*, Cheltenham: Edward Elgar, 307–33.

IMF (2007) *Direction of Trade Statistics Yearbook 2006*, Washington, DC: IMF.

IMF (2016) *Direction of Trade Statistics Yearbook 2015*, Washington, DC: IMF.

IMF (2017) *Direction of Trade Statistics Yearbook 2016*, Washington, DC: IMF.

Isham, J., Woolcock, M., Pritchett, L. and Busby, G. (2005) The varieties of resource experiences: Natural resource export structures and the political economy of economic growth, *World Bank Economic Review* 19(2): 141–74.

Luong, P.J. and Weinthal, E. (2010) *Oil Is Not a Curse: Ownership Structure and Institutions in Soviet Successor States*, Cambridge: Cambridge University Press.

Ministry of Economy, Trade and Industry, Japan (METI) (2013) Supporting industries and companies with potential to advance into foreign markets, *White Paper on International Economy and Trade 2013*, www.meti.go.jp/english/report/downloadfiles/2013 WhitePaper/2-3.pdf, accessed on August 1, 2014.

Mori, A. (1997) Economic development strategy and tax reform: A comparative analysis of the reform in the four ASEAN countries in the 1980s, *The Economic Review (Kyoto University)* 160(1): 28–57 (in Japanese).

Sachs, J.D. and Warner, A.M. (1997) The big push, natural resource booms and growth, *Journal of Development Economics* 59: 43–76.

Sachs, J.D. and Warner, A.M. (2001) The curse of natural resources, *European Economic Review* 45: 827–38.

Torik, R. (2001) Learning by doing and the Dutch disease, *European Economic Review* 45: 285–306.

van der Ploeg, F. and Poelhekke, S. (2009) Volatility and the natural resource curse, *Oxford Economic Papers* 61: 727–60.

van Wijinbergen, S. (1984) The 'Dutch disease': A disease after all? *Economic Journal* 94: 41–55.

Venables, A.J. (2016) Using natural resources for development: Why has it proven so difficult? *Journal of Economic Perspectives* 30(1): 161–84.

World Bank (2017) *World Development Indicators Databank*, as of April 27, 2017.

Yeung, Y. and Howes, S. (2015) Resources-to-cash: A cautionary tale from Mongolia, *Development Policy Centre Discussion Paper #42*, Crawford School of Public Policy, Australian National University, Canberra.

Zhao, H. (2011) China–Myanmar energy cooperation and its regional implications, *Journal of Current Southeast Asian Affairs* 30(4): 89–109.

9 Economic and carbon impacts of China's NDC and the Paris Agreement on Asian energy-exporting countries

Hikari Ban and Kiyoshi Fujikawa

Introduction

By January 2018, a total of 173 of 197 parties, including China, had ratified the Paris Agreement. Specific rules have been advanced to make the agreement effective, and climate policies were and/or are going to be implemented according to the Nationally Determined Contributions (NDCs) in each party.

However, several problems plague equitable international distributions of burden.[1] Table 7.2 reveals that annual targets for reducing CO_2 impose considerable differences in burden, even on developed economies. In addition, countries participating in the Paris Agreement include exporters and importers of energy, and predicted paths of economic development vary for each participant.

Satisfying the principle of equity is fundamental to the formation of international and domestic consensus. Although simulation analysis cannot resolve problems of equity, its assessments may provide clues. Chapter 7 discussed the impacts of China's peak-out and the Paris Agreement on China. This chapter studies the global impact of climate policies using the model, data, and simulation scenarios in Chapter 7. We focus on production of coal and gas and trade among China's bordering countries.

Table 9.1 shows the top eight countries'/regions' shares of China's energy imports in 2011 measured by toe (percent). Indonesia accounts for nearly half of China's coal imports, followed by Australia and Mongolia. China imports oil primarily from the Middle East, Africa, and Russia. The category Rest of Former Soviet Union, which includes Tajikistan, Turkmenistan, and Uzbekistan, accounts for nearly 90% of gas imports. Generally, China imports oil mainly from the Middle East and Africa, while it imports coal and gas from its bordering countries. We focus on coal and gas sectors because China's carbon policy likely will affect their output and trade remarkably, as Chapter 7 suggests. Regions covered in this chapter include Oceania, Indonesia, Vietnam, Other Asia, Russia, and sub-Saharan Africa (SSA) for coal and Oceania, Indonesia, Malaysia, Russia, Turkestan, and the Middle East and North Africa (MENA) for gas.

Structural changes in baseline scenario

We begin by describing structural changes to industry and in factor endowments of each country in the baseline scenario. We do so because the effects of carbon policy depend on trends in the baseline, as shown later.

Table 9.1 China's import share measured in toe (%)

Coal		Oil		Gas	
Indonesia	45.5	South Central Africa	14.8	Rest of Former Soviet Union	88.2
Australia	13.6	Saudi Arabia	12.5	Qatar	4.8
Mongolia	12.9	Iran	12.3	Rest of Western Asia	1.3
Russia	6.6	Russia	10.7	Australia	1.1
South Africa	6.2	Oman	8.2	Indonesia	1.1
Rest of East Asia	5.6	Rest of Western Asia	7.8	Russia	1.1
Vietnam	4.6	Kazakhstan	5.2	Malaysia	0.7
Rest of World	5.1	Rest of World	28.5	Rest of World	1.7

Source: Authors' calculations with the GTAP 9 Data Base.

Note: Rest of East Asia includes the Democratic People's Republic of Korea and Macao. South Central Africa is Angola and the Democratic Republic of the Congo. Rest of Western Asia includes Iraq, Lebanon, Occupied Palestine, the Syrian Arab Republic, and Yemen. Rest of Former Soviet Union includes Tajikistan, Turkmenistan, and Uzbekistan.

In 2030 of the baseline, compared with 2020, production rises in all industries in China, Taiwan, Thailand, Indonesia, Malaysia, Vietnam, Other ASEAN, India, Mexico, Russia, MENA, and SSA. Indonesia's coal (125.6% compared with 2020), India's coal (161.2%), MENA's coal (92.4%) and gas (117.2%), and SSA's coal (181.9%) and gas (218.4%) show growth rates considerably above the GDP.

Comparatively many industries in Oceania, Japan, and Singapore show negative growth rates in 2030 compared with 2020. In Oceania, production of coal (−38.8%) and gas (−43%) decline remarkably. Production of textiles and clothing, chemical products, iron, transportation equipment, electronic equipment, and other manufactures also decline. The service sector expands in Oceania. Japan shows slightly less negative growth in the industries noted for Oceania. Singapore shows negative growth in agriculture, forestry, fishing, coal, oil, and gas with low production volume and relatively high growth in petroleum and coal products, electricity, chemical products, nonmetallic minerals, and iron. Results imply that Singapore becomes more industrialized.

Supplies of land and natural resources remain constant, but prices change with demand. Natural-resource rental prices rise universally and dramatically (300%) in Other Asia, SSA, and Latin America. They decline in Japan and Singapore. Supply of unskilled labor declines in China, Japan, Korea, Taiwan, Singapore, Thailand, Canada, the US, the EU, Other Europe, Russia, and Turkestan, but wages rise universally. Supply of skilled labor rises in all regions, but the growth rate is high in Indonesia, Malaysia, Vietnam, Other ASEAN, India, Other Asia, MENA, and SSA. Wages for skilled labor decline in Other ASEAN, MENA, and SSA. Capital stock increases in all countries, and its growth is high in China (110.6%), Taiwan (90.9%), Indonesia (94.9%), India (119.7%), and Other Asia (115.2%). Capital rental rates rise in Oceania, Japan, Vietnam, Canada, and the US but decline in other countries.

Analysis of macro impacts

We now examine China's NDC (C-NDC) scenario in which only China achieves its peak carbon target in 2030, and the Paris Agreement (PA) scenario, in which major countries including China achieve their NDCs (see Chapter 7).

This section discusses the macro impact of carbon restrictions. Table 9.2 illustrates China's NDC scenario. China's carbon policy exerts a slightly positive effect on other countries' GDP as measured by the difference rate from the baseline in 2030. Indonesia is highest (0.5%) through a relatively large increase in capital stock (Table 9.4). CO_2 emissions decline in China and Taiwan but rise slightly in other regions. Comparing the percentage differences of CO_2 emissions from the baseline with those of GDP, we can see that CO_2/GDP deteriorates in many regions where GDP increases.

Table 9.2 Macro impacts under the C-NDC scenario (differences from the baseline, 2030)

	GDP	EV*		Terms of trade	Domestic equity income**	Foreign equity income***	Carbon price of CO_2 ($/ton)		CO_2
	(%)	(Billion $)	(%)	(%)	(Billion $)	(Billion $)	Nominal	Real	(%)
Oceania	0.1	−12.9	−1.7	−1.9	−3.0	−1.4			0.0
China	−1.1	−138.3	−1.2	−0.0	−191.9	55.4	3.2	3.3	−28.5
Japan	0.2	8.5	0.9	0.4	6.8	−7.2			0.2
Korea	0.2	3.1	1.2	0.2	1.5	−1.8			0.2
Taiwan	0.0	−1.3	−0.4	−0.1	−0.9	−0.6			−0.3
Indonesia	0.5	11.1	1.5	0.9	7.8	−0.0			0.4
Malaysia	0.2	0.5	0.3	0.0	0.1	−0.3			0.2
Singapore	0.2	0.2	0.1	0.1	0.3	−0.7			0.3
Thailand	0.3	1.3	0.8	0.1	−0.0	−0.0			0.4
Vietnam	0.3	0.4	0.6	0.0	−0.0	0.0			0.3
O_ASEAN	0.1	0.3	0.3	−0.1	−0.1	0.0			0.4
India	0.2	10.2	0.5	0.2	1.7	0.0			0.9
O_Asia	0.2	4.8	1.2	0.4	0.3	−0.0			0.2
Canada	0.1	0.0	−0.0	−0.1	0.9	−1.6			0.2
US	0.1	12.7	0.3	0.2	−3.5	−2.3			0.2
Mexico	0.1	1.6	0.5	0.1	−0.9	0.0			0.1
Latin	0.3	1.2	0.1	−0.5	2.6	−0.0			0.6
EU28	0.2	22.1	0.9	0.1	9.3	−12.6			0.3
O_Euro	0.1	−0.5	−0.2	−0.1	0.5	−1.9			0.3
Russia	0.2	0.6	0.1	−0.2	3.2	−3.3			0.3
Turkestan	0.2	−0.3	−0.2	−0.3	0.1	−0.3			0.4
MENA	0.2	9.4	0.4	0.0	8.5	−5.4			0.3
SSA	0.2	2.0	0.2	−0.2	0.8	−0.0			0.6

Sources: Authors' simulations with GDyn and the GTAP 9 Data Base.

Note

  * EV is the total difference from the baseline of equivalent variation from 2020 to 2030.

  ** Income on equity paid to regional households by domestic firms.

*** Income on equity paid to regional households by the global trust.

Equivalent variations (EV) increase slightly in many countries except in China, and the rate of increase in Indonesia is relatively high. Percentages for Oceania seem worse than in China. Factorial decomposition of EV reveals that the main influences are terms of trade in Oceania (−1.8%) and Indonesia (0.5%).[2]

Under the Paris Agreement scenario, the GDP of most carbon-constrained countries is below the baseline (Table 9.3). It is remarkably lower for Russia and Taiwan, followed by the EU and Singapore. China and Japan are slightly positive. GDP is above the baseline in all regions that have no carbon-reduction commitments.

The EV of most carbon-restricted countries are below the baseline but higher in Singapore and Thailand. Among carbon-restricted countries, relatively large negative impacts appear in Taiwan, Canada, the EU, and Russia. Canada and Russia are

Table 9.3 Macro impacts under the PA scenario (differences from the baseline, 2030)

	GDP	EV*	Terms of trade		Domestic equity income**	Foreign equity income***	Carbon price of CO$_2$ ($/ton)		CO$_2$
	(%)	(Billion $)	(%)	(%)	(Billion $)	(Billion $)	Nominal	Real	(%)
Oceania	−2.0	−27.5	−3.7	2.5	−29.4	−8.3	57.2	48.3	−50.0
China	0.3	−236.1	−2.1	−0.4	−325.6	−307.8	3.6	3.8	−28.5
Japan	0.3	−20.8	−2.7	2.8	−64.6	−70.7	17.9	18.1	−24.0
Korea	−2.5	−10.4	−4.3	2.4	−50.6	−1.8	20.3	20.5	−37.0
Taiwan	−9.1	−42.2	−11.8	2.8	−51.4	9.0	59.4	60.5	−65.7
Indonesia	−1.6	−20.7	−2.6	−1.3	−37.3	0.0	12.9	13.0	−29.0
Malaysia	−0.8	−9.1	−4.8	−1.1	−9.5	−2.9	4.0	4.3	−17.9
Singapore	−4.1	6.6	7.4	4.6	−26.6	2.4	72.4	69.5	−45.1
Thailand	−0.3	9.2	5.3	0.8	−7.8	−0.1	6.6	6.9	−20.0
Vietnam	−0.5	−3.7	−4.2	−1.9	−1.4	0.0	1.9	1.9	−8.0
O_ASEAN	1.1	6.2	4.0	−0.8	−3.4	0.0			8.2
India	2.7	139.2	6.5	2.9	−12.8	0.0			4.2
O_Asia	1.4	42.6	10.1	2.6	−0.9	0.0			4.6
Canada	−2.9	−79.5	−13.9	−2.1	−51.4	8.2	42.5	42.0	−54.2
US	−2.1	−307.8	−7.4	1.2	−232.7	−75.0	37.1	37.0	−52.2
Mexico	−0.6	−14.4	−3.6	−1.5	−30.2	0.0	8.2	8.5	−22.0
Latin	3.0	203.4	9.0	3.1	28.1	−0.0			8.8
EU28	−4.4	−527.2	−20.4	2.5	−427.7	−70.0	69.6	68.8	−51.1
O_Euro	1.4	−31.7	−7.0	−1.9	−3.7	−43.8	0.0	0.0	15.5
Russia	−9.2	−229.0	−29.8	−10.7	−251.1	84.0	17.6	17.2	−43.8
Turkestan	0.1	−21.6	−14.2	−7.6	−3.9	−8.2			4.0
MENA	0.4	−266.7	−10.8	−7.0	−160.8	−34.6			5.8
SSA	1.3	−18.8	−1.1	−4.0	−23.6	−0.0			8.1

Source: Authors' simulations with the GTAP 9 Data Base.

Note
 * EV is the total difference from the baseline of equivalent variations from 2020 to 2030.
 ** Income on equity paid to regional households by domestic firms.
*** Income on equity paid to regional households by the global trust.

important energy exporters, and these four regions have high carbon targets. The EV for Turkestan and the Middle East deteriorate despite their absence of carbon constraints.

Terms of trade improve in Singapore, but deteriorations in Russia, Turkestan, and MENA are remarkable. These are also reflected in rates of change for EV. Factorial decomposition of EV reveals that contributions by terms of trade in Singapore, Russia, Turkestan, and MENA are 21.7%, −12.9%, −10.2%, and −8.3%, respectively.

Differences in financial income from the baseline are negative in most countries. Carbon price is high in Singapore, the EU, Taiwan, Oceania, and Canada and cheap in Vietnam, China, and Malaysia. We attribute the industrialization in heavy chemistry and relatively severe carbon reductions as factors underlying high carbon prices in Singapore. Reductions in CO_2 emissions from the baseline exceed 50% in Taiwan, Canada, the US, the EU, and Oceania.

Table 9.4 shows percentage differences from the baseline for capital stock and capital rental rates in 2030. Under China's NDC scenario, rental prices and capital stock fall in China and rise in Indonesia. Under the Paris Agreement scenario, rental rates are relatively high and capital stock increases in China and Japan despite being carbon-constrained countries. Declines in Russia and Taiwan are remarkable.

Table 9.5 reports the initial share of energy among total exports and imports, and percentage differences from the baseline for the export price index and the import price index. Oceania's export index deteriorates notably under China's NDC scenario. This is the cause of the deterioration of EV in the Oceanian region under China's NDC scenario. We discuss the decline in Oceania's export price later.

Under the Paris Agreement scenario, the export price index falls in Russia, Turkestan, MENA, and SSA, which have high shares of energy exports. The import price index falls in Japan, Korea, Taiwan, Singapore, Thailand, and the US. All of them have high shares of energy imports, which explains the trend in terms of trade in Table 9.3.

Table 9.4 Impact on capital stock and rental prices (differences from the baseline, 2030, %)

	C-NDC		PA			C-NDC		PA	
	Output	Price	Output	Price		Output	Price	Output	Price
Oceania	0.2	−1.0	−1.8	−3.3	O_Asia	0.4	0.6	2.7	1.2
China	−1.7	−2.1	1.9	−4.6	Canada	0.3	0.0	−3.2	−7.3
Japan	0.4	0.1	1.8	−2.3	US	0.3	−0.1	−2.7	−6.0
Korea	0.4	0.0	−2.4	−5.4	Mexico	0.1	−0.0	0.3	−3.2
Taiwan	0.1	−0.5	−11.3	−10.6	Latin	0.5	0.2	6.2	3.0
Indonesia	1.0	1.5	−2.1	−5.1	EU28	0.4	0.1	−3.4	−7.2
Malaysia	0.4	−0.1	−0.8	−4.2	O_Euro	0.3	−0.0	3.1	−2.4
Singapore	0.3	−0.1	−4.3	−6.6	Russia	0.5	0.1	−14.7	−14.9
Thailand	0.4	−0.0	0.2	−2.6	Turkestan	0.4	−0.0	0.9	−6.8
Vietnam	0.5	−0.1	−0.5	−4.2	MENA	0.4	0.2	0.7	−4.1
O_ASEAN	0.3	−0.1	2.4	−1.9	SSA	0.5	0.2	3.0	−3.0
India	0.5	0.1	5.6	−0.4					

Source: Authors' simulations with the GTAP 9 Data Base.

Table 9.5 Energy share (%, 2011) and export/import price index (differences from the baseline, 2030, %)

	Energy share		C-NDC		PA	
	Export	Import	Export	Import	Export	Import
Oceania	16.1	5.4	−2.0	−0.1	2.6	0.1
China	0.2	12.0	−0.5	−0.5	−0.4	−0.0
Japan	0.0	21.2	0.1	−0.3	1.6	−1.2
Korea	0.0	22.5	−0.1	−0.3	0.7	−1.7
Taiwan	0.0	15.7	−0.3	−0.2	2.0	−0.8
Indonesia	25.7	4.0	0.7	−0.2	−1.6	−0.3
Malaysia	6.8	4.0	−0.1	−0.1	−0.9	0.2
Singapore	0.0	15.4	−0.1	−0.1	2.6	−2.0
Thailand	0.1	15.5	−0.0	−0.1	0.2	−0.6
Vietnam	8.0	0.1	−0.1	−0.2	−1.3	0.6
O_ASEAN	11.6	6.4	−0.3	−0.2	−0.5	0.3
India	0.0	29.4	−0.0	−0.2	0.9	−2.0
O_Asia	5.3	5.6	0.3	−0.1	2.0	−0.6
Canada	13.9	3.2	−0.2	−0.0	−1.7	0.5
US	1.1	12.8	0.0	−0.1	0.2	−1.0
Mexico	9.3	1.5	−0.0	−0.1	−0.9	0.5
Latin	12.9	5.2	−0.6	−0.1	3.3	0.2
EU28	0.5	8.0	0.1	−0.0	2.5	−0.0
O_Euro	13.0	8.1	−0.0	0.0	−1.9	0.0
Russia	43.7	1.2	−0.2	−0.1	−10.1	0.6
Turkestan	63.1	3.3	−0.4	−0.1	−7.7	−0.1
MENA	52.3	4.9	−0.0	−0.1	−6.8	0.3
SSA	47.6	4.9	−0.3	−0.1	−4.1	−0.2

Source: Authors' calculations with the GTAP 9 Data Base.

Note: Energy share means the share of total export of coal, oil, and gas in total export amount.

Analysis of sectorial impact

We now investigate the results of scenario analysis by industry, focusing on energy. Results in Chapter 7 suggest that an increase in China's imports of coal and gas caused by its carbon policy affect economies of energy-exporting countries. Therefore, we begin by examining coal and gas. Tables 9.6 and 9.7 show percentage differences from the 2030 baseline of the production and export in major coal- and gas-exporting regions under China's NDC scenario. Exports to China increase for all countries, and exports to Japan decline for some countries. Differences in behavior relate to differences of initial energy trade structure and of price responses to carbon policy among energy-exporting countries.

In Oceania, for example, coal and gas supply prices decline and exports to Japan and China increase, boosting production. The drop in supply prices in Oceania is attributable to declining wages (unskilled labor −0.6%, skilled labor −0.7%)

Table 9.6 Coal prices, output, and export under the C-NDC scenario (differences from the baseline, 2030, %)

	Share in coal exports		Supply price	Output	Exports		
	China	Japan			Total	China	Japan
Oceania	9.4	32.4	−0.1	5.4	8.4	46.4	4.9
Indonesia	29.8	13.5	1.8	6.8	7.4	33.0	−4.8
Vietnam	59.3	17.2	1.1	9.5	23.3	37.6	−1.4
O_Asia	97.3	0.1	1.0	25.8	36.8	38.0	−1.8
Russia	11.2	14.6	0.4	2.0	5.4	42.5	2.2
SSA	16.4	1.4	0.2	4.5	7.8	44.4	3.3

Source: Authors' calculations with the GTAP 9 Data Base.

Note: Share means the share of China or Japan in total export amount of coal (2011, %).

Table 9.7 Gas prices, output, and exports under the C-NDC scenario (differences from the baseline, 2030, %)

	Share in gas exports		Supply price	Output	Exports		
	China	Japan			Total	China	Japan
Oceania	2.9	78.2	−0.1	2.9	27.2	57.7	19.3
Indonesia	0.9	52.7	0.7	−2.3	−3.7	21.9	−6.4
Malaysia	1.1	56.2	0.4	2.5	5.0	34.1	2.3
Russia	0.3	14.1	0.3	0.3	4.3	38.9	5.2
Turkestan	47.8	0.4	0.6	1.6	10.2	26.3	−4.4
MENA	0.9	12.9	0.5	1.3	2.1	32.4	1.1

Source: Authors' calculations with the GTAP 9 Data Base.

Note: Share means the share of China or Japan in total export amount of gas (2011, %).

and capital rents (−1%). Under the baseline scenario, Oceania's output of coal and gas declines. Furthermore, its trade and service sector which are labor and capital intensive expand, and wages and capital rents rise. However, China's carbon policy is likely to reverse the direction of changes in Oceania's industrial structure (trade −0.1%, services −0.1%). In Oceania, 62.6% of capital, 55.9% of unskilled labor, and 74.8% of skilled labor are employed in trade and services, so shrinkage in these sectors prompts declines in wages and capital rents.

Indonesia shows relatively higher rates of difference from the baseline for coal and gas supply prices than other countries. This finding relates to rising wages (unskilled labor 2.1%, skilled labor 1.9%) and capital rents (1.5%). The share of coal in Indonesian industry measured by value added (3.7%) surpasses Oceania (1.8%), Vietnam (1.9%), Other Asia (0.7%), Russia (0.7%), and SSA (0.5 %). Export dependency in Indonesia's coal industry (export value/production value) exceeds 90% (GTAP 9 Data Base). Exports to China exceed 50% of the total Indonesian exports, so exporting more to China significantly affects Indonesia's coal production. In addition, Indonesia shows remarkable expansion of coal production under the baseline scenario. China's NDC scenario likely will boost it, raising wages and capital rents.

Indonesia's gas industry is relatively dependent on exports (55%). However, the share of export to China in Indonesia's gas exports is not so high (0.9%) but the share of export to Japan is relatively high (52.7%). Therefore, gas production in Indonesia is more affected by declining exports to Japan. Given rising wages and capital rents, exports and production in most manufacturing industries are below the baseline.

Increases in coal exports to Japan from Russia and SSA and gas exports to Japan from Malaysia, Russia, and MENA are also evident. Increases in supply prices are relatively small in these regions. Coal exports to Japan from Vietnam and Other Asia and gas exports to Japan from Turkestan decline, but their output may increase because price increases are less than in Indonesia and the share of exports to China is considerably large.

For industries other than coal and gas, most departures from the baseline under China's NDC scenario are below 1%. However, Oceania exhibits relatively high positive differences in rates for iron (3.2%), other manufacture (3%), machinery (2.9%), transportation equipment (2.1%), chemicals (2%), and nonmetallic minerals (1.3%). This finding arises because wages and capital rents decline in Oceania and benefit exports. China's output of nonmetallic minerals declines notably,[3] leading to positive impacts elsewhere (Indonesia 2.9%, Latin 1.8%, India 1.6%). Increases exceeding 1% are evident in the construction industry via increases in investment (e.g., 3.5% in Indonesia).

We now discuss the Paris Agreement scenario. Tables 9.8 and 9.9 show differences from the baseline for production and exports by major exporters of coal and gas to China under the Paris Agreement scenario in 2030. Coal exports to China exceed the baseline, but coal production except for Other Asia is below it because of less demand from carbon-constrained regions. There are two possible reasons for findings concerning Other Asia: It has a high share of coal exports to China, and domestic demand does not fall because it is not a carbon-restricted

Table 9.8 Coal prices, output, and exports under the PA scenario (differences from the baseline, 2030, %)

	Supply price	*Output*	*Exports*		
			Total	*China*	*Japan*
Oceania	−5.3	−28.3	−8.1	78.5	−28.2
Indonesia	−4.4	−5.9	−1.6	60.7	−34.9
Vietnam	−2.2	−4.6	13.9	45.3	−41.4
Other Asia	2.5	7.8	10.7	12.8	−52.2
Russia	−10.7	−40.0	−2.7	145.5	−1.6
SSA	−2.1	−10.8	−22.2	32.2	−41.7

Source: Authors' simulations with the GTAP 9 Data Base.

Table 9.9 Gas prices, output, and exports under the PA scenario (differences from the baseline, 2030, %)

	Supply price	Output	Exports		
			Total	China	Japan
Oceania	−4.0	−46.7	−63.8	−41.0	−69.7
Indonesia	−5.9	−33.1	−35.2	25.3	−47.4
Malaysia	−7.2	−20.0	−16.6	89.3	−22.6
Russia	−15.3	−36.6	664.2	3,251.9	1,872.7
Turkestan	−5.9	−2.0	−20.2	22.2	−28.1
MENA	−6.4	−13.1	−24.5	46.9	−38.7

Source: Authors' simulations with the GTAP 9 Data Base.

region. Although Russia likely will export substantially more gas, output declines because of a collapse in domestic demand. The absence of carbon constraints mitigates declines in gas production in Turkestan and MENA.

We now briefly describe how the Paris Agreement scenario affects other industries. In carbon-constrained countries, the greatest reductions appear in the electricity sector. However, the electricity sector's share of total industrial CO_2 reductions varies regionally: Malaysia (86.2%), Korea (80.0%), China (75.5%), Taiwan (75.6%), Russia (74.8%), Japan (74.8%), Oceania (67.6%), the US (65.7%), Indonesia (63.7%), Thailand (56.8%), the EU (53.0%), Mexico (49.0%), Singapore (44.1%), Vietnam (43.8%), and Canada (30.6%). Three factors can be inferred: the electricity sector's initial share of total industrial CO_2 emissions, its initial share of coal consumed, and changes in international competitiveness caused by carbon policies. For example, the electricity sector's share of industrial CO_2 emissions is 51.2% worldwide, but it is 67.8% in Russia, 63.7% in Taiwan, 59.8% in China, and 58.7% in Korea. It is low in Canada (24.5%), Singapore (30.4%), Vietnam (35.5%), and Thailand (36.3%).

The share of electricity generated by coal (toe) is 60.1% for the world overall, but it is 93% in China and 73.1% in Oceania. It is 0% in Singapore, 17.8% in Mexico, and 36% in Vietnam. The higher the percentage of coal, the greater are expectations for reductions by the electricity sector. In Thailand and Vietnam, nonmetallic minerals account for 14.6% and 19.8%, respectively, of industrial CO_2 emissions. Coal accounts for 81.7% and 91.3%, respectively, of energy consumption there. The nonmetallic minerals sector's share of total industrial CO_2 reduction under the Paris Agreement scenario is high in Thailand and Vietnam (30.0% and 42.6%, respectively).

Malaysia and Japan are comparatively less burdened by carbon policy, so there are some industries where output increases (Japan: air transportation, 6.2%; construction, 5.3%; water transport, 3.9%; nonmetric minerals, 0.8%; Malaysia: air transport, 13.4%; water transport, 5.2%; chemical products, 3.6%; other transport, 3%). Then much more CO_2 reduction in the electricity sector, basically a non-tradable sector for Japan and Malaysia, is necessary.

Sensitivity analysis

This section discusses whether the global impact of carbon restrictions depend on the extent of substitution between coal and non-coal energy in China. We report the global impact obtained via sensitivity analysis in Chapter 7.

Table 9.10 shows the relation between China's elasticity of substitution between coal and non-coal energy composites (σ_{NELY} in Figure 7.1) and real carbon prices for countries with carbon constraints. As elasticity increases, real carbon prices decline in countries other than Oceania but to a degree less than in China.

Figures 9.1 and 9.2 illustrate the relation between elasticity (σ_{NELY}) and exports of coal or gas to China under China's NDC scenario. The horizontal axes in Figures 9.1 and 9.2 are σ_{NELY} and the vertical axes are the percentage difference from baseline coal or gas exports under China's NDC scenario. Figure 9.1 shows that the greater the elasticity, the lower are exports to China from coal-exporting regions. Figure 9.2 shows that the greater the elasticity, the higher are exports to China from gas-exporting regions. These behaviors are consistent with the substitution of coal for non-coal energy in China's electricity sector evident in Table 7.9. Under the Paris Agreement scenario, the same occurs under China's NDC scenario.

Table 9.11 shows differences from the baseline for GDP, EV, and CO_2 in 2030 when elasticities are 0.1, 0.5, and 1. As elasticity increases, GDP increases only in Russia and Turkestan and declines slightly elsewhere. Among countries not in the table, GDP declines everywhere except in China as elasticity increases.

A high elasticity exerts a positive influence on EV in Oceania, Malaysia, Vietnam, Russia, Turkestan, MENA, SSA. Its effect is negative in Indonesia and

Table 9.10 Elasticity of substitution between coal and non-coal energy and real carbon prices under the PA scenario (2030, US$)

	0.1	0.2	0.3	0.4	0.5	0.6	0.7	0.8	0.9	1.0
Oceania	48.3	48.3	48.3	48.3	48.3	48.3	48.3	48.3	48.3	48.3
China	4.7	4.4	4.2	4.0	3.8	3.6	3.5	3.3	3.2	3.1
Japan	18.5	18.4	18.3	18.2	18.1	18.1	18.0	18.0	17.9	17.8
Korea	20.8	20.7	20.7	20.6	20.5	20.5	20.4	20.4	20.3	20.3
Taiwan	60.8	60.7	60.6	60.6	60.5	60.5	60.4	60.4	60.3	60.3
Indonesia	13.3	13.2	13.1	13.1	13.0	12.9	12.9	12.8	12.8	12.8
Malaysia	4.4	4.3	4.3	4.3	4.3	4.2	4.2	4.2	4.2	4.2
Singapore	69.9	69.7	69.7	69.6	69.5	69.4	69.3	69.3	69.2	69.2
Thailand	7.0	7.0	6.9	6.9	6.9	6.8	6.8	6.8	6.7	6.7
Vietnam	2.0	2.0	2.0	1.9	1.9	1.9	1.9	1.9	1.9	1.9
Canada	42.1	42.1	42.0	42.0	42.0	42.0	41.9	41.9	41.9	41.9
US	37.1	37.1	37.0	37.0	37.0	36.9	36.9	36.9	36.9	36.8
Mexico	8.5	8.5	8.5	8.5	8.5	8.5	8.4	8.4	8.4	8.4
EU	69.3	69.1	69.0	68.9	68.8	68.7	68.6	68.5	68.5	68.4
Russia	17.2	17.2	17.2	17.2	17.2	17.1	17.1	17.1	17.1	17.1

Source: Authors' simulations with the GTAP 9 Data Base.

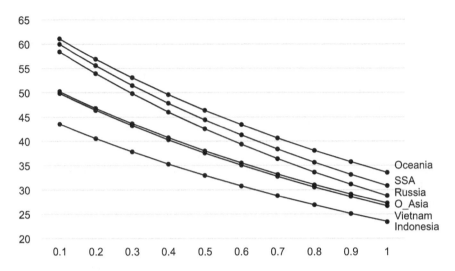

Figure 9.1 Difference in rates from the baseline coal exports to China under the C-NDC scenario (2030, %)

Sources: Authors' simulations with GDyn and the GTAP 9 Data Base.

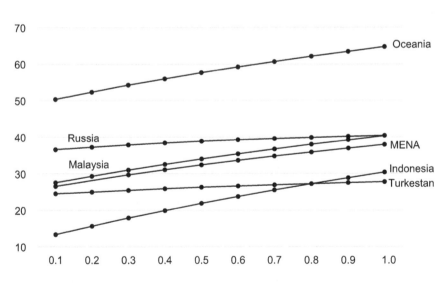

Figure 9.2 Difference in rates from the baseline gas exports to China under the C-NDC scenario (2030, %)

Sources: Authors' simulations with GDyn and the GTAP 9 Data Base.

Table 9.11 Elasticity and macro impacts under the C-NDC scenario (2030)

	0.1	0.5	1	0.1	0.5	1	0.1	0.5	1
	Oceania			Indonesia			Malaysia		
GDP	0.09	0.07	0.06	0.64	0.53	0.43	0.22	0.20	0.19
EV	−14.3	−12.9	−11.8	13.8	11.1	8.6	0.4	0.5	0.7
CO_2	0.11	0.03	−0.03	0.46	0.37	0.31	0.23	0.16	0.10
	Vietnam			Other Asia			Russia		
GDP	0.28	0.26	0.24	0.28	0.24	0.19	0.20	0.24	0.27
EV	0.4	0.4	0.5	6.1	4.8	3.6	−3.4	0.6	4.4
CO_2	0.42	0.33	0.26	0.28	0.24	0.22	0.30	0.25	0.22
	Turkestan			MENA			SSA		
GDP	0.19	0.21	0.22	0.22	0.21	0.21	0.26	0.24	0.22
EV	−1.1	−0.3	0.4	1.7	9.4	16.7	0.0	2.0	3.9
CO_2	0.45	0.41	0.38	0.39	0.31	0.25	0.71	0.58	0.49

Sources: Authors' simulations with GDyn and the GTAP 9 Data Base.

Note: For GDP and CO_2: percentage differences from the baseline in 2030 (%). For EV: total differences from the baseline of EV 2020–30 (billion $).

Other Asia, both of which are highly dependent on coal exports to China. CO_2 emissions decline everywhere else, including unlisted regions, as elasticity increases.

Trends identical to those mentioned in Table 9.11 appear in the sensitivity analysis results under the Paris Agreement scenario.

Concluding remarks

This chapter analyzed the global impact of carbon policy based on the NDCs of China and other countries using the GDyn-E model and the GTAP 9 Data Base. The main findings from simulation results are as follows.

Under China's NDC scenario, Oceania's and Indonesia's exports of coal and gas to China are considerably but oppositely affected. There seem to be differences between changes in industrial structure at the baseline and in the initial trade structure. In Oceania, where the service economy is expected to advance in the baseline scenario, China's carbon policy generates a higher output for many industries through lower factor prices and expanded exports. However, the decline in export prices exacerbates Oceania's economic welfare. Higher coal exports to China seem to bolster Indonesia's economy and welfare, although its gas production declines.

Under the Paris Agreement scenario, the stringency of carbon-reduction targets significantly influences GDP. Relatively large negative effects appear for Russia, Taiwan, the EU, and Singapore, where reduction targets are large. China and Japan exhibit a slight positive influence. Economic welfare relates strongly to changes in terms of trade. Relatively large deteriorations in terms of trade were observed in energy-exporting countries.

The extent to which China substitutes between coal and non-coal energy can affect the global economy, although not as greatly as it can affect China itself. If substitutability is large, reducing CO_2 emissions is likely to increase a little and the real carbon tax is likely to decline. However, economic welfare declines in some coal-exporting regions.

Our simulations suggest three results concerning international equity. First, the burden of meeting reduction targets differs, even among developed countries. Second, carbon policy likely impairs terms of trade among energy exporters and enhances them for importers. Third, differences in industrial structure at the baseline, differences in industrial and trade structures, and differences in fuel used to produce electric power alter the effects of carbon policy.

Our analysis suggests that further international consultation and cooperation are necessary for equitable burden-sharing. Future studies should compare scenarios under various reduction targets. This chapter followed the carbon tax imposition method based on conventional production standards. Given the deterioration in economic welfare among energy exporters, it may be necessary to reconsider the attribution of carbon tax revenues. Analyses of conversion to renewable energy, a subject not addressed here, are also indispensable.

Notes

1 For equity and burden-sharing, see Fleurbaey et al. (2014).
2 See Chapter 7 for factorial decomposition of EV.
3 See Table 7.5 for China's output.

Reference

Fleurbaey, M., Kartha, S., Bolwig, S., Chee, Y.L., Chen, Y., Corbera, E., Lecocq, F., Lutz, W., Muylaert, M.S., Norgaard, R.B., Okereke, C. and Sagar, A.D. (2014) Sustainable development and equity. In: Climate Change 2014: Mitigation of Climate Change, in Edenhofer, O., Pichs-Madruga, R., Sokona, Y., Farahani, E., Kadner, S., Seyboth, K., Adler, A., Baum, I., Brunner, S., Eickemeier, P., Kriemann, B., Savolainen, J., Schlömer, S. von Stechow, C., Zwickel, T. and Minx, J.C. (eds.) *Contribution of Working Group III to the Fifth Assessment Report of the Intergovernmental Panel on Climate Change*, Cambridge, UK and New York: Cambridge University Press.

10 Impact of the China-induced coal boom in Indonesia

A resource governance perspective

Akihisa Mori

Introduction

Indonesia has been evaluated as one of the four resource-rich developing countries that has escaped the resource curse. It attained both long-term investments exceeding 25 percent of the Gross Domestic Product (GDP) on average from 1970 to 1998, (equal to that of various successful industrial countries lacking raw materials) and per capita gross national products (GNP) growth exceeding four percent per year on average during the same period (Gylfason 2001).

Indonesia's escape from the resource curse is explained by the three positive characteristics: its priority to sound macro-economic management, control of rent-seeking activity, and explicit concern for the welfare of the rural poor. Three institutions facilitated the achievement of these positive features: the capital fund that smoothed the absorption of rent into the economy; the espousal of the Extractive Industries Transparency Initiative, which can shrink the scope of rent-seeking activity; and a public sector investment evaluation unit that objectively compares the prospective returns of offshore assets with those of government domestic investments (Auty 2007).

The Asian Economic Crisis and the subsequent political and economic turmoil changed the landscape of Indonesia. While real GDP growth exceeded four percent except during the crisis period, and the share of gross domestic fixed capital formation declined to less than 20 percent in the post crisis period, the latter recovered to 25 percent in 2009. From 2000 to 2008, domestic investments did not exceed US$6 trillion, and foreign direct investments (FDI) did not exceed US$15 billion. It was not until China's FDI reached US$5 billion per year that the inflow of FDI regained momentum. China's FDI was, however, concentrated toward the mining sector. China accounts for 17 percent of the FDI in the mining sector and 3 percent of the total FDI (Figure 10.1). Since then, Indonesia has rapidly increased coal exports to China. Coal exports and production in 2013 more than doubled compared to 2008 (Figure 10.2). China's share of Indonesian coal exports increased to 30 percent during 2011 and 2013 (Figure 10.3).

Corruption and illegal natural resource exploitation became rampant in resource-rich provinces in Indonesia (Resosudarmo 2004). The democratic decentralization accompanying the Asian Economic Crisis raised conflicts over authority and responsibility between central and local governments. It gave the

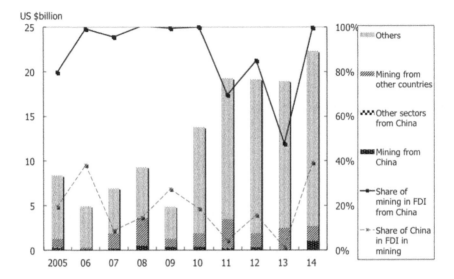

Figure 10.1 FDI from mining sector from China to Indonesia

Source: Author complied based on Hong and Sambodo (2015: 6).

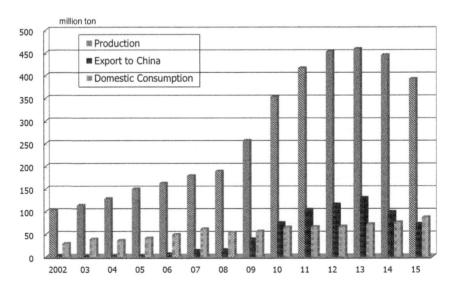

Figure 10.2 Indonesian coal production, domestic consumption, and export to China

Sources: Author compilation based on *Statistik Indonesia*, each year.

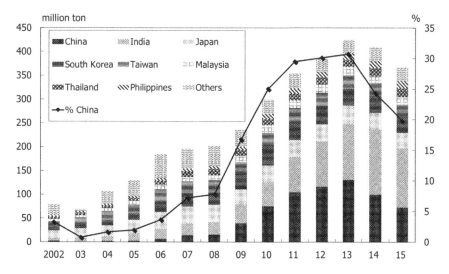

Figure 10.3 Indonesian coal export by destination

Sources: Author compilation based on *Statistik Indonesia*, each year.

latter wider discretion for granting concessions and obscured legal and illegal logging and mining practices (Casson and Obidzinski 2002). Local councils did not work effectively to prevent such destructive activities.

Hong and Sambodo (2015) showed that deepening collaboration with China offered Indonesia an opportunity for resource-dependent development. However, is Indonesia enjoying the China-induced coal boom and the subsequent resource-dependence without cost? If not, what policies and measures have the Indonesian government taken to address the side effects of resource-dependence? If the government is performing poorly, what prevents them from working effectively?

Garnaut (2015) points out that Indonesia is suffering from a resource curse due to a lack of natural resource funds; but its counter-cyclical fiscal policy (including fuel subsidy cuts) has prevented the curse from being as serious as in Brazil and South Africa with their pro-cyclical fiscal policy. However, the Indonesian government did not cut its fuel subsidy for the purpose of escaping the curse. Rather, it was a large fiscal burden that had squeezed the government's budget spending for development priorities, which, linked with the rise in world oil price, stimulated the government to reform its fuel pricing policy (Yusuf and Resosudarmo 2014). While Indonesia has also enhanced its domestic market obligation (DMO) for resource sales and divestment requirements for foreign investors, these were intended to increase the domestic consumption of domestic resources and not to escape the curse. In the meantime, regulatory capture and environmental degradation have accelerated at the local level during the China-induced coal boom. Junita (2015) points out that poor performance arises from inconsistent laws and their poor enforcement. Still, to present a balanced view, it is indispensable to grasp how China has capitalized on weak resource gover-nance in Indonesia to earn profit and bring about the curse.

Thus, this chapter explores how China's massive coal imports and investments in the coal sector have affected Indonesia's environment and resource governance, which had been destabilized by democratic decentralization. It employs the relationship between ownership structure and fiscal regime demonstrated by Luong and Weinthal (2010) to analyze how China capitalized on resource gover-nance to increase profits in the sector.

The remainder of this chapter is organized into five sections. The second section describes the analytical method. The third section analyzes the changes in the extent of resource governance in Indonesia, while the fourth section analyzes the impact the China-induced coal boom and Chinese investments had on resource governance. The fifth section then discusses the results and implica-tions of both analysis, and the sixth section concludes the chapter.

Analytical framework

China's methods of intrusion

The Chinese government usually follows three strategies to secure energy and food: first, purchasing them from the global market; second, acquiring shares in international resource companies in order to control them; and third, buying land in other countries. It regards buying energy and food in the global market as the least desirable option for security reasons and pushes Chinese companies to invest in international companies and acquire foreign land with resources (Cardenal and Araujo 2014: 137). Moreover, it uses the China Development Bank (CDB) and Export-Import Bank of China (CEXIM) as financial vehicles for long-term import contracts and foreign investments.

The Chinese government is proactive in building strategic bilateral relation-ships with key energy producers and resource-rich countries in Central Asia, Africa, and Latin America. It especially targets countries whose leaders want to reduce the influence of the United States or which the United States has lost political interest in since the Cold War. Chinese state oil and gas companies have exploited their long-standing ties with the Communist Party of China (CPC) to advance their corporate interests in foreign countries (Patey 2014).

China's demand in conjunction with the corruption and negligence of local elites allow for extensive overexploitation of natural resources around the world in two ways. First, resources are exported to China without any kind of processing that might generate little wealth at the local level in terms of employment or investments. The complete lack of interest Chinese authority shows toward monitoring the origin of resources complements this mode of operation (Cardenal and Araujo 2014: 207). While the CDB and CEXIM set out environmental and social safeguard standards, they rarely enforce these standards for their customers (Economy and Levi 2014). The Chinese national oil companies of CNOOC, Petro China, and Sinopec are less likely either to promote transparency or to implement environmental and social welfare programs (Luong and Weinthal 2010: 211).

Second, Chinese businessmen capitalize on corruption to gain easy access to large quantities of natural resources without having to comply with the local laws or production method. They provide financing to local companies and people to get them to act as 'straw men', even in countries where the state does not grant concessions to foreign investors.

Type of natural resource governance

The analytical framework presented by Luong and Weinthal (2010) can be adopted to assess whether a country has strong or weak natural resource governance.

It disaggregates ownership and control into four possible resource development strategies: state ownership with control (S_1), private domestic ownership with control (P_1), state ownership without control (S_2), and private foreign ownership without control (P_2).

S_1 is a strategy in which the state must own its rights to develop the majority of stakes (more than 50 percent) in the extractive sector. Foreign involvement is limited to either participating in contracts that restrict their managerial and operational control (such as carried interest or joint ventures) or operating as service contractors. It fosters a weak fiscal regime by creating low transaction costs for governing elites to derive income from resource rents, while high social expectations for the population that the state should have an enlarged role in generating and allocating resource rents. This directs the state to rely increasingly on indirect and implicit taxation for revenue and make the wide distribution of resource rents as visible as possible, undermining budgetary stability and transparency in the end.

Under P_1, private domestic companies can own the rights to develop the majority of petroleum deposits and hold the majority of shares (more than 50 percent) in the extractive sector. Contrary to S_1, it fosters strong fiscal regimes: it generates high transaction costs, as governing elites must negotiate with private companies to increase their stake. The population perceives the role of the state as confined to collecting and redistributing resource rents and, thus has lower social expectations. The combination of high transaction costs and low social expectations provides domestic private miners, governing elites, and the general population with an incentive to establish direct and explicit taxation that ensures predictable revenue streams for private miners and governing elites and convinces the general population to extract a fair share. This combination also makes it easier for governing elites to convince the general population to agree to a broad-based tax regime across sectors and give up populist-style social spending to save the share of resource rents during booms in order to cover budgetary shortfalls during the burst and/or invest them in more productive uses.

S_2 is a strategy where the state owns the rights to develop the majority of mining deposits and hold the majority of shares (more than 50 percent), yet foreign investors are allowed to participate through more permissive contracts – such as production-sharing agreements (PSAs) – which grant them significant managerial and operational control. Under P_2, private foreign companies can own the rights to develop the majority of mining deposits and hold the majority of shares (more than 50 percent) usually through concessionary contracts. Under S_2 and P_2, the effects of the ownership structure on transaction costs, social expectations, and power relationships are mediated through the international system where these foreign investors operate.

P_2 has the greatest potential to foster fiscal stability and transparency both within and outside the extractive sector while improving the daily lives of citizens and the development prospects of resource-rich countries. The ability of foreign investors to essentially minimize their fiscal burden reinforces the governing elites' incentives to adopt broad-based tax reforms. High social expectations vis-à-vis the state under S_2 instead dampen such incentives. Likewise, the ability of foreign investors to maintain stable and transparent expenditures directed toward reducing poverty and promoting socioeconomic development is more likely to foster budgetary reform under P_2 than S_2 because of differing levels of societal expectations vis-à-vis the state.

Still, P_2 can foster fiscal stability and transparency only where foreign investors are supported and pressured by international financial institutions (IFIs) and international non-governmental organizations (INGOs). As long as they make a serious commitment to corporate social responsibility (CSR) in addressing the economic and social needs of affected communities, they exercise an ability to minimize their fiscal burden on the government. Otherwise, governing elites are likely to direct the spending of foreign investors toward their own pet projects either at the national level (under S_2) or at the subnational level (under P_2), where they can unilaterally revoke contracts with foreign investors not committed to CSR.

Impact of ownership structure on institutions and governance

Change in ownership structure

In the 1960s, the Indonesian government changed its ownership structure from private ownership without control (P_2) to state ownership without control (S_2). In the Dutch colonial period with foreign dominance over natural resources, Indonesia obtained minimum resource rent, as it had to rely on foreign capital, technology, and expertise to explore and produce natural resources. To regain state control, the Indonesian government established Pertamina in 1966 as a state monopolized company that conducted integrated upstream and downstream business and implemented profit-sharing agreements (PSAs) in the oil and gas sector (Luong and Weinthal 2010: 191). Under a PSA, investors undertake exploration and production and in return for carrying the initial risk, receive a share of the oil and gas produced as payment.

In the coal-mining sector, foreign participation was allowed in the form of contractors to PT Bukit Asam Tbk, a state-owned coal-mining company (Presidential Decree 49/1981), through a Contract of Work (CoW) system. While the contract system ensured the security of tenure (*Conjunctive Title*) and security of investment (*Lex Specialis* treatment),[1] it was discriminative against foreign companies in that only Indonesian companies were allowed to obtain ownership of mines under the local indigenous mining permits (KP) framework (Mining Law of 1967).

This ownership structure enabled Indonesian political elites to gain significant oil and gas rent for spending at their own discretion. The government obtained 85 percent of the after-tax share of oil, 30 percent of output from gas projects, and 13.5 percent of sales revenue from mining projects (PT Adaro Indonesia 2014). In addition, the government could mobilize Pertamina as a source of financing to pursue its political agenda, as Pertamina was granted exclusive powers to appoint private companies as contractors and to issue and administrate production-sharing contracts (PSC) in exchange for 2 percent of its sales earnings as commission (Law 8/1971). Political intervention increased after Pertamina's financial crisis in 1975, which allowed the state to incorporate Pertamina's earnings into its budget (Kato 2005).

Democratic decentralization, coupled with underinvestment and the natural maturation of producing oil fields, prompted the Indonesian government to shift to private ownership without control (P_2). Pertamina's monopolistic position in the oil and gas business was terminated, and it has since become a state limited-liability company subject to the same contracts as other private companies. Private participation was allowed under the PSA with BP Migas and BPH-Migas, both of which were established to take over Pertamina's authority in issuing and administrating PSAs as well as supervising day-to-day operations (The Oil and Natural Gas Law of 2001). They are also officially permitted to make contracts directly with buyers.

While fruitless explorations directed foreign oil companies to prop up output from existing fields instead of discovering new ones,[2] the change in ownership structure, coupled with fruitful exploration in recent years, have allowed foreign investments to resurge in gas production. The BP-led consortium started operations at Tangguh LNG in West Papua in 2009 (BP 2017), and a Mitsubishi Corporation-led consortium did so at Donggi Senoro LNG in Central Sulawesi in 2015. The change in ownership structure also prompted foreign contractors and the National Gas Company (PGN) to develop a gas pipeline to Singapore. As a result, foreign companies have become dominant in Indonesian oil and gas production.[3]

Meanwhile, the government is facing difficulties in satisfying the high social expectations for poverty alleviation and development. The transaction costs for charging oil and gas rent has become too high to obtain additional revenue through Pertamina.

These difficulties increased the pressure to shift the ownership structure back to S_2. Foreign investors are subject to restrictive regulations, including: a domestic market obligation (DMO) that mandates contractors to supply 25 percent of the produced oil and gas to the domestic market (GR34/2004); an import duty and VAT on imports of capital goods needed for production even during the exploration period; a restriction on foreign workers and encouragement of the employment of Indonesian workers, in addition to the transfer of knowledge, skills, and expertise to the local workforce (MEMR Decree 31/2013); and a negative investment list that restricts foreign shareholdings in several business activities that includes drilling, pipeline development, and oil and gas survey services (Presidential Decree 39/2014), while implementing nationwide gas pipeline network development projects. Pertamina is still influential in concessions due to a lack of coordination among MEMR, BP Migas, and Pertamina during the Reformasi, when supervisory capacity collapsed and the behavior of technocrats became increasing irresponsible (Kanekiyo and Inoue 2006). The Constitutional Court decision on the dissolution of BP Migas further opened the way for Pertamina to gain the right to first refusal of any contract along with the right to issue upstream business licenses[4] (Adelman et al. 2015).

In the coal and mineral resource-mining sector, the government implemented a mining business license (IUP) and a single area-based licensing system in the Mining Law of 2009 as an alternative to the KP framework and CoW system, both of which had collapsed during the Asian Economic Crisis.[5] As new licenses are issued through a tender process instead of direct appointment, the new system seems to provide non-discriminative mining business opportunities for both foreign and domestic investors (Junita 2015). Still, it imposes several restrictions on foreign IUP holders. These include a divestment requirement to compensate for untaxed resource rents (GR 23/2010, amended by GR 24/2012),[6] an export ban on raw minerals (GR 7/2012), and (after the ban was canceled by a Supreme Court decision) progressive rates of export duty. This also links divestment requirements with progressive rates of export duty to encourage foreign companies to start domestic processing and refining (GR 77/2014 and MEMR Regulation 8/2015). Also included in the restrictions on foreign IUP holders is a coal DMO (Law 4/2009) to satisfy increasing domestic demand for the 35 GW Electrification Program. The government set the target of 92.3 million tons of coal supply in 2015 and raised it to 111 million tons in 2016. To secure a stable and cheap coal supply, the government requires coal miners to supply coal that satisfies quality standards for mine mouth power plants at a cheaper price in 2016 and mine owners to hold a minimum 10 percent of the equity of power plant companies.

All of these policies and measures have reinforced the shift in ownership structure in the coal and mineral resource-mining sector from state ownership without control (S_2) to private ownership with control (P_1).

Impact on the fiscal regime of the central government

The change in the ownership structure has prompted the central government to shift its fiscal regime toward a stronger one: a broad-based tax regime across sectors. To increase oil and gas revenue, the central government has reduced the tax rate and increased its flexibility in favor of contractors to stimulate investment, while maintaining the basic framework of PSA intact. It announced a plan to raise the 'unfairly low' royalty rate of 3 to 7 percent and 2 to 6 percent of sales proceeds for open-pit and underground mining to 13.5 percent under the

CoW system[7] (Indonesia Investments 2015b). It has also implemented measures to formalize resource revenue, including: redefining oil and gas revenue as Government Share and Corporate and Branch Profit *Tax* (C&D Tax) in order to remit them to the State Treasury account instead of the Oil and Gas accounts (GR 79/2010); implementing the Cost Recovery and Income Tax (GR 79/2010); and imposing an additional royalty on net profit by 10 percent for mining license-holders who conduct business activities in state forest reserve areas (IUPK), which is expected to enhance government monitoring over capital expenditure and mining operating costs of IUPK mining companies (PwC 2016b: 37).

These tax measures have increased government revenue from direct and explicit taxation. The revenue from income tax surpassed non-tax resource revenue in 2006 and the gap has widened (Figure 10.4). While non-tax revenue from coal increased from 4.5 trillion to 37.6 trillion IDR in 2014 (Figure 10.5), it amounted to only 17 percent of non-tax revenue from oil and gas and 4 percent of central government revenue. Accordingly, the share of royalties declined from 79 percent in 2006 to 61 percent in 2014.

Nonetheless, an ad valorem royalty – as well as widespread under-reporting of production volumes, under-invoicing, and other evasion mechanisms – have brought insufficient collection of non-tax coal revenue. Weak compliance was to blame for the estimated 22 to 46 percent of potential non-tax revenue (16 to 51 trillion IDR) from reported coal sales that was not collected 2010 to 2012 (World Bank 2015: 44). The government set a benchmark price to serve as the

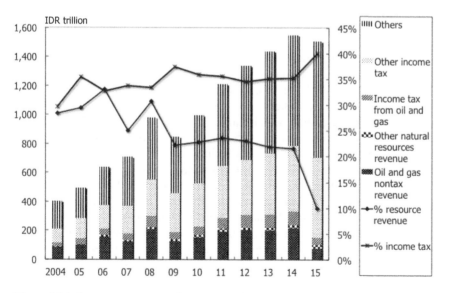

Figure 10.4 Government revenue by source 2004–15

Sources: Republic of Indonesia, Laporan Keuangan Pemerintah Pusa Audite (Audited Statement of Government Fiscal Accounts), each year.

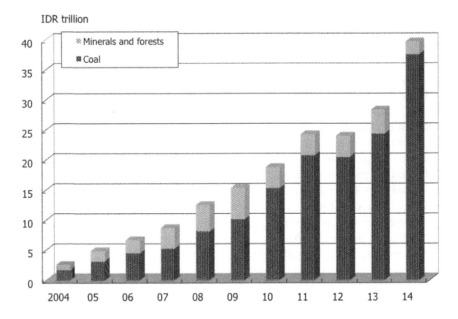

Figure 10.5 Government revenue from minerals and forests 2004–15

Sources: Republic of Indonesia, *Laporan Keuangan Pemerintah Pusa Audite (Audited Statement of Government Fiscal Accounts)*, each year.

floor price for royalty calculations in order to stabilize resource revenue at a time of price collapse.

On the expenditure side, central expenditure reflects the features of a distributive state despite the government's pledge to remove energy price controls by 2007 as a condition of the emergency loans from both the IMF and ADB (Sakamoto 2006: 20). Subsidies and personnel expenditures have shared a significant and increasing portion, which squeezed capital investments (Brodjonegoro 2004). Fuel subsidy was cut in 2005 and 2008 with temporary impact, partly because it noted Suharto's step-down after implementing the IMF-led fuel subsidy cut, worried that a fuel subsidy cut might trigger social unrest. It was not until 2015 when the government withdrew its gasoline subsidy and linked the domestic price of diesel and kerosene with the international market that the share and amount of subsidy was significantly reduced (Figure 10.6).

To complement a shortage of capital investments, the central government has attempted to mobilize foreign capital. It called on foreign investors for tender in the first fast-track programs (FTP), which aim to increase the power generation capacity of the National Power Company (PLN). It adopted a public-private partnership (PPP) scheme for accepting independent power producers (IPPs) in the second FTP – which aimed to increase power generation capacity by 10 GW – while PLN projects still accounted for a majority. To attract FDI in PPP projects, the central government obtained a World Bank loan to establish the Infrastructure

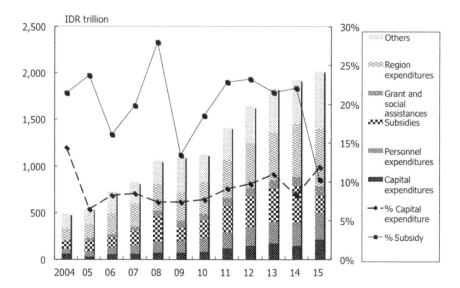

Figure 10.6 Government expenditure by type 2004–15

Sources: Republic of Indonesia, Laporan Keuangan Pemerintah Pusa Audite (Audited Statement of Government Fiscal Accounts), each year.

Guarantee Fund, an independent state-owned enterprise (SOE) for providing business viability guarantees for infrastructure PPP projects. The detailed procedures and steps for land acquisition shown in the Infrastructure Guarantee Fund enable easier land acquisition for developers (Law 2/2012).

Nonetheless, government infrastructure spending did not increase as planned, and actual disbursement fell to 72 percent in 2015 from 78 percent in 2014 (Amirio 2016). SOEs did not always have the management capacity and funding for their projects. A lack of nationwide land tenure data hampered effective enforcement of the Land Acquisition Law of 2012, and thus prolonged the process. A decline in fiscal revenue has squeezed the amount of saved budget generated by the scrap of the energy subsidy for infrastructure development.

Impact on the fiscal regime at the local government level

Democratic decentralization changed the transfer system from one dominated by earmarked grants to one largely relying on general grants, revenue sharing, and local original revenue. Four types of commodities are designated as shared non-taxes: oil and gas, along with mining, forestry, and fishery products. Local governments of the place of origin receive the most revenue, with 6 percent of non-tax oil revenue and 12 percent of non-tax gas revenue, whereas the central government retains 85 and 70 percent, respectively (Ardiansyah et al. 2015). Additional shares are allocated to both local and provincial governments (Law 33/2004, as amended to Law 25/1999). Mining royalties were redistributed to local governments in the same province. Because revenue sharing deteriorated into fiscal disparity among local governments, the central government created the General Allocation Fund (DAK) to set aside at least 25 percent of net revenue as regional expenditure – of which provincial governments receive 10 percent and local governments 90 percent. Taking political issues into account, distribution among local governments is decided by the fiscal gap defined in Law 25/1999.

The rearrangement of the fiscal allocation rule gives room for local political elites to pursue their own economic benefits. First, they set the local tax and charge systems and establish local government enterprises, the latter of which handle business activities previously operated by big private companies or exploit natural resources. Second, local political elites establish new local governments to gain resource revenue and general allocation funds in their disposal. This holds especially true for natural resource-rich provinces, such as Riau where the Siak regency was established, and East Kalimantan where the Bontang municipality was established, and several regencies became independent to establish the North Kalimantan province. Third, local political elites exert political influence on the central government to gain additional budget, allowing a soft budget constraint (Brodjonegoro 2001). Finally, they issue CoW, coal CoW (CCoW), and KP to a large number of companies to increase local government revenue.

This strengthens the characteristics of a rentier and distributive state in the fiscal regime of local governments in the coal-producing provinces of East and South Kalimantan and South Sumatra (Figure 10.7). Local governments at the

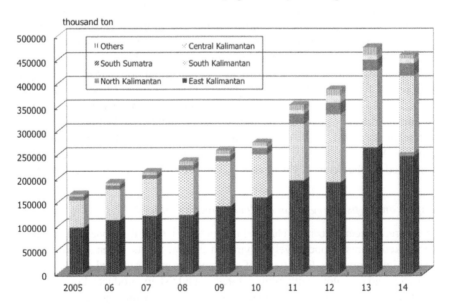

Figure 10.7 Coal production by province

Sources: Author compilation based on Ministry of Energy and Mineral Resources (2016) and JOGMEC (2016).

place of origin for oil, gas, and coal have capitalized on the new income-generating opportunity to obtain significantly higher tax shares and non-tax natural resource revenue. This is especially so for East Kalimantan, where all local governments at the regency and municipality level enjoy increasing revenue from the mining business (Table 10.1). Furthermore, local governments in East Kalimantan obtain

Table 10.1 Local government revenue and expenditure by category

	2005–08	*2009–13*	*2014–15*
Original tax revenue			
East Kalimantan	5%	6%	9%
South Kalimantan	7%	7%	10%
South Sumatra	4%	6%	9%
Throughout Indonesia	7%	9%	13%
Tax share			
East Kalimantan	21%	9%	8%
South Kalimantan	10%	5%	4%
South Sumatra	13%	11%	9%
Throughout Indonesia	9%	7%	4%
Non-tax natural resources			
East Kalimantan	47%	54%	52%
South Kalimantan	8%	20%	18%
South Sumatra	23%	24%	23%
Throughout Indonesia	9%	9%	8%
General allocation funds			
East Kalimantan	15%	13%	13%
South Kalimantan	60%	46%	45%
South Sumatra	49%	42%	41%
Throughout Indonesia	60%	53%	51%
Personnel expenditure			
East Kalimantan	25%	30%	31%
South Kalimantan	43%	49%	44%
South Sumatra	37%	44%	41%
Throughout Indonesia	44%	50%	48%
Subsidies, grants, and aid			
East Kalimantan	7%	6%	4%
South Kalimantan	6%	3%	2%
South Sumatra	4%	3%	2%
Throughout Indonesia	5%	5%	3%
Capital expenditure			
East Kalimantan	46%	40%	40%
South Kalimantan	31%	27%	28%
South Sumatra	39%	31%	30%
Throughout Indonesia	30%	23%	24%

Sources: Author calculation based on *Financial Statistics of Regency/Municipality Government*, each year.

larger amounts and a higher share of non-tax natural resource revenue, which dominated the majority of their revenue during the coal boom (2009–13). While not comparable to those in East Kalimantan, the local governments in South Kalimantan and South Sumatra also gained significantly higher non-tax natural resource revenue than the national average during the boom.

These local governments have capitalized on increased revenue to expand personnel expenditure rather than capital investment in the boom, as they are free to spend the transfers or unconditional transfers given to local governments. While the capital expenditure on paper is larger than the national average and more than 25 percent of the budget that the Widodo administration mandated all local governments to earmark for infrastructure development,[8] in-depth securitization is required to ensure their spending is really productive and helps economic diversification. Even when local governments spend it for infrastructure development, local political elites may intervene in the process to gain political and economic rent from the project, slowing down progress (Morishita 2016).

Impact on resource governance

In the oil and gas sector, the shift back to state ownership with control (S_2) has been associated with corruption. Pertamina's regained power in concessions often prolongs negotiations over ownership structure with foreign contractors.[9] It also enables Petral – a Pertamina's energy trading unit – to conduct fuel smuggling and corruption, which was under investigation in 2016. Strong internal protesting led the Widodo government to fail in reforming Pertamina's corporate governance.

Decentralization in the mineral licensing system has also spread corruption by linking political confusion with a widespread concern over illegality (Tsing 2005; Indonesia Investments 2014). Local governments at the regency are delegated the authority to regulate and issue KP in their jurisdictions for all minerals – including the strategic minerals of oil and coal – without consulting the central government (GR 75/2000 and Mining Law of 2009). This broke the nationally uniform cadastral rules to pieces, disabling the ability of local governments to effectively use a nationally unified licensing database, and thus weakening property rights. While the central government attempted to determine specific mining areas through detailed mapping after consultation with local governments, the Constitutional Court ruled against this demarcation, deciding that local governments had the authority to designate the areas. Besides, detailed mapping was lagging far behind schedule. This made local governments lack responsible control, while letting mining licenses overlap (Spiegel 2012), favoring local investors who shared their desire for revenue maximization. The Ministry of Energy and Mineral Resources (MEMR) admits that more than half of the 8,475 mining licenses issued from May 2011 to May 2014 did not comply with the standard procedures and resulted in overlapping concession areas. In Jambi, 99 mining licenses were revoked due to overlaps in mining area and maladministration, followed by 83 in South Sumatra and 2 in South Sulawesi (Indonesia Investments 2014).

This has forced legal investors to spend a significant amount of time and money to identify promising areas for license applications and check the licensing regime for compliance with the rules. Large miners have hesitated to invest in order to avoid the risk of overlapping licensing and impartiality of local decision-making (Venugopal 2014). No new CoW has been developed since 2000 (Bhasin and Venkataramany 2008). Informal miners, in contrast, are unwilling to leave the illegal spectrum, bribing security officers of mining companies or cooperating with local authorities to prevent their resources from being swallowed up by large mining companies (Lestari 2013).

The inability of the local population to hold local politicians accountable for their decisions has also left room for local rent seekers to capture profits by securing privileged positions. As political parties have no trust from the general public and thus cannot collect membership fees, they rely heavily on mining industries to finance their political campaigns in return for mining licenses at the district level in Kalimantan.

In this context, the mining industry can easily disguise profits and wriggle out of paying taxes, as a lack of transparency has made it difficult for tax authorities to obtain good and reliable information about contracts, production, and the cash flow of the companies (Jorde 2013).

Local political elites and officials have become prone to corruption. For example, in the Kutai Kertanegara district in East Kalimantan that issued 687 KP permits by 2009, eight senior district government officials were jailed between 2005 and 2010 on corruption charges, and the district head of that period is in jail for corruption of IDR124 billion (US$13 million) (Down to Earth 2010). The number of small miners that operated with the KP was boosted from 650 in 1999 to more than 8,000 in 2010 (Ives 2015). US$1.8 billion of government revenue is estimated to be lost annually by local governments' illegal mining license allotments on state forest areas in the four provinces in Kalimantan (Human Rights Watch 2013). Also, 22 to 46 percent of potential non-tax revenue (IDR16 to 51 trillion) is estimated to be eroded from reported coal sales (World Bank 2015).

To overcome the duplicate licensing authority, the Director General of Minerals and Coal (DGMC) built the Minerba One Map Indonesia (MOMI), a web-based Geographical Information System (GIS) that covers all the data of the IUP. The DGMC employed the MOMI to announce a Clear and Clean IUP List (CnC List) and to issue a Clear and Clean certificate (CnC certificate) for IUP holders who demonstrate that they are free of competing claims (MEMR Regulation 2/2013). While this encouraged more than 40 percent of IUP holders to obtain a CnC certificate (Indonesia Investments 2015a), illegal coal mining was estimated at 50 to 80 million tons per year (Coaltrans Conferences 2014), amounting to 11 to 18 percent of the yearly production. In the end, the central government took over the legal authority of issuing mining business licenses from local governments (Law 23/2014, an amendment to the Law 32/2004 on Regional Government).

Impact on livelihood and ecology

Open cast or surface mining is responsible for extreme and irreversible environmental destruction within mined areas, with especially detrimental impacts on local water resources. Groundwater needs to be pumped out of mine pits in order to access the seams, lowering groundwater levels over a large area. Forests need to be cleared, and fertile topsoil is removed in order to access coal. In these processes, open cast coal mining can contaminate valuable underground aquifers, streams, and rivers. Contaminated water may contain high levels of salts, sulfate, iron, aluminum, and toxic heavy metals such as cadmium and cobalt. Many heavy metals bio-accumulate in tissue, and if they reach high enough concentrations, they can cause health and reproductive problems in wildlife and humans. As metals settle and persist at the bottom of streams, past operations can threaten human health and the environment for many years to come, even if current miners comply with regulations (Greenpeace Southeast Asia 2014).

Nonetheless, inconsistent and contradictory rules between the Mining Law of 2009 and the Forest Law of 1999 allow coal mining in forests and accelerate deforestation (Resosudarmo 2004). While the Forest Law of 1999 prohibited open cast mining in forest conservation areas, the prohibition was not incorporated into the Basic Forestry Law of 1967. Besides, Megawati revised the law (Law 19/2004) to exclude from the prohibition 13 major companies out of 150 concessionaires that had conducted open cast mining within protected forest before the enactment of the 1999 Forestry Law. Despite a group of non-governmental organizations (NGO) and environmentalists blaming Megawati for justifying these operations and demanding revocation of the revision, the Constitutional Court decided not to violate the Constitution (Saraswati 2005).

Then, the Ministry of Forestry issued 842 licenses for underground mining from 2005 to 2011, covering 2.03 million hectares of forest (Ministry of Forestry 2011). The regulation has been further loosened to allow underground mining in protected forests where they are deemed strategically important (GR 10/2010), along with non-forestry activities subject to a 'borrow-and-use' permit (IPKH) from the Ministry of Forestry in both production forests and protected forests (GR 24/2010, amended by GR 61/2012). The 'borrow-and-use' permit requires holders to pay various non-tax state revenues for their activities, and undertake reforestation activities upon ceasing their use of the land (PwC 2016b).

Meanwhile, the Ministry of Environment requires contractors to obtain an environmental license as part of an environmental impact assessment (AMDAL) and/or the environmental management (UKL) and environmental monitoring efforts (UPL) process, since an environmental license has become a prerequisite to obtaining other relevant business permits (GR 23/2010). They are also mandated to periodically submit environmental audits and set aside funds as an environmental bond in a government-designated bank to be spent on environmental rehabilitation and recovery. In addition, contractors are required to obtain the Leasing Forest Area License (IPPKH) for projects within and/or adjacent to protected areas (production and/or protected forest) and/or a Conversion Permit for projects in conservation forests. To enhance regulatory and enforcement functions, the Ministry of Forestry and Ministry of Environment were integrated to become the Ministry of Environment and Forestry (MoEF), which, in addition to provincial governors, and regents/mayors, is considered to have the responsibility to formulate a more systematic and integrated environmental management and protection plan (Prasetyo 2016).

Nonetheless, AMDAL is not considered to be effective due to the absence of transparency in the mining industry information and of local community involvement in the decision-making process (Junita 2015). Furthermore, it is critically dependent upon how license-holders react, as these measures deprive license-holders of their vested interest in local governments (World Bank 2014; Suzuki 2016).

MEMR instead requires contractors and license-holders to comply with relevant laws and regulations concerning occupational health and safety, environmental management, and local Community Development (CD). For PSA contracts executed on or after 2008, contractors and license-holders have become explicitly responsible for conducting CD programs without cost recovery in the duration of a PSA (MEMR 22/2008) (PwC 2016b).

In response, major coal miners such as Adaro Indonesia, Bumi Resources, and Berau Coal launched community development and environmental management programs, including mine water management, land reclamation, and rehabilitation of biodiversity. They have been rewarded green or blue awards in the environmental rating program (PROPER), gold awards in Aditama, and/or good performance in the mining sector award from MEMR (Table 10.2).

Nonetheless, INGOs and local environmentalists have uncovered a number of extreme and irreversible cases of environmental destruction at and around coal mines. Such was the case for within and around the PT Kaltim Prima Coal (KPC) project site, the second largest production site in Indonesia, and included discharge of untreated wastewater that was contaminating downstream river water, which villagers rely on for daily needs; frequent flooding, affecting at least three villages and a main road downstream; serious dust and noise pollution from blasting; and forced relocation of local villagers from ancestral homelands, causing distress due to insufficient land for cultivation and hunting (Johansyah et al. 2014). The Arutmin project site, the third largest, has also been criticized for its reclamation of post-mining land, in addition to forest destruction and toxic water contamination (Greenpeace Southeast Asia 2014). Small miners are also responsible for destruction. Some of them have abandoned

Table 10.2 Environmental and CSR program of major coal mines

ISO 14001	Adaro Indonesia	Bumi Resources	Berau
	Obtained	Obtained (KPC, Arutmin)	Obtained
PROPER	Green (2006/7, 2009, 2010/11, 2015)	Green (KPC, 2014/15) Blue (Arutmin 2014/15)	Green (Binungan and Sambarata, 2014, Provincial level), Gold (Lati, 2014, Provincial level)
Awards	Aditama (gold) for environmental management (2013)	Culture-Based Community Empowerment (Arutmin, 2015), Aditama (KPC, 2014), Mining Environmental Management (First Prize, Arutmin, 2014)	Aditama (silver) for environmental management (2013/14)
Mine Water Management	Settling pond	Sedimentation pond with dredgers and dump drainage rehabilitation	–
Reclamation	Planting commercial crops and shrubs in reclamation area	Plant growing and community-based eco-tourism in the reclaimed land (KPC)	Cumulatively re-vegetated 3055 ha out of 9650 ha disturbed land by 2014
Biodiversity	Post-mining rehabilitation	Conservation farming at Kutai National Park, Mangrove-based coastal preservation	–
Community Development program	Community rubber plantation, Clean water access, Community business	Community-based waste bank, Empowerment of resettled community	Village electrification, Post resettlement community program

Sources: Author compilation based on PT Adaro Indonesia (2014, 2017), PT Berau Coal Energy Tbk (2015) and PT Bumi Resources Tbk (2016).

their operations, leaving behind poorly managed waste ponds and untreated mining sites (Fiyanto 2014).

Short summary

Democratic decentralization changed the ownership structure from S_2 to P_2 in the oil and gas sector and from S_2 to P_1 in the coal and mineral resource sector. However, Indonesia faces declining oil and gas production and slower growth in royalty revenue in the coal and mineral resource sector. High social expectations in the name of resource nationalism have forced the government to take the maximum resource rent from foreign investors, which discourages them from exploring new oil fields. A duplicated licensing system, inconsistent and contradictory rules between the Mining Law and the Forest Law, and corruption at the local level make the distinction between legal and illegal mining ambiguous, allowing miners to pay smaller royalties than for the actual production.

The government is responding differently in the two sectors. In the oil and gas sector, it is shifting the ownership structure back to S_2 in order to gain maximum resource rent from Pertamina while enhancing its corporate governance. In contrast, the government is enhancing the tax regime to increase non-tax resource royalties in the coal and mineral resource sector and pressuring miners to make a serious commitment to CSR programs to improve livelihood and ecology. Nonetheless, the government inaction toward abandoning open cast mining offsets the effectiveness of CSR programs.

Impact of the China-induced coal boom and Chinese investments

China's coal imports and investments have several implications on upstream and downstream business in the extractive sector in Indonesia.

Disruption of livelihood and ecology

The end of the coal boom is likely to pose environmental risks as a number of local small-scale miners – who directly or indirectly export coal to China – often expose land and poorly maintain tailing dams and sediment ponds after abandoning their operations (PT Berau Coal Energy Tbk 2015: 130).

Chinese purchasers have provided low-cost capital to support the expansion of mining companies and let them act as 'straw men' in Indonesia (Garnaut 2015). Chinese and Hong Kong purchasers also buy coal from IUP holders, who have increased their coal production and exports since 2005 and raised their share to one-third of coal exports (Figure 10.8). Twenty percent of them directly export to China and Hong Kong, and the rest export through Indonesian traders (Figure 10.9). In addition, there are thousands of small local KP miners outside the control of MEMR. They may collude with local political elites and/ or officers in coal smuggling. This is why the government designated seven ports in Kalimantan and Sumatra as coal export ports and required registration from coal exporters as a way of improving supervision of coal export sales and optimizing government revenue from them (Minister of Trade 49/M-DAG/ PER/8/2014).

Meanwhile, purchasers often capitalize on their massive purchasing power to achieve favorable terms in contracts. This makes Indonesian coal miners susceptible to price fluctuations and causes them to abandon their operations during times of low market prices.

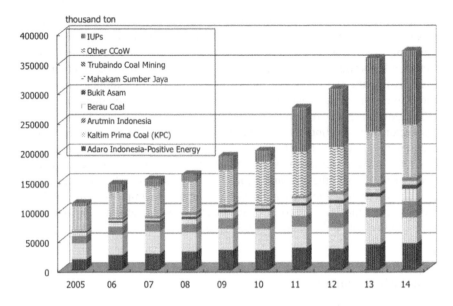

Figure 10.8 Coal export by company

Sources: Author compilation based on Ministry of Energy and Mineral Resources (2016) and JOGMEC (2016).

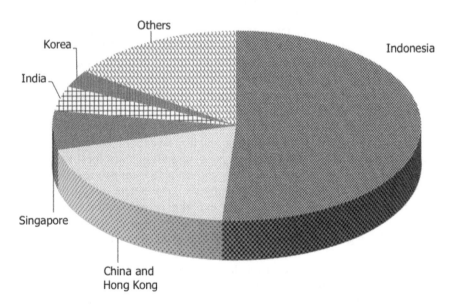

Figure 10.9 Sales destinations of IUP holders in 2015

Source: Author compiled based on Ministry of Energy and Mineral Resources (2016).

A typical example is CNOOC's gas purchasing price from Tangguh LNG. Capitalizing on its purchasing power, CNOOC forced Tangguh LNG to compete with Australia over the long-term supply contract to Guangdong province in China. As it eventually picked Australia, it instead offered Tangguh LNG a contract with neighboring Fujian province in China but with unattractive terms and conditions: a significantly lower fob price of US$2.4 per MMBTU for 2.6 million tons of LNG export per annum for 25 years in 2002 (Kato 2005). This triggered a race to the bottom over terms and conditions, losing potential export earnings from both new and existing customers. It took more than ten years for the Indonesian government to raise the price up to US$8, which is still lower than the spot price sold to Japan (Cahyafitri 2014).

Low export prices can trigger overexploitation and low-cost production that does not include social and environmental costs. China's coal import tariff and declining coal demand since 2014 have further dropped the coal price for Indonesian miners, forcing them to abandon their operations and leave polluted water and soil untreated.

Manipulation of Indonesian policies

To protect its vested interests, China enhances its political influence in Indonesian policymaking by increasing its economic influence on major coal miners that have political power to get them to act as their local agents.

PT Berau Coal has grown to be the fifth-largest coal producer due to massive exports to China, which accounts for about 44 percent of the company's total sales. China Huaneng Group, which owns Guangdong Yudean Group jointly with the Guangdong provincial government, has purchased a 51 percent stake of PT Berau Coal (Wang and Ducruet 2014).

The Qinfa Group and Yuehe have become among the top 10 customers of Arutmin Indonesia, and Huaneng Power International and China Light & Power have become among top 10 customers of KPC (Bumi Resources 2012). Arutmin Indonesia and KPC expanded their production to be the fourth and second largest coal producers in Indonesia respectively, after Bakrie Group's Bumi Resources acquired stakes in the early 2000s (Bumi Resources 2015). When the Bakrie Group faced financial distress in the 2008 Global Financial Crisis, China Investment Corporation (CIC) officially obtained a 19 percent stake (worth US$950 million) in KPC in exchange for providing US$1.9 billion in debt instruments (Bumi Resources 2015). When the coal price drop worsened the group's financial status in 2015, the CIC increased its stake up to 22.9 percent of Bumi Resources – the parent company of Arutmin Indonesia and KPC – in exchange for accepting its new share issuance (Timmerman 2017).

This investment enabled Chinese investors to protect their vested interests from policy changes, as major Indonesian coal miners have acquired political power under the democratic decentralization regime. Aburizal Bakrie, ex-chairman of the Bakrie Group, was appointed as the Coordinating Minister for Economy and then the Minister of People's Welfare under the Yudoyono government and became the chairman of the Golkar Party. Chinese purchasers increased coal imports from the Bakrie Group. These major coal miners provide funding for political parties and play leading roles in the parties, thus they are well placed to protect themselves from unfavorable policy changes. This makes it difficult for the government to effectively enforce environmental regulation and tax the mining industry (Garnaut 2015) – especially projects with Chinese investments, despite criticism for environmental and social disruption.

Chinese investors also take advantage of the transformation of coal miners into coal power to expand business. Indonesian coal miners are suffering from recently volatile coal prices (Singgih 2017), more stringent quality standards, and a requirement to hold a minimum of 10 percent of the equity of power plant companies. In response, they are looking for opportunities to transform their businesses into coal power plants in Indonesia and foreign countries (Wibaba 2015). Few Indonesian coal miners, however, have enough capacity and adequate technology to construct and manage coal power plants. Thus, Chinese investors establish joint companies with them to assist this transformation. PT Bukit Asam (PTBA), the third largest coal producer in Indonesia, agreed to a US$1.2 billion (IDR15.6 trillion) loan from the CEXIM when it joined a coal power plant project, despite its refusal of China's financing for its mining activities. It created PT Hudian Bukit Asam Power (HBAP), a consortium with China Hudian Hong Kong Company to develop the PLTU Banko Tengah coal power project (2 units, 620 MW each). Under the project, a coal supply agreement of 5.4 thousand tons annually for 25 years, an EPC contract with PT HBAP and China Hudian Hong Kong Company, and an O&M contract with PT HBAP and China Hua Dian Corporation were executed. This contractual arrangement implies that Chinese construction workers, operators, and PTBA will profit for 25 years at the expense of an electricity tariff paid by the Indonesian population (Suzuki 2015).

To win the support of the Indonesian government and to ensure Chinese companies' entry into the coal power business, the Chinese government reached an agreement with the Indonesian government regarding cooperation in the construction of power plants through environmentally sustainable technologies on a mutually beneficial basis, as well as in the planning, construction, operation, and maintenance of electrical grids (People's Republic of China and the Republic of Indonesia 2015). Under this pressure, the Indonesian government is forced to take responsibility for its coal power business.

High carbon development

Chinese investments in the electricity sector will perpetuate greater carbon emissions for the next 20 to 30 years. Chinese companies have won engineering, procurement, and construction (EPC) contracts for 36 coal power projects

(Hervé-Mignucci and Wang 2015), which would satisfy the capacity increase target in the first FTP. In addition, the CEXIM pressured the Indonesian government to accept an unconditional government guarantee for credit. This de facto shifts the business risks – including land acquirement and stable supply of coal – for the PLN.

In the second FTP, the government expected IPPs and renewable energy to share the majority. This resulted in three coal power projects with a number of proposals for infrastructure development projects (Bappenas 2015). The government had no choice but to increase the share of coal power up to 60 percent in the revised program and 55–65 percent in the 35 GW program.

This power development, however, contradicts the Nationally Determined Commitment (NDC) that pledges a greenhouse gas (GHG) emissions reduction of 29% by 2030 compared with business as usual. The government is looking for opportunities to gain credits through the Clean Development Mechanism from foreign countries by suspending issuance of palm oil plantations in peatland and tropical rainforests and recovering peat soil to prevent forest fires – both measures that reduce emissions. Nonetheless, coal power will increase emissions more than the offset from forest fire prevention.

Discussion

Indonesia stands at a crossroads between industrialization with a heavy reliance on Western countries and resource-based development with an increasing reliance on China. For many years, miners from Western countries have required the security of tenure and investment for their mining businesses. Despite the divestment requirement backed by the rising resource nationalism, Freeport Indonesia has insisted that these securities fail the requirement. Meanwhile, Western countries are importing and making investments in the footwear, garments, and textile industries, which gives strength to the Indonesian manufacturers to compete in the world market. The export earnings have enabled Indonesia to reduce its resource dependency, providing enough fiscal revenue to produce more a stable fiscal regime as well as transparency to make Indonesia less vulnerable to a resource boom and burst. These industries have gradually controlled their heavily polluted wastewater (Mori 2008).

Meanwhile, basic labor rights for workers, including the freedom to organize and collectively bargain, are frequently denied, and decent wages at factories in Indonesia are constellated as labor-intensive production points in the global supply chain of the world's most profitable Western transnational companies with brand names (Connor et al. 2016). It is still a standard practice for factory employees to work seven days a week without overtime or proper benefits (Hodal 2012). While the expanding political influence of the union in local executive elections has provoked massive strikes over minimum wage hikes every year (Moestafa 2013), the government set out Regulation No. 78/2015 on the Policy of Wage, which excludes unions from annual negotiations over the minimum wage and restricts the minimum wage hike to within the total percentage achieved by adding percentage inflation and percentage growth of GDP each fiscal year.

China offers an alternative development pathway. The Chinese government ostensibly respects the priority of the host country government and seeks business opportunities for Chinese companies, especially state-owned enterprises that can earn maximum profit with low risk. In Indonesia, it respects the divestment require-ment and chooses to provide low-cost capital to support the expansion of local miners, instead of forcing the participation of Chinese companies. As the minor partner in line with the coal DMO and the requirement of holding a minimum 10 percent of the equity of power plant companies, it also chooses to support Indonesian coal miners in expanding the downstream power generation industry.

However, our analysis demonstrates that China's provision of low-cost capital to local small miners and their investments in major coal miners strengthen its vested interests and political power. This increases abandonment of open cast mining with poor management – the underlying cause of notorious disruption to livelihood and ecology – raises GHG emissions, and brings difficulties for the Indonesian government to prevent disruptions and to uphold its pledge on GHG emissions in its NDC.

In addition, China has deprived Indonesia its industrial competitiveness during the coal boom, as shown in Chapter 8. This holds especially true for electrical appliances that led the rapid industrialization in Indonesia before the Asian Economic Crisis. This led the country to resource-dependent development, vulner-able to resource price shocks and China's demand while deprived of opportunities to enhance the human capital essential in advancing development (Gylfason 2001).

In this regard, stronger resource governance is indispensable for Indonesia to minimize the tradeoff between foreign controlled mining with low wage manu-facturing exports and resource-dependent development with trade, social, and environmental deficits. A series of policy reforms under the Widodo government is heading in this direction. The Detailed Procedures for Granting Operation Production to IUPs and IUPKs was amended so that the government can rene-gotiate CCoWs (PerMen 32/2015). A tax amnesty program is also ongoing to improve tax compliance and encourage the repatriation of offshore assets.

To enhance credibility and simplify administrative procedures, the Corruption Eradication Commission (KPK) has been mobilized to investigate mining firms in 12 provinces and the Supervision Coordination of Mineral Coal Governance (Korsup Minerba) has been established to ensure compliance with basic laws, such as not overlapping with other mines, assessing environmental impact, and preventing payment leakage to the government, as well as to collect data and improve information systems (PWYP Indonesia 2016). Indonesian banks have been required to stop all lending to coal-mining projects in East Kalimantan (Greenpeace Southeast Asia 2016) when the Korsup Minerba released that local governments revoked around 40% in permits (Burton 2016).

These reforms have seen mixed results so far. While the government obtained trillions of rupiah from a number of mining firms that previously had not paid their full royalty payments (Cahyafitri 2015), the total amount in arrears still remains worth IDR5.07 trillion (US$380.2 million) as of February 2017 (Amianti 2017a). Moreover, the unattractive terms and conditions in the amnesty program has brought about disappointing results, with IDR136.5 trillion (US$10.5 billion) or 13.6 percent of the full target for repatriation (Indonesia Investments 2017). In Kalimantan, 1,041 out of 6,041 taxpayers in the mineral and coal-mining industry joined the amnesty, with total payments reaching IDR228.6 billion (US$17 million), and 78 out of 1,114 taxpayers in oil and gas joined, with payments totaling IDR40.8 billion (Adri 2016). The MEMR warns that it will revoke operating permits of mining and coal companies with arrears in non-tax revenue payments.

Nonetheless, Indonesia is heading toward formalization of resource revenue under private ownership with control (P_1) and thus, toward stronger resource governance. It is possible to reduce the disruption to livelihood and ecology, as the government faces smaller protests and transaction costs in revocation permits for companies with arrears in non-tax revenue payment than for noncompliance with environmental and social regulations – the latter of which imposes the heavier burden of proof on the government and requires wider support. More importantly, the Chinese government and investors can hardly oppose reform openly even if they are in jeopardy.

Conclusions

This chapter treats Indonesia as a case study to analyze how the China-induced coal boom has affected resource governance, which was destabilized by democratic decentralization. Findings can be summarized as follows.

First, democratic decentralization shifted the ownership structure from state ownership without control (S_2) to private ownership without control (P_2) in the oil and gas sector and private ownership with control (P_1) in the coal sector. This shift has enabled the government to battle for a stronger fiscal regime: a broad-based tax system with productive and transparent expenditures.

Second, China has capitalized on the duplicate licensing system, obscured property rights, and local corruption caused in the change of ownership structure in order to accelerate open cast mining. The results of this were not only huge profits for Chinese purchasers, but also negative impacts on the quality of livelihood and ecology in Indonesia. It also increased economic impacts of Chinese purchasers on major miners that have strong political power, protecting their vested interests from policy changes. This makes it difficult for the Indonesian government to enforce more stringent environmental and social safeguard policies, including the phasing-out of open cast mining, and the shift toward low GHG emissions development.

Third, a series of mining policy reforms the Widodo government has implemented to eradicate illegal mining and increase government revenue can be evaluated as the right direction to get out of the tradeoff between the Western country-induced foreign controlled mining with manufacturing export and the China-induced resource-dependent development with trade, social, and environmental deficits.

Notes

1 Security of tenure empowers the investor to obtain proceeds from a general survey through exploration all the way through mine development, production, processing, and marketing. Security of investment is an assurance that there will be no effect on the investment from changes in government laws or policies after signing for the period in force.
2 Almost half of the 750 oil and gas exploration wells drilled between 2002 and 2012 were dry, leading to a surrender of blocks following fruitless exploration in recent years (Global Business Guide Indonesia 2014).
3 In 2016, Chevron Pacific Indonesia shares 35 percent of national crude oil output, followed by Mobile at 23 percent and Pertamina at 15 percent. CNOOC SES and Petro China share 4 and 2 percent, respectively. In gas output, Total shares 26 percent, followed by ConocoPhillips at 22 percent, BP at 18 percent, and Pertamina at 17 percent (PwC 2016a).
4 These provisions are described in the draft revision to the Oil and Gas Law of 2001. The draft, however, raises concerns about too much strong power given to Pertamina, and less pragmatic and more susceptible issuance and administration of PSAs to parliamentary lobbying and resource nationalism (PwC 2016a), prolonging discussion in parliament.
5 More than 170 exploration projects had been either suspended, withdrawn, or rendered inactive, and only 12 of the 268 CoWs were in operation by 2000.
6 This requires a reduction of foreign ownership of up to 49 percent after ten years of operation. While the government reduced the requirement by 60 or 70 percent and extended the period of divestment by GR 77/2014, it was reversed to the original requirement by GR 1/2017.
7 The CoW covers all tax, royalties, and other fiscal charges, including: dead rent in the contract area, production royalties, income tax payable by the company, employees' personal income tax, withholding taxes on dividends, land and building tax, regional taxes and retributions, and so on (PwC 2016b).
8 In 2015, nearly 67 percent of 542 regions nationwide failed to spend 25 percent of their budget to spur infrastructure development (Amianti 2017b).
9 This resulted in it taking eight years for Exxon Mobile to start operation at Cepu oil bloc.

References

Adelman, D., Carswell, C.J., Beale, P.A. and Barthe-Dejean, J. (2015) *Update: Indonesia's New Draft Oil & Gas Law*, www.reedsmith.com/en-US/UPDATE-Indonesias-New-Draft-Oil-Gas-Law-07-22-2015, accessed on February 3, 2017.

Adri, N. (2016) Jokowi to 2,000 mining businesspeople: Evade tax? We'll catch you, *Jakarta Post*, December 6, 2016.

Amianti, G.D. (2017a) Government to revoke permits of delinquent miners, *Jakarta Post*, March 8, 2017.

Amianti, G.D. (2017b) Indonesia tightens watch on regional spending, *Jakarta Post*, January 9, 2017.

Amirio, D. (2016) Deeply rooted problems hinder private funding of infrastructure, *Jakarta Post*, October 12, 2016.

Ardiansyah, F., Marthen, A.A. and Amalia, N. (2015) Forest and land-use governance in a decentralized Indonesia: A legal and policy review, *Occasional Paper 132*, Bogor: CIFOR.

Auty, R.M. (2007) Natural resources, capital accumulation and the resource curse, *Ecological Economics* 61: 627–34.

Bappenas (2015) *Public Private Partnership: Infrastructure Projects Plan in Indonesia 2015*, https://www.bappenas.go.id/files/9314/8767/3599/PPP_BOOK_2017.pdf, accessed on May 5, 2018.

Bhasin, B. and Venkataramany, S. (2008) *Mining Law and Policy: Replacing the 'Contract of Work' System in Indonesia*, www.eisourcebook.org/cms/Mining%20Law%20and%20 Policy%20Evolution%20in%20Indonesia.pdf#search=%27Mining+law+and+policy%3 A+Replacing+the+%E2%80%98Contract+of+Work%E2%80%99+system+in+Indon esia%27, accessed on January 22, 2017.

BP (2017) *Tangguh LNG*, www.bp.com/en_id/indonesia/bp-in-indonesia/tangguh-lng.html, accessed on February 14, 2017.

Brodjonegoro, B. (2001) Indonesian intergovernmental transfer in decentralized era: The case of General Allocation Fund, Presented paper at the *International Symposium on Intergovernmental Transfers in Asian Countries: Issues and Practices*, Asian Tax and Public Policy Program, Hitotsubashi University.

Brodjonegoro, B. (2004) The Indonesian decentralization after law revision: Toward a better future? Presented paper at the *International Symposium on Fiscal Decentralization in Asia Revisited*, Asian Tax and Public Policy Program, Hitotsubashi University.

Bumi Resources (2012) *1H 2012 Financial Results*, www.bumiresources.com/index. php?option=com_financialinfo&task=download&id=357&Itemid=115, accessed on February 22, 2017.

Bumi Resources (2015) *Annual Report 2015*, www.bumiresources.com/index. php?option=com_financialinfo&task=download&id=541&Itemid=52, accessed on February 22, 2017.

Burton, B. (2016) Corruption and illegalities in the mining sector in Indonesia: A ranking of 12 provinces involved in Korsup Minerba, *Endcoal*, http://endcoal.org/2016/02/ media-briefing-corruption-and-illegalities-in-the-mining-sector-in-indonesia-a-ranking-of-12-provinces-involved-in-korsup-minerba/, accessed on July 14, 2016.

Cahyafitri, R. (2014) Tangguh LNG price raised after deal, *Jakarta Post*, July 1, 2014.

Cahyafitri, R. (2015) Revenue target from coal & mineral sector raised, *Jakarta Post*, February 5, 2015.

Cardenal, J.P. and Araujo, H. (2014) *China's Silent Army: The Pioneers Traders Fixers and Workers Who Are Remaking the World*, London: Penguin.

Casson, A. and Obidzinski, K. (2002) From new order to regional autonomy: Shifting dynamics of "illegal" logging in Kalimantan, Indonesia, *World Development* 30: 2133–51.

Coaltrans Conference (2014) Indonesian government tightens regulatory screws in the coal industry, http://www.coaltrans.com/articles/3352741/indonesian-government-tightens-regulatory-screws-in-the-coal-industry.html, accessed on June 1, 2018.

Connor, T., Delaney, A. and Rennie, S. (2016) *Non-Judicial Mechanisms in Global Footwear and Apparel Supply Chains: Lessons from Workers in Indonesia*, Non-Judicial Redress Mechanisms Report Series 14, Jakarta.

Down to Earth (August 2010) Deadly Coal – coal exploitation and Kalimantan's blighted generation, *Down to Earth Newsletter* 85–6.

Economy, E.C. and Levi, M. (2014) *By All Means Necessary: How China's Resource Quest Is Changing the World*, Oxford: Oxford University Press.

Fiyanto, A. (2014) *Devastation from Coal Mining in South Kalimantan, Indonesia*, www. greenpeace.org/international/en/news/Blogs/makingwaves/devastation-from-coal-mining-in-south-kaliman/blog/51571, accessed on June 22, 2016.

Garnaut, R. (2015) Indonesia's resources boom in international perspective: Policy dilemmas and options for continued strong growth, *Bulletin of Indonesian Economic Studies* 51(2): 189–212.

Global Business Guide Indonesia (2014) *Indonesia's Oil and Gas Sector – Upstream Challenges*, www.gbgindonesia.com/en/energy/article/2014/indonesia_s_oil_and_gas_sector_upstream_challenges.php, accessed on January 18, 2017.

Greenpeace Southeast Asia (2014) *Coal Mines Polluting South Kalimantan's Water*, www.greenpeace.org/seasia/id/PageFiles/645408/FULL REPORT Coal Mining Polluting South Kalimantan Water_Lowres.pdf, accessed on June 22, 2016.

Greenpeace Southeast Asia (2016) Indonesian coal market update – Regulatory crackdown on coal mining, *Financial Briefing Update*, 22 February 2016, www.banktrack.org/manage/ems_files/download/20160222_indonesian_coal_market_update_pdf, accessed on June 22, 2016.

Gylfason, T. (2001) Natural resources, education, and economic development, *European Economic Review* 45: 847–59.

Hervé-Mignucci, M. and Wang, X. (2015) Slowing the growth of coal power outside China: The role of Chinese finance, *A CPI Report*, Climate Policy Initiative.

Hodal, K. (2012) Nike factory to pay $1m to Indonesian workers for overtime: Shoe plant workers clocked up nearly 600,000 hours of overtime without pay over two years, *The Guardian*, January 12, 2012.

Hong, Z. and Sambodo, M.T. (2015) *Indonesia-China Energy and Mineral Ties Broaden*, Singapore: Institute of Southeast Asian Studies.

Human Rights Watch (2013) *The Dark Side of Green Growth: Human Rights Impacts of Weak Governance in Indonesia's Forestry Sector*, www.hrw.org/report/2013/07/15/dark-side-green-growth/human-rights-impacts-weak-governance-indonesias-forestry, accessed on March 18, 2017.

Indonesia Investments (2014) *Weak Governance in Indonesian Mining Sector: Overlapping Mining Areas*, www.indonesia-investments.com/news/todays-headlines/weak-governance-in-indonesian-mining-sector-overlapping-mining-areas/item2114? accessed on February 8, 2017.

Indonesia Investments (2015a) *Government in Search of Unpaid Bills*, www.indonesia-investments.com/zh_cn/news/todays-headlines/coal-mining-industry-indonesia-government-in-search-of-unpaid-bills/item5892, accessed on January 18, 2017.

Indonesia Investments (2015b) *Higher Royalties for IUP-Holders*, www.indonesia-investments.com/business/business-columns/coal-mining-industry-indonesia-higher-royalties-for-iup-holders/item5195, accessed on January 18, 2017.

Indonesia Investments (2017) *Tax Amnesty Program Indonesia*, www.indonesia-investments.com/finance/tax-system/tax-amnesty-program/item7124? accessed on February 7, 2017.

Ives, M. (2015) *Indonesian Coal Mining Boom Is Leaving Trail of Destruction*, http://e360.yale.edu/features/indonesian_coal_mining_boom_is_leaving_trail_of_destruction, accessed on January 23, 2017.

JOGMEC (2016) A survey of coal and mining industry in Indonesia, *A Survey Report on Enhancing Exploration of Oversees Coal 2016* (in Japanese), http://coal.jogmec.go.jp/content/300318148.pdf, accessed on May 5, 2018.

Johansyah, M., Agustiorini, S., Sebastian, S. and Maimunah, S. (2014) *PT KPC/Bumi Resources Deadly Coal: Ecological and Social Crisis Caused by KPC/Bumi Resources' Coal Production*, JATAM East Kalimantan, www.banktrack.org/download/

jatam_infosheet_final_20_aug_pdf/jatam_infosheet_final_20_aug.pdf, accessed on February 13, 2017.

Jorde, S. (2013) Coal and climate in Kalimantan: Norwegian interests in Indonesia's environmentally damaging coal expansion, *Working Paper*, Framtiden, www.framtiden. no/rapporter/rapporter-2013/698-report-coal-and-climate-in-kalimantan-2013/file.html, accessed on August 30, 2016.

Junita, F. (2015) The foreign mining investment regime in Indonesia: Regulatory risk under resource nationalism policy and how international investment treaties provide protection, *Journal of Energy and Natural Resources Law* 33(3): 241–65.

Kanekiyo, K. and Inoue, T. (August 2006) Current state and challenges of oil and gas in Indonesia, *IEEJ* 1–26 (in Japanese).

Kato, M. (2005) Oil and gas industry in Indonesia: Perspectives and challenges amid liberalization, in Ishida, M. (ed.) *Indonesia: Challenges for Revitalization*, Chiba: Institute of Developing Economies, 171–93 (in Japanese).

Lestari, N.I. (2013) Mineral governance, conflicts and rights: Case studies on the informal mining of gold, tin and coal in Indonesia, *Bulletin of Indonesian Economic Studies* 49(2): 239–40.

Luong, P.J. and Weinthal, E. (2010) *Oil Is Not a Curse: Ownership Structure and Institutions in Soviet Successor States*, Cambridge: Cambridge University Press.

Ministry of Energy and Mineral Resources (2016) *Indonesia Mineral and Coal Information 2015*, https://www.esdm.go.id/assets/media/content/Statistik_Mineral_Dan_ Batubara_2015-ilovepdf-compressed.pdf, accessed on May 5, 2018.

Moestafa, B. (2013) Two million workers strike in Indonesia wage protest, group says, *Bloomberg*, October 31, 2013.

Mori, A. (2008) Environmental soft loan program in Asian countries: Industrial pollution control or mal-use of foreign aid resources? *Journal of Cleaner Production* 16(5): 612–21.

Morishita, A. (2016) Political dynamics of foreign-invested development projects in decentralized Indonesia: The case of coal railway projects in Kalimantan, *Southeast Asian Studies* 5(3): 413–42.

Patey, L. (2014) *The New Kings of Crude: China, India and the Global Strategies for Oil in Sudan and South Sudan*, London: C. Hurst & Co. Ltd.

People's Republic of China and the Republic of Indonesia (2015) *Joint Statement on Strengthening Comprehensive Strategic Partnership between the People's Republic of China and the Republic of Indonesia*, March 27, 2015, https://www.kemlu.go.id/ Documents/joint%20statement%20RI-Tiongkok/Joint%20Statement.pdf, accessed on May 5, 2018.

Prasetyo, W. (2016) *Environmental Law in Indonesian: Recent and Possible Future Changes*, www.lexology.com/library/detail.aspx?g=916c9632-1fe4-4bea-8827- ca02d05e4650, accessed on February 13, 2017.

PT Adaro Indonesia (2014) *Sustainability Report 2012–13: Delivering Positive Energy Sustainably*, www.adaro.com/pages/read/9/51/Sustainability%20Reports, accessed on March 18, 2017.

PT Adaro Indonesia (2017) *Adaro Awards*, www.adaro.com/pages/read/6/20/Award#Awards for Adaro, accessed on March 18, 2017.

PT Berau Coal Energy Tbk (2015) *Efficiency & Optimization, Performance for Stable Achievement: Annual Report 2014*, http://www.indonesia-investments.com/upload/ bedrijfsprofiel/221/Berau-Coal-Energy-Annual-Report-2014-Company-Profile-Indonesia-Investments.pdf, accessed on May 5, 2018.

PT Bumi Resources Tbk (2016) *Maintaining Growth in a Changing World: Annual Report 2015*, www.bumiresources.com/index.php?option=com_financialinfo&task=download&id=541&Itemid=52, accessed on May 5, 2018.

PwC (2016a) *Oil and Gas in Indonesia: Investment and Taxation Guide May 2016–7th Edition*, https://www.pwc.com/id/en/energy-utilities-mining/assets/May%202016/PwC%20Indonesia-oil-and-gas-guide-2016.pdf, accessed on May 5, 2018.

PwC (2016b) *Mining in Indonesia: Investment and Taxation Guide May 2016–8th Edition*, https://www.pwc.com/id/en/energy-utilities-mining/assets/May%202016/PwC%20Indonesia-mining-in-Indonesia-survey-2016.pdf, accessed on May 5, 2018.

PWYP Indonesia (2016) *Coordination and Supervision in Energy Sector*, http://pwyp-indonesia.org/en/activities/advocacy/coordination-and-supervision-in-energy-sector-2, accessed on January 31, 2017.

Resosudarmo, I.A.P (2004) Closer to people and trees: Will decentralization work for the people and forest in Indonesia? *European Journal of Development Research* 16(1): 110–32.

Sakamoto, S. (2006) LNG and gas industry in Indonesia: Why they become stagnant, and how they can get out. *Oil and Natural Gas Review* 40(6): 15–27 (in Japanese).

Saraswati, M.S. (2005) Mining in protected forests legalized, *Jakarta Post*, July 8, 2005.

Singgih, V.P. (2017) Adaro wants more power plants to shift core business, *Jakarta Post*, February 10, 2017.

Spiegel, S.J. (2012) Formalisation policies, informal resource sectors and the de-/re-centralisation of power: Geographies of inequality in Africa and Asia, *Report*, Bogor: CIFOR.

Suzuki, J. (2016) Local government 'disloyalty' blamed for Indonesia's sudden stall, *Nikkei Asian Review*, June 8, 2016, http://asia.nikkei.com/Politics-Economy/Policy-Politics/Local-government-disloyalty-blamed-for-Indonesia-s-sudden-stall, accessed on July 14, 2016.

Suzuki, W. (2015) Indonesian coal producer gets $1.2B loan from China, *Tambang Batubara Bukit Asam*, March 28, 2015.

Timmerman, A. (2017) Bumi Resources gets nod to raise $2.6b via rights issue, *Deal Street Asia*, February 7, 2017, www.dealstreetasia.com/stories/indonesia-bumi-resources-gets-nod-to-raise-2-6b-via-rights-issue-64377, accessed on February 8, 2017.

Tsing, A.L. (2005) *Friction: An Ethnography of Global Connection*, Princeton: Princeton University Press.

Venugopal, V. (2014) Assessing mineral licensing in a decentralized context: The case of Indonesia, *Briefing, Natural Resource Governance Institute*, October 2014.

Wang, C. and Ducruet, C. (2014) Transport corridors and regional balance in China: The case of coal trade and logistics, *Journal of Transport Geography* 40: 3–16.

Wibaba, A.A. (2015) *Coal Business Is Dim, PTBA Lights Power Plants*, www.ptba.co.id/en/detail/index/138/coal-business-is-dim-ptba-lights-power-plants, accessed on March 13, 2017.

World Bank (2014) *Indonesia Economic Quarterly March 2014: Investment in Flux*, www.worldbank.org/content/dam/Worldbank/document/EAP/Indonesia/IEQ-March2014-english.pdf, accessed on July 12, 2016.

World Bank (2015) *Indonesia Economic Quarterly March 2015: High Expectations*, www. worldbank.org/content/dam/Worldbank/document/EAP/Indonesia/IEQ-MAR-2015-EN. pdf, accessed on July 12, 2016.

Yusuf, A.A. and Resosudarmo, B.P. (2014) Is reducing subsidies on vehicle fuel equitable? A lessons from Indonesian reform experience, in Sterner, T. (ed.) *Fuel Taxes and the Poor: The Distributional Effects of Gasoline Taxation and Their Implications for Climate Policy*, Oxon: RFF Press, 171–80.

11 Upper Mekong region energy development impacts on Myanmar's socio-ecological systems

Hydropower, environmental change, and displacement

Lynn Thiesmeyer

Introduction

Energy project sites and the Southeast Asian environment: China and other transnational investments in hydropower in Myanmar

Since the year 2000, the East Asia-Pacific nations of Thailand, Japan, and most notably China have continued to channel sizable amounts of their corporate investments as well as their Overseas Development Assistance into energy supply and extraction in Southeast Asia. China's search for, and extraction of, energy resources to be found within the reach of quick and low-cost (overland) transport from its neighbors are intensifying. It comes as no surprise that with or without China's policy for CO_2 emissions reduction, its overseas energy procurement has led to environmental consequences in its energy-supplying neighbors. What is less understood, however, is the way in which the energy-exporting country's environmental impacts quickly lead to both economic and political impacts. This has become apparent in Southeast Asia's Upper GMS (Greater Mekong Subregion), where proximity to China and dependence on Chinese investment have facilitated an increasing number of Chinese energy projects, especially in mining, fossil fuels, and hydropower.

In 2013 the Institute for Developing Economies (Japan) pointed out that "54% of China's total investment in Myanmar was focused on the energy area, with oil and natural gas accounting for 31%" (Bi Shihong 2014: 180). In that year approximately a further 33% was invested for the planning and construction of hydropower dams (Urban et al. 2013). The two operational large-scale dam sites in northern Myanmar that are closest to the Chinese border have been transmitting high volumes of electricity to China since 2008. The foremost is Shweli I dam in northern Shan State, which can generate up to 3,022 million KWH annually. The second is the Dapein I and II dam cluster in Kachin State, having already sold billions of kilowatts of electricity to China.[1]

Here, I focus on the impacts of energy-resource extraction in the northern Myanmar states of Shan and Kachin under Chinese investment and construction, particularly large-scale hydropower dams. In this still economically underdeveloped but resource-rich region, Chinese and other foreign investment including joint ventures with Myanmar SOEs pose a risk, through their uses of vast land areas, to the transboundary ecosystems and livelihoods of Myanmar's economy and to those of the Mekong Region. There are at least 25 planned and operating dams. While the newest are being built under Build-Operate-Transfer schemes, those that are Chinese-financed are planned on average to transmit 50–90% of the first several years of electricity back to China.

The vast Upper Mekong regions of Yunnan Province, Laos, Thailand, and Myanmar enjoy a natural environment, resources, and habitats that remain somewhat more intact than those of the more developed Lower Mekong. Yet in recent years it has also become the target of rapid development. There is an economic quadrangle promoted by the governments of China, Laos, Thailand, and Vietnam, and financed by other Asian as well as EU partners, based around the former "Triangle" areas:

> the Golden Triangle, composed of Laos, Myanmar and Thailand [and] . . . [a]nother triangle area upstream on the Mekong River is composed of China, Laos and Myanmar and it is called the "Green Triangle". . . . The combined area of the Golden Triangle and the Green Triangle is called as the "Golden Triangle Area" or the "Quadrangle Economic Zone."[2]

Specifically,

> The Greater Golden Triangle Cooperation [was] originally proposed by the Chiang Rai Chamber of Commerce in 1990 and later promoted again by the Chiang Mai Chamber of Commerce in 2000 . . . [which] could cover the Golden Triangle and bordering Chinese provinces. . . . Other triangle areas include . . . the **economic quadrangle** area to extend the Greater Golden Triangle.[3]

This area, consisting of China's Yunnan Province, northern Laos, northern Thailand, and north and northeastern Myanmar, has been under development since 1993. It has been the recipient of ongoing investments in hydropower planning and development from Japan, Thailand, Singapore, Norway, Austria, and China. Japan's ODA agency JICA was placed in charge of hydropower development planning and its Strategic Environmental Assessment with Myanmar's Ministry of Electricity and Energy (MOEE, [which merged the MOE and MOEP in March 2016] 2016).[4] Chinese investments in Myanmar hydropower project construction in Myanmar's northern states, however, as well as its consumption of hydro-energy for Chinese projects both in Myanmar and in China, still exceed those of other nations.

Chinese investment provided for the blasting of the Upper Mekong for deeper-draught shipping and has helped emplace the North-South and East-West Corridors of the Asian Highway Network for overland transport. This has made it possible for the Upper Mekong region to become the site of large-scale development projects, and this in turn has made it necessary to develop large-scale energy resources. The most copious resource that is immediately available in Myanmar is water and water power. It contributes to the vast Greater Mekong Subregion power grid both in-country and to its neighbors, as will be discussed below.

Like the majority of development projects, these have impacted the local and regional environment, whose ecosystems are particularly important for an agricultural-export economy like that of Myanmar. The relevant ecosystem productivity and its economic benefits to human communities grow, shrink, or otherwise change with the introduction of large-scale projects. The discussion which follows the analysis of data and findings in the final section of this chapter relates the socio-ecological systems (SES) issues to the impacts within the particular area under study (northern Myanmar) as derived from the localized environmental and economic survey data presented in this chapter.

Energy resources and supply in the Upper Mekong region (China and Myanmar)

Hydropower energy supply, as well as the large-scale, large-volume supply of other resources in the Upper GMS has concentrated in areas surrounding the rivers shared between China and Myanmar. These are China's Nu Jiang (Myanmar's Thanlwin, called Salween along the Thai border), China's Longchuan Jiang (Myanmar's Shweli or Nam Mao), China's Lancang Jiang (the Mekong River), and China's Dulongjiang (Myanmar's N'mai), Myanmar's Ayerawaddy and Nam Mali, and their tributaries and hydrology/limnology. These projects' ecosystem changes or disruptions have brought about losses of carbon capture and other ecosystem services, and resulted in some degradation of soil, air, and water as well as land transfer away from the local economic activities of cropping and forestry. In these remote and traditional areas, damage to the ecosystem and loss of land mean loss of productivity and income. In these less-developed regions of Asia, ecosystems' primary "services" should be understood as those of food, income and livelihood.

Within this region, the economic quadrangle development seeks to provide cross-border highways, power grids, and industrial development, all of which in part seek to extract, generate, or use exponentially larger quantities of energy than in recent decades. These are rapidly taking a toll on the environment and thus on the livelihoods of the nearly 2 billion rural dwellers in the region. On the national level, Myanmar is a country where over 30% of the GDP is currently occupied by agriculture. Tampering with the environment means economic losses in this sector. Myanmar's numerous new hydropower projects have not only impacted the environments of their dam sites, but have also made water resources the object of competition between two economically important sectors: an energy sector that includes transboundary energy projects with China, and the agricultural sector that provides not only export earnings but also livelihoods for the over 15 million residents of Myanmar's northern and eastern states. Massive withdrawals of groundwater and diversion or pooling of rivers for hydropower mean that renewable energy, typically thought to include water power, may become non-renewable.

Since 2000, Myanmar's annual demand for water for agriculture was nearly 90% of total freshwater water withdrawal; including the burgeoning industrial sector, the withdrawal was at least 739 m³ per year (FAO/Aquastat 2012, 2016) and has risen steadily. The construction or land transfer during the planning stages of large-scale dams since 2008, as well as the capture and diversion of water resources to energy projects, results in lower volumes of water for other uses, lower carbon capture regionally, and loss of human livelihood and living space with the potential for greater carbon emissions from displacement to and employment in denser, higher-emissions locales and activities. Under rapid economic development, energy resources that were localized commodities soon become sought and traded globally. More importantly, their mode of use and level of consumption also have global effects. China's extraction of energy resources within the reach of quick and low-cost transport from its overland neighbors is intensifying. Before and after China's 2015 plan for CO_2 emissions, its energy procurement's potential impacts on the environment within China and within its neighbors have become more visible. What is less understood, however,

Map 11.1 Salween Dams
Source: IRN (2012).

is the way in which the energy-exporting country's environmental impacts lead to socio-ecological, socio-economic, and socio-political impacts.

These have become apparent in Southeast Asia's Upper Mekong region, where proximity to China and dependence on Chinese investment have facilitated an increasing number of Chinese energy projects, especially in mining, fossil fuels, and hydropower. The unique nature of hydropower facilities, with their location and resource capture along moving rivers, makes them a significant case by which energy extraction and transport outside China and their eco-social stresses on the host country can be studied.

In Myanmar, many of the larger Chinese-funded dams are located in areas of northern and eastern Myanmar, in Shan and Kachin States. These are currently host to 18 existing or commissioned dams and seven known planned dams near or with transmission lines extending within Myanmar as well as to the China border. Many are along the Shweli River (three), along the Upper Salween (at least seven), and along their northern tributaries into Myanmar's major river, the Ayerawaddy. Of the 50 planned dams, however, there are a significant number of smaller dams (under 280 MW planned capacity) on smaller rivers and on tributaries of the three large rivers mentioned above.[5] Among other issues, the requisitioning of large tracts of productive and inhabited land for hydropower dam construction is a driver of political unrest and livelihood loss along with long-term ecosystem losses. These are now placing an economic burden on agriculture, which begins to occupy a shrinking place in the GDP but *not* in the share of population – still over 65% – which it supports (World Bank 2016), making it a serious socio-economic concern in all of the relevant local areas hosting the planned dams.

An increase in carbon and other greenhouse-gas emissions is known to occur with already-built dams and their reservoirs.[6] Major known environmental impacts in Myanmar include air contaminants and water and soil pollutants. There is now less carbon capture in Myanmar's ecosystem, which is already carbon-overloaded because commercial and residential cooking are fueled with wood charcoal throughout the country. There is a widespread loss of watershed ecosystem services, especially those providing livelihood access and options because dams even in the planning and construction stages occupy anywhere from 50 sq. km to 870 sq. km of formerly forested or farmed land, leading to much higher carbon release.

The surveys in this research were mixed method, with the quantitative environmental sampling data on air, water, and soil taken on site, and qualitative household interviews on socio-economic data were made with rural residents in the impacted areas. They were conducted between 2013 and 2016 with interdisciplinary and international teams consisting of an environmental chemist, a biodiversity specialist, socio-economic and rural economy researchers, and a public health specialist. The team members and assistants included Myanmar, Chinese, Thai, and Japanese nationals. Samples were taken on-site and were chemically analyzed. Sites were exclusively rural and chosen for their location along development project "clusters."

There is no meaning in talking about energy (supply) unless we also talk about what it is energy *for*. In this case it is for large, geographically clustered development projects, including plantations, mines, pipelines, highways, and hydropower facilities in Myanmar and in China. Energy supply projects are located in "clusters" because they supply energy for these other, multi-sectoral projects in and beyond those clusters. With the large land area diverted from agricultural production through the construction of hydropower dams and reservoirs, there is also a loss of watershed and its ecosystem services. Of especial concern here is irrigation from watersheds, as there have been two massive droughts in 2010 and 2016, leading to high rural unemployment and up to 30% reductions in agricultural productivity, as discussed below.

Socio-ecological systems issues in hydropower development

Socio-economic systems approaches, with their concern with ecosystem services in the interaction of humans with, and upon, their ecosystem and its resilience, have frequently been used in environmental and human-ecological research on Asian rural development (Ostrom 2009; Berkes et al. 2003). Where the resilience and productivity of an environment and its ecological services can be presumed to rely on sustainable management and use by humans, the result should be economic and ultimately political stability (Ostrom 2009; Bruckmeier 2016b). If insecurity is the concern, a socio-ecological systems approach should be able to identify breakdowns in particular ecosystems' provision of basic needs to their human communities and the links to insecurity in food, income (livelihood), environment, and the socio-political order. Both a breakdown in some ecosystem service provisions as well as the potential for sustainable environmental management can be applied to rural areas hosting development projects in Myanmar (Nassl and Loffler 2015).

The commodification of energy resources can be seen as both cause and result of rapid industrialization and the post-industrial processes now taking place in the less-developed areas of Myanmar, Laos, and southern China. The procurement of an energy mix including natural gas, petroleum, and other hydrocarbons, biofuels, and hydropower – their extraction, refining, and transport (transmission) – take very different forms and involve very different costs and benefits according to the type of resource. They do, however, share similarities in terms of their impacts on the environment from which they are extracted or captured, which is normally in rural areas dependent on cropland and forest for the local economy. They also share in the increasing breadth of their ecological footprint and their related potential either to enhance or to shut down local livelihoods. In Myanmar and the rest of the Upper GMS (Yunnan Province, northern Myanmar, northern Laos, and northern Thailand) between one-third and one-half of the local and regional economies' share of GDP is in agriculture. Energy projects' loss and rendering unusable of previously productive areas means a direct impact on up to 50% of the local and provincial economies.

With or without China's policy for CO_2 emissions reduction, it has been evident for some time that its cross-border energy procurement is leading to new environmental consequences within its own territory and that of its neighbors. What is less understood, however, is the way in which environmental impacts in the neighboring energy-exporting country lead to regional, national, and local economic impacts in the region's economically important sectors. These impacts have become apparent in Southeast Asia's Upper Mekong region along the border of China, in northern Laos and particularly in Myanmar. Northern and eastern Myanmar's proximity to China and dependence on Chinese investment have helped facilitate an increasing number of Chinese energy projects, especially in mining, fossil fuels, and hydropower. The unique nature of hydropower facilities, with their location and resource capture along moving rivers, also offers a significant case by which energy extraction and transport to and from China and their eco-social stresses on host countries can be studied. Further, the unique nature of hydro-energy is that is it based on a resource that moves. The flow of rivers within Asia almost inevitably crosses nation-state boundaries, making both the economic and political significance of hydropower projects loom much larger.

Balancing the economic development benefits of energy projects with their negative impacts and costs is proving difficult. The Golden Quadrangle Development Scheme includes several infrastructure and energy projects. A regional electricity grid reaching from southern China to Vietnam, Laos, Thailand, and Myanmar, as well as the additions to the Asian Highway Network and proposed rail lines in the area, provide the basic infrastructures. The electricity grid will be supplied in large part by the 30 hydropower dams in Yunnan Province, the 20 hydropower dams in Myanmar, and the seven hydropower dams in Laos.

Socio-ecological stresses resulting from such large and land-gobbling projects are numerous and widespread, and are just beginning to be surveyed. These include, first, greater carbon release (loss of carbon capture) from the deforestation that accompanies large-scale land clearing for large-scale dams. Second is the related issue of the desertification and salinization of the soil which has for centuries provided cropland, pasturage, and forest products for the regional economy and the resultant warming and drying. With it comes biodiversity loss and loss of sustainable and saleable biomass. Third comes the widespread disruption of the hydrology within the entire region, making it likely that the current drought-flood cycles will occur more frequently and with more severity. Other significant socio-ecological system stresses include the severe reduction in livelihoods that leads to massive displacement – including political conflict refugees, which include hydro-power dam areas; there already are over 90,000 displaced persons living in camps in northern Myanmar alone – and the actual issue of severe drought and flooding in 2015–16 which have caused high losses of agricultural output and rural jobs, and contributed to a high inflation rate of 9.5%, surpassing GDP growth.

Any discussion of rural environmental or ecosystem impacts, especially their economic impacts, must take into account not only the proportion of GDP coming from agriculture, but also the proportion of workers and livelihoods currently supported by the agricultural sector. As with other data in Myanmar, the relevant statistics vary. But most economic indicators show that although 32%–38% of recent years' GDP came from agriculture, it employs at least 60%–70% of the labor force.[7] Further, although the financial and other economic burdens, both local and national, can be understood and quantified, the rural areas under discussion bear a large proportion of the non-financial resource costs and environmental costs in the region.

Hence the quantifiable economic changes coming from the socio-ecological system impacts in Myanmar, occur particularly in the largest sector, agriculture. A visible consequence is a greater reliance on more costly and more hazardous inputs to compensate for the reduced agricultural output. These inputs include new irrigation systems, and also agricultural chemicals, causing drying and thus indirectly resulting in greater carbon release. There are also tens of thousands of cultivators being displaced within northern Myanmar now residing in primitive displacement camps, directly resulting in greater atmospheric carbon emissions into much smaller, denser areas. These are now placing an economic burden on agriculture, which as we have seen, while occupying a shrinking portion of the GDP, continues to predominate in the share of national population that it supports. Specifically, the disadvantageous economic changes and risks derive from the two issues below.

The first is from the exploration, extraction/capture construction and maintenance of energy resources; in the case of hydropower, this necessitates impounding very large tracts of productive land, as indicated by the abbreviation "LS" inin Table 11.1. Chiefly, there is a loss of access to productive land within the facility's immediate area due to submergence and construction areas, and also for

Table 11.1 Name of dam, name of river, and location(s)

Name of dam		Name of river and location(s)/Used area where known
Shweli 1 Dam; planned Shweli 2 and 3 (LS)		Shweli (Nam Mao), northern Shan, and Ruili, China
Namkham Dam, northern Shan State		Shweli, northern Shan, and Jiegao, China
Chibwe Nge (feeder dam to Myitsone)		Shweli, northern Shan, and Jiegao, China, Myanmar
Chibwe Dam (LS)		Nam Mai, Kachin State
Myitsone mega-dam (P/C) (LS)		Nam Mali, N'Mai, and Ayerawaddy, Kachin State
Kaunglanphu Dam (LS)		N'mai River, northern Kachin State
Laiza (LS)		Mali River, northern Kachin State
Dapein I		N'Mai River, Bhamo, southern Kachin State
Noung Pha (P/C)		Salween, northern Shan State
Mong Wa (P/C)		Salween and Nam Lwe, eastern Shan State
Kunlong (P/C) (LS)		Salween, northern Shan State, Kokang region
Zedawgyi 2		Mandalay
Yeywa (LS)		Myitnge, Mandalay Division/59.0 sq. km
Upper Keng Tawng (Nam Lat) (P/C)		Salween feeder Nam Tein, Langkhio, southern Shan State
Mong Ton (Tasang)	Mega-dam (P/C)(LS)	Salween, southern Shan State/640 sq. km

Sources: Compiled from ASEAN Centre for Energy (2004) and the Myanmar Ministry of Electricity and Energy's "Hydropower Development Plans" (2016).

Note: LS ("Large-scale") here refers to dams with a planned generating capacity of at least 500 MW. P/C means planned, with some land transfer, clearing, and construction having been implemented.

some distance around it due to the need to securitize the facility. This land loss occurs prior to the actual completion and operation of dams. The result is a loss of agricultural and forest products and of livestock. Following from this large-scale land loss is the loss of the ecosystem services: those that capture CO_2 and those that retain moisture, moderate its evaporation and rainfall, and moderate the surrounding temperatures. These in turn make agriculture more difficult and where agriculture is continued, require much more costly inputs for chemicals as well as for irrigation to replace the lost or impounded moisture. Mechanical irrigation creates some amount of GHG emissions, while the synthetic fertilizers, herbicides, and insecticides in use in northern Myanmar are usually imported from neighboring countries and are not used at the levels of international safety standards, creating more atmospheric emissions from the already-dry soil and chemicals (see Thiesmeyer 2010). Also following from extensive land loss are the movement and re-grouping of, in the case of Myanmar, tens of thousands of displaced persons from project areas. In economic terms this means both far higher welfare costs and lost labor – China's border areas of Yunnan Province, which used to accept thousands of displaced Myanmar nationals, ceased to do so in 2017, making the burden Myanmar's and that of other neighboring countries as well. The hundreds of displacement camps along the areas of new dam construction, which fall within short distances from Myanmar's border with China, host thousands of families in small areas with few or no amenities, meaning that cooking, building, and other processes that emit carbon-based atmospheric pollutants are also further concentrated and increased. Finally, there is the economic instability for cultivators themselves: loss or irregularization of work and income. In the areas of planned and completed hydropower dam construction in Kachin and northern Shan State, the numbers of impacted persons who were actually displaced into camps totaled 99,638 as of November 2016, with more along the Kachin-China border by the end of that year.[8]

The second economic impact comes indirectly from the CO_2 emissions associated with large-scale dam construction and operation, and with the loss of carbon capture (leading to carbon release) resulting from them.[9] As discussed in the Analysis of findings section, below, there has been a rapid rise in forest loss and concurrently a rise in CO_2 emissions, which may include carbon release (loss of the carbon capture that forests could have performed) in all of Myanmar since the year 2000.

The socio-ecological systems approach shows that, as mentioned above, the proportion of GDP in agriculture is also important because of the proportion of workers and their livelihoods in the general population that it represents. The stages of energy supply, which include construction, extraction, and transmission or transport, all impact the ecosystem and the livelihoods and regional GDP that the ecosystem supports. Rivers automatically have cross-boundary impacts, economically and politically as well as ecologically. In a region such as the Upper GMS and particularly in northern Myanmar, the environment is the economy. The chief environmental damage of large-scale projects like hydropower dams comes from the amount, and prior use, of the land area that they take up.

In addition to the hundreds of square kilometers of cropland and productive forest that they make inaccessible for livelihoods, they also require the land to be cleared. Such deforestation naturally causes carbon release (loss of carbon capture), while the land area loss leads to food insecurity and income insecurity. The ecological disruption thus caused then brings warming, drying, and drought-flood cycles: the 2015–16 drought in mainland Southeast Asia extended into 2017 at the same time that it caused an "agricultural supply shock" (World BankMyanmar Economic Monitor, May 2016a) that lowered GDP growth.

An SES explanation would show that the direct and indirect effects above would fall into the category of slow-onset disasters, which also heighten the risk of rapid-onset disasters such as natural disasters and economic collapse. The slow-onset problems will result from the gradual but progressive drying, contamination, and non-productivity associated with these projects' land-use changes and also from the resulting large-scale mobility and displacement of low-income, low-educated populations.

Survey data and indications

The specific on-site survey findings and secondary data used in this research fall into the following categories:

1) Major dam sites in Shan State and Kachin State
2) Loss of forest cover in Myanmar/Calculable carbon release from deforestation and carbon release rate
3) Potential for worsening drought
4) Hydro-electricity transmission to Chinese investment projects and industries within Myanmar (industrial parks and mining)
5) Human displacement in relation to development projects, and effects of displacement on the climate and carbon release.

The areas of the surveys and the secondary data in the Upper GMS used here focus on northern and eastern Myanmar. Quantitative data from these sources indicate correlations among large-scale energy projects and observable impacts on the socio-ecological system, as shown below.

Some Chinese-invested dam projects for northern Myanmar and area of construction

Below are some of the dams entered on the Myanmar ministries' lists of planned and currently operating dams in Shan and Kachin States, northern Myanmar. It is well to bear in mind that "Chinese-invested" does not mean that the entire hydropower project, from planning to surveying to building, is financed and conducted by Chinese firms. Several of the dams and their areas have, throughout the relatively contorted history of their planning and construction, been financed and assessed by consortia including those from China, Japan,

Thailand, the U.S., World Bank's International Finance Corporation (IFC), and the ADB.[10]

Several of the dams have occupied, or begun construction by clearing, areas of hundreds of square kilometers. The locations of the particularly large dam sites (Myitsone and Mong Ton) are within rural cropland and forested land. The deforestation and de-vegetation involved from the initial stages of construction cause carbon release. Over large areas like these, the contribution to the increase in atmospheric carbon as well as other GHGs adds up to millions of tons. (See Xu 2012.) This is further shown below.

Large-scale deforestation and carbon release

Decrease in forested area/increase in CO_2 emissions

Hydropower dams are, in terms of the land area they occupy, the largest of large-scale energy projects. Along with large plantations, they require a significant area to be deforested around and beyond the area of the dam's operation. The negative impact of such forest area loss can be calculated in terms of tons of carbon capture loss (carbon release).

The World Bank's datasets show the following information related to forested land loss and increase in CO_2 emissions in Myanmar:

1) Decrease in forest area (whole country) during the period 2000 to 2015
   348,680 sq. km in 2000 $\Rightarrow$ 290,000 sq. km in 2015
2) Increase in CO_2 emissions, in kilotons (whole country) during the period 2000 to 2013
   10,088 in 2000 $\Rightarrow$ 12,603 in 2013.

World Bank (2018)

Carbon release rates (calculations on loss of carbon capture)

As energy projects are typically located within rural areas of the country, the land area and its ecosystem services have been particularly reduced within forests, pastureland, cropland, and watersheds or wetlands. This can be converted into amount of carbon capture capacity that has been lost, or released carbon. In other words energy requires deforestation which leads to greater atmospheric carbon. The United Nations Environmental Program conducted a survey on deforestation in Myanmar, showing that carbon capture or release can be calculated by

> multiplying the annual deforestation in Myanmar, estimated to be **372,250 ha** per year, with 98 tC/ha, which is the approximate amount of tons of carbon stored per ha in the country's forests annually. Based on this data,

and the conversion of 1 ton of biomass carbon to the equivalent of 3.67 tCO27, avoiding deforestation, alone, in Myanmar has **the potential to contribute to approximately 133 million tons in CO$_2$ emission** reductions every year.

(UNEP 2013: 8)

This calculation shows that conversely, the current rate of deforestation may be responsible for up to 133 million tons of CO$_2$ release every year. Further, as we have seen, Myanmar is a nation whose GDP is 30% occupied by agriculture, and nearly 70% of whose employment is in the agricultural and forestry sectors. Myanmar's land loss to energy projects points to a risk of uneven growth or stagnation due to lack of sustainability.

The loss of forest cover, the change in primary productivity (release) of carbon, including the intensification of carbon release in the areas of large-scale dams, can be corroborated using the work of Soe W. Myint (2016) and Wang and Myint (2017). They show that both the percent of tree cover and the primary productivity changed markedly within (though not only in) the areas of the planned dams in Kachin and Shan States in the period from 2001 to 2010, a period coinciding with rapid construction and deforestation for planned hydropower projects. Ecosystem services, and thus the socio-ecological system's resilience, are heavily dependent on forests and the watersheds they protect. The loss of forest cover has led to a decrease in ecosystem productivity as shown in the maps above. It also leads to temperature changes, especially warming, and rainfall changes, especially drought or a flood-drought cycle, in the deforested areas.

Correlations to areas of worsening drought and changes in precipitation

It has not been possible until recently for scientific observation and measurement to show precisely the rate of impact of any one *specific* human activity on changes in the environmental indices of warming, drying, precipitation (or moisture generally), soil degradation, and loss of productivity. In Myanmar as elsewhere, there are several components of environmental shifts, including global shifts from outside of Myanmar like El Niño/El Niña. For this reason, we indicate only the possible correlations; it remains for future research to determine more exact measurements and assessments. Given the risk of an increasing correlation between warming/drying of soil and higher CO$_2$ emissions in some ecosystems (Zeng and Gao 2016: 5), however, arguably much of the increased carbon in the northern Myanmar atmosphere is carbon release from deforestation and other causes around construction sites, as well as from the reservoirs around operational dams (Chanudet, Descloux, Harby, Sundt, Hansen, Brakstad, Serça, and Guerin, ibid.).

Use of Myanmar hydropower for Chinese industries in Myanmar

The dams in the two northern states of Myanmar are providing electricity to new and existing industrial zones around the urban centers of Mandalay.

Industrial parks

The so-called "border trade" with China has rapidly increased its share within the GDP of Myanmar and has brought in much greater Chinese investment in Lashio and Mandalay, the northern cities now majority-occupied by Chinese investors and landowners. According to Myanmar Marketing Research and Development Company's Myinmo Zaw and the Institute of Developing Economies-Japan External Trade Organization's Toshihiro Kudo, Chinese investors in the Mandalay industrial parks are in the majority, and

> as border trade between Myanmar and China grows year by year, businesses in Mandalay are on the rise because of the export-import goods passing through the city. In 2009, the volume of Myanmar-China border trade was US$1,059 million. . . . There is a possibility the border trade between Myanmar and China could reach US$1,500 million in the near future.
>
> (Myinmo Zaw and Kudo 2011: 256)

This required, and helped to build, the energy facilities within northern Myanmar, and the portion of the relevant hydropower staying in Myanmar is currently transmitted mainly to these industries, which then transfer their products to China. The products are then trucked overland on the Chinese-built Highway No. 4 to Ruili in Yunnan Province across the border from Muse; and they are also sold within Myanmar.

In particular, Mandalay Metro area currently has three industrial parks whose investors are majority Chinese. Nearby Yaradanapon Cyber City to the northeast and the planned Myotha Industrial Park to the southwest also provide manufacturing and service for the Chinese market. The Asian Highway No. 4 passing through the two northern states has already made overland export from this area to China much faster and easier. The manufacturing within the parks requires much higher voltages than Myanmar was previously capable of providing. New Chinese-funded dams at Yeywa (southwest of Mandalay) and at Shweli (northeast of Mandalay near the Chinese border) transmit electricity to the industrial parks over 230-kilovolt (KV) double transmission lines.

Mining

As industry financed by China has rapidly increased, so has mining, providing high economic growth figures. As shown above there are three new or renovated industrial parks in Mandalay, the gateway to the north, which has been targeted for industrial development by China, Japan, Thailand, and Indian investors. It is estimated that although industries locating in the industrial parks are locally registered, 80% of their owners are Chinese. The nearby dams in Yeywa (a large-scale dam) and Zedawgyi will provide some of the necessary electric power. But it is Chinese investment that has also provided a 356-km long transmission line to connect the large Shweli River dam to the Mandalay industrial parks and the main Myanmar grid.

In Shan State, there are two newly expanded mining operations using Chinese-built hydropower:

1) Ngwe Kabar Kyaw silica mining operation, powered by the Namkham Dam
2) Nam Tu non-ferrous mining operations, powered by the Shweli I Dam.

While foreign-invested, large-scale mining produces some of the same socio-ecological system stresses as other development projects, including hydropower, the main issue is that it is using energy-for-energy. Some of the mines, such as those for lignite, other hydrocarbons, and some non-ferrous metals, will be used in energy generation themselves. Added to this, the intensive extraction and refining processes consume large amounts of electricity for its extractive and refining processes, and also to support the considerable number of workers, both cross-border and domestic, at the mine. The contribution of mining, especially surface mining, to airborne pollution and atmospheric carbon is a corollary to the export of development and energy projects to Myanmar.

Correlation of large-scale projects to areas of displacement in northern Myanmar (Shan and Kachin States)

The dam sites in particular are producing a high number of displaced persons, who whether through settlement in primitive camps or movement to urban areas then engage in higher-carbon-emission activities. Further, among the displaced who had traditionally accessed the land near dams is a high number of stateless persons, those born without birth certificates or lacking other identification. Statelessness is common in northern Myanmar for a number of reasons including illiteracy, lack of hospitals, or transportation to township centers for registration, lack of understanding of the legal necessity of registering, and frequent move-ment back and forth across nearby borders. Their lack of identification means that they can be easily moved away from land required for new hydropower facilities, making them part of the large number of displaced persons in camps in Myanmar. Recent statistics for displaced persons and their geographical break-down indicate that there were 99,036 persons in 188 Internally Displaced Person sites as of January 2018. Of these, the largest numbers of sites and persons since the year 2016 can be seen in the areas of Kachin State hosting the planned Myitsone Dam (Myitkyina) and the commissioned Dapein Dam (Bhamo), and the Shweli Dams in the Nam Hkam (Namkham) area of northern Shan State (UNHCR 2016; UNOCHA 2018).

Analysis of findings

Impacts of energy for China, ASEAN, and Chinese export industries in Myanmar

The recent data in the Survey data and indications section above show that the hydro-energy planned hydro-energy sites and projects discussed here form one part of a "clustering" of multi-sectoral development projects over the larger GMS that include plantation agriculture, oil and gas pipelines, dams, mines, highways, and industrial parks. Their physical connections between energy sources and final product producers (manufacturers that use the energy) are also expanding over vaster areas of land and changing the environment beyond the territories and the nations where the energy is sourced. Further, the livelihoods within these environments are disappearing too rapidly in this economically as well as politically dangerous shift, given that the environment is the economy for highly agricultural-export-dependent nations in the GMS.

Several specific issues, both conceptual and practical, can be identified through the findings above:

- It is not only the operation of projects such as electricity generation which impact on the environment and the local economy, but their earliest stages of land transfer and construction as well.
- Within China's investments in Myanmar, there is a "clustering" of current and future projects that is multi-sectoral (plantations, pipelines, dams, mines, and highways), and the same is true on a slightly smaller scale with current Japanese and Thai infrastructure investments.
- There is also the spiraling issue of energy resources being needed in order to produce energy itself – energy for energy. This accelerates not only the exploration and extraction of the target resources, but also of the ecological space which houses them.
- The requisite connections from energy projects to their delivery terminals, including highways, transmission lines, and pipelines, are also causing environmental and economic setbacks.
- Environmental impacts are not only economic impacts in the source areas and project-hosting areas, but throughout the nation.
- Economic impacts, that is, livelihood impacts, from these development projects are rapid and acute, involving large populations, their movements and densification in contaminable and high-emission areas and activities. Deforestation for building, fuel, and sale is common, leading to greater localized carbon release. Household-level cottage industries and cultivation can pollute air and water, and lead to over-pumping of local groundwater ($\Rightarrow$ greater drying and warming as well as soil degradation), overharvesting and densification of small stock (poultry). There is also exporting and re-exporting of these environmental problems to neighboring countries along the border. "Among the most significant problems associated with

refugee-affected areas are deforestation, soil erosion, and depletion and pollution of water resources."[11]

- Energy resources are among the locally sourced goods now sought and traded globally. But unlike cultivated or manufactured products, most energy resources are still tied to place, and thus tied to the citizenry's socio-ecological systems and economies of place. All large countries and many smaller ones now import or export energy or such energy sources as fuel minerals. Consequently, the present and projected style of use and levels of consumption of energy resources also have global (cross-border) effects.
- In Myanmar, notwithstanding the transition to democratic forms of governance, the local regions in which Chinese-funded development projects are locating themselves continue to be the regions where armed conflict and ruptures of cease-fire agreements occur.
- Although the construction of projects is based on land transfer, which has led to local conflict, it is also true that from the outset local-conflict areas can be more easily sold or transferred for large-scale, outside-investor-based projects. Within the "Special Regions," those heavily manned by the military because the Myanmar government has designated them as restricted zones due to violent conflict and the presence of displaced person camps (see also IRN 2011), we find the planned Kunlong and Noung Pha dams in the Kokang area; the Mong La and Nam Lwe dams in the Mong La area (both in northern and eastern Shan); and in numerous areas of Kachin State, including the areas around Waing Maw (south of the suspended Myitsone Dam area) and Chibwe (near the two Chibwe dams feeding the construction at Myitsone Dam).

The conflict areas of northern and eastern Myanmar are currently host to at least 18 existing or commissioned dams and seven known planned dams in Shan and Kachin states. Conflict areas have spread along Myanmar's Mekong at the China border, along the Shweli River, and along the Salween in southern Shan State all in locations where planned dams have already incurred land transfer and some displacement. The conflicts are also found along northern tributaries of all of these rivers and those of Myanmar's major river, the Ayerawaddy.

Finally, energy projects have a great impact on population displacement and ecological disruption. Unlike agro-clusters, where the main associated infrastructures are road (and perhaps some water) transport and localized intra-sectoral communication, energy and other hard resource clusters need transmission lines, their facilitating geography, and their securitization, and regional/transboundary communications, requiring much vaster amounts of land. These are now found in "marginal environments": drylands (or drying lands at risk of slow-onset disaster) and forestry-supporting mountains. They have also led to large-scale displacement with its attendant socio-ecological stresses and high release of GHGs. "Population mobility in drylands is a very common household livelihood strategy, composed of different types of movements (permanent, temporary and seasonal) into, outside and within arid lands" (de Sherbinin et al. 2012: 2–3).

Such environmentally displaced persons move either to urbanized areas, or to campsites. A sudden influx of population to an urban area means increased density and inadequacy of infrastructure, leaving a greater environmental footprint from more and dirtier emissions of various kinds in neighborhoods with little or no treatment of them. Displacements to existing camps or self-constructed forest camps also occur with little or no access to sanitation, water treatment, garbage or waste treatment. Due to their compact nature, camps tend to densify or concentrate carbon-emitting production and waste activities in small spaces with few or no outlets. In other words, just as non-environmental migration to urban areas brought about an increase in carbon emissions and warming, so will the more rapid-onset migrations of development project-evicted populations.

Concluding remarks

An important caveat here is that not all the planned or built dams in Myanmar originate from Chinese investment or construction projects. Currently large-scale hydropower is planned, funded, and implemented through consortia of several country donors along with private sector investors. It is well to bear in mind that while national and local government representatives may agree on the need for bi- and multilateral projects in economic growth that will not harm the environment, the proposal, planning, and implementation of such projects are performed by outside actors like those shown here.

Further, not all the Chinese-funded hydropower dams under contract with Myanmar's government or its state-owned enterprises have been fully built or put into operation as yet, nor have those funded or built by Japan, Thailand, or other partners. However, the environmental impacts discussed here can result from the existing construction sites as well as from the building of the transmission lines,

Table 11.2 List of other-funded planned or constructed dams

List of important other-funded (Japanese, Thai, EU) planned or constructed dams in northern and eastern Shan State

Name	Location	Investor(s)
Mobye	Border of Shan and Kayah States	Japan
Lawpita	Kayah State, from Datawcha Dam	Japan
Lawpita 2	(Rebuilt Lawpita) Balu Chaung, Kayah State	Japan
Upper Paunglaung	Southern Shan State	Switzerland, Germany, UK
Mong Ton	Southern Shan State	Thailand (China)

Sources: ASEAN Centre for Energy (2004), Ministry of Electricity and Energy, Japan International Cooperation Agency, and International Finance Corporation (2016), Myanmar Times (20 August 2012), and Japan International Cooperation Agency (2014).

which are on land that has already been transferred away from agricultural livelihoods and deforested. These are causing most of the high carbon release in the area of dams. Secondly, they also contribute to the risk of higher future emissions due to acute livelihood changes and denser population resettlement in the rural area.

From the standpoint of policy reform vis-à-vis the socio-ecological system, we may identify three issues that call for improvement. Local actors and residents facing the possibility of land conversion, resource loss, eviction/displacement, and project-related livelihood loss/ecological services loss, are often *not*:

- Well-informed or in agreement with the initial project proposal and plans.
- In a position to choose in terms of livelihood resources.
- In agreement with the national government or its governance.
- Both the planned and completed dam sites have also been contributors to droughts, deforestation, and population movement, all of which directly or indirectly add to the greenhouse gases in Myanmar.
- Further, the clustering of development projects within the same or adjacent areas has the potential to cause greater land loss, economic loss, and other ecosystem disruptions resulting from widespread carbon release.

Hydropower projects along tributaries of the Mekong, Salween, and Ayerawaddy in Myanmar have been, and will continue providing, a necessary source of hydroelectric power for China as well as for neighboring Thailand and to Myanmar itself. As mentioned in the Introduction, a mere two of the present dam sites in northern Myanmar have already sold at least 750 billion KWH to China since 2008. Other dams such as those nearer to Mandalay and those still in the planning stages will also provide agreed ratios of their generated power to domestic consumers within Myanmar. Equally necessary to the region are the rural resources of cropland, forest, watersheds, stable temperatures, and other ecosystem services, and permanent habitation and livelihoods. In order for these to be sustained, their vulnerability and in some cases non-renewability must first be recognized, and included in more rigorous and accurate impact assessments.

Notes

1 Between December 2008 and April 2013, Shweli [I] power station has sold 7.4 billion Kwh to the Yunnan grid. And between August 2010 and June 2011 (when the Kachin conflict stopped its operation), Dapein power station sold 513 million Kwh to the Yunnan grid [resumed in May 2013]. (Sun Yun 2013: 271)
2 Ishida (2013: 1–2).
3 Nolintha (2013: 149–50).
4 See the presentation by the Ministry of Electricity and Energy (MOEE), October 2016 (prepared with JICA and the IFC).
5 Ministry of Electricity and Energy et al. (2016).
6 Chanudet et al. (2011: 5385–8); Varis, Kummu, Härkönen, and Huttenen (in Tortajada et al. eds. 2012: 71–3 and 75–7).
7 "It contributes 32% of the GDP, 17.5% of the total export earnings and employs 61.2% of the labour force (FAO 2009–2010)" MIMU (2016); "Agriculture is the main source of livelihood for over 70 % of Myanmar population" FAO (2017).

8 United Nations Office for the Coordination of Humanitarian Affairs (2018).
9 See Chanudet et al. (2011) and Varis, Kummu, Härkönen, and Huttenen (in Tortajada et al. eds. 2012)
10 From Japan these include JICA and the energy companies Kansai Electric Power and its subsidiary NEWJEC.
11 United Nations High Commissioner for Refugees, Engineering and Environmental Services Section, "Refugees and the Environment" (2001).

References

ASEAN Centre for Energy (2004) *Completed and Ongoing Projects (Myanmar)*, https://web.archive.org/web/20060105151324/www.aseanenergy.org/energy_sector/electricity/myanmar/completes_on_going_projects.htm accessed on March 2, 2018.

Berkes, F., Colding, J. and Folke, C. (2003) *Navigating Socio-Ecological Systems: Building Resilience for Complexity and Change*. Cambridge: Cambridge University Press.

Bi Shihong (2014) The economic relations of Myanmar – China, in Lim, H. and Yasuhiro, Y. (eds.) *Myanmar's Integration with Global Economy: Outlook and Opportunities*, Bangkok: Bangkok Research Center IDE-JETRO, 174–199.

Bruckmeier, K. (2016a) *Social-Ecological Transformation: Reconnecting Society and Nature*, London: Palgrave Macmillan. doi:10.1057/978-1-137-43828-7_5

Bruckmeier, K. (2016b) Social-ecological systems and ecosystem services, in Bruckmeier, K. (ed.) *Social-Ecological Transformation: Reconnecting Society and Nature*, London: Palgrave Macmillan, 183–234. doi:10.1057/978-1-137-43828-7_5

Chanudet, V., Descloux, S., Harby, A., Sundt, H., Hansen, B.H., Brakstad, O., Serça, D. and Guerin, F. (15 November 2011) Gross CO_2 and CH_4 emissions from the Nam Ngum and Nam Leuk sub-tropical reservoirs in Lao PDR, *Science of the Total Environment* 409(24): 5382–91.

de Sherbinin, A., Levy, M., Adamo, S.B., MacManus, K., Yetman, G., Mara, V., Razafindrazay, L., Goodrich, B., Srebotnjak, T., Aichele, C. and Pistolesi, L. (November 2012) Migration and risk: Net migration in marginal ecosystems and hazardous areas, *Environmental Research Letters* 7(4): 1–14, http://iopscience.iop.org/article/10.1088/1748-9326/7/4/045602/pdf doi: 10.1088/1748-9326/7/4/045602, accessed on March 2, 2018.

Food and Agriculture Organization of the United Nations (FAO) (2017) *Family Farming Knowledge Platform: Myanmar*, www.fao.org/family-farming/countries/mmr/en/, accessed on March 2, 2018.

Food and Agriculture Organization of the United Nations (FAO) AQUASTAT (2012, 2016) *Water Use (Myanmar)*, www.fao.org/nr/water/aquastat/countries_regions/MMR/index.stm, accessed on March 2, 2018.

International Rivers (ed.) (2013) *Independent Expert Review of the Myitsone Dam EIA*, Uploaded 30 September 2013, www.internationalrivers.org/sites/default/files/attached-files/independent_expert_review_of_the_myitsone_dam_eia.pdf, accessed on February 22, 2018. International Rivers (IRN) (2011) *The Myitsone Dam on the Irrawaddy River: A Briefing*, www.internationalrivers.org/resources/the-myitsone-dam-on-the-irrawaddy-river-a-briefing-3931, accessed on March 2, 2018.

International Rivers (IRN) (2012) *The Salween River Basin Fact Sheet*, www.internationalrivers.org/resources/the-salween-river-basin-fact-sheet-7481, accessed on March 2, 2018.

Ishida, M. (ed.) (2011) Intra- and inter-city connectivity in the Mekong region, *BRC Research Report No. 6, IDE-JETRO*, Bangkok.

Ishida, M. (ed.) (2013) Five triangle areas in the Greater Mekong subregion, *Palgrave Macmillan IDE-JETRO Series, Research Report No. 11*, Bangkok, www.ide.go.jp/ English/Publish/Download/Brc/11.html, accessed on March 2, 2018.

Japan International Cooperation Agency (JICA) (2014) Japan-Myanmar renewed 60-year long ties over historic power station, *JICA Press Release*, June 28, 2014, www.jica. go.jp/myanmar/english/office/topics/press140628.html, accessed on March 2, 2018.

Lim, Hank, and Yamada Yasuhiro, eds. (2014) Myanmar's Integration with Global Economy: Outlook and Opportunities, Bangkok: Bangkok Research Center IDE-JETRO.

Ministry of Electricity and Energy of Myanmar (MOEE), Japan International Cooperation Agency (JICA), and International Finance Corporation (IFC) (2016) Overview of hydropower potential and energy sector in Myanmar and sustainability of the sector, *Nay Pyi Taw: Strategic Environmental Assessment Workshop*, 6 October 2016, www.ifc.org/wps/ wcm/connect/c7302c68-f34f-40bd-99b3-6ad04c0cfe0b/IFC%27s+SEA+Workshop. pdf?MOD=AJPERES

Myanmar Information Management Unit (MIMU) (2016) *Agriculture Sector*, www. themimu.info/sector/agriculture, accessed on March 2, 2018.

Myanmar Times (2012) Current development of major hydropower projects, 20 August 2012, www.mmtimes.com/special-features/151-energy-spotlight/2943-current-development-of-major-hydropower-projects.html, accessed on March 2, 2018.

Myinmo Zaw and Kudo, T. (2011) A study on economic corridors, industrial zones, ports and metropolitan and alternative roads in Myanmar, in Ishida, M. (ed.) *Intra- and Inter-City Connectivity in the Mekong Region*, BRC Research Report No. 6, Bangkok, Thailand: Bangkok Research Center, IDE-JETRO, 240–87.

Myint, S.W. (2016) Deforestation in Myanmar: Land and atmospheric effects, Paper presented at *International Land Cover/Land Use Changes Regional Sciences Meeting in South and Southeast Asia (Yangon, January 2016)*, http://lcluc.umd.edu/sites/default/ files/lcluc_documents/Deforestation_Soe_Myint.pdf

Nassl, M. and Loeffler, J. (December 2015) Ecosystem services in coupled social-ecological systems: Closing the cycle of service provision and societal feedback, *Ambio* 44(8): 737–49. doi:10.1007/s13280-015-0651-y, accessed on March 2, 2018.

Nolintha, V. (2013) Triangle area development: Prospects and challenges for Lao PDR, in Ishida, M. (ed.) *Five Triangle Areas in The Greater Mekong Subregion*, BRC Research Report No. 11, Bangkok, Thailand: Bangkok Research Center, IDE-JETRO, 133–68.

Ostrom, E. (24 July 2009) A general framework for analyzing sustainability of social-ecological systems, *Science* 325: 419–22. doi:10.1126/science.1172133

Sun, Y. (2013) China's relations with Myanmar: National interests and uncertainties, in Bae, J.-H. and Ku, J.H. (eds.) *China's Internal and External Relations and Lessons for Korea and Asia*. Seoul: Korea Institute for National Unification (South Korea), 249–90.

Thiesmeyer, L. (2010) *Informal and Illegal Movement in the Upper Greater Mekong Subregion*. Bangkok: Center for Research on Contemporary Southeast Asia, www. irasec.com/ouvrage24

Tortajada, C., Altinbilek, D. and Biswas, A.K. (eds.) (2012) *Impacts of Large Dams: A Global Assessment*. Berlin: Springer.

United Nations Environmental Program (UNEP) Riso Centre (2013) *Emissions Reduction Profile: Myanmar*, Denmark: Roskilde, www.acp-cd4cdm.org/media/363090/emissions-reduction-profile-myanmar.pdf

United Nations High Commissioner for Refugees, Engineering and Environmental Services Section, "Refugees and the Environment" (2001). http://www.unhcr.org/protection/ environment/3b039f3c4/refugees-environment.html

United Nations High Commissioner for Refugees (UNHCR) (2016) *Global Focus: Myanmar*, http://reporting.unhcr.org/node/2541#_ga=1.241475782.574973682.146493 8256

United Nations Office for the Coordination of Humanitarian Affairs (UNOCHA) (2018) *Myanmar: IDP Sites in Kachin and Northern Shan States (*31 December 2017*)*, Creation date 20 January 2018, https://reliefweb.int/sites/reliefweb.int/files/resources/Kachin-Shan_Snapshot_IDPS_A4_31Dec17.pdf

Urban, F., Nordensvärd, J., Khatri, D. and Wang, Y. (2013) An analysis of China's investment in the hydropower sector, *Environment, Development and Sustainability* 15: 301–24. doi:10.1007/s10668-012-9415-z

Varis, O., Matti Kummu, Saku Härkönen, and Jari T. Huttunen (2012) "Greenhouse Gas Emissions from Reservoirs." In Tortajada, C., Altinbilek, D. and Biswas, A.K. (eds.), 69–94.

Wang, C. and Myint, S.W. (2017) Environmental concerns of deforestation in Myanmar 2001–2010, *Remote Sensing* 8(728): 1–15. doi:10.3390/rs8090728

World Bank (2016a) Myanmar Economic Monitor, May 2016. http://www.worldbank.org/en/country/myanmar/publication/myanmar-economic-monitor-may-2016, accessed on March 2, 2018.

World Bank (2016b) *Rural Population (Myanmar) Percent of Total Population*, https://data.worldbank.org/indicator/SP.RUR.TOTL.ZS?locations=MM, accessed on February 22, 2018.

World Bank (2018) *CO$_2$ Emissions (metric tons per capita), Myanmar*, https://data.worldbank.org/indicator/EN.ATM.CO2E.PC?locations=MM&view=chart

Xu, X. (2012) Terrestrial biodiversity, climate change, in International Rivers (ed.) (2013), *Independent Expert Review of the Myitsone Dam EIA*. Oakland, CA: International Rivers. https://www.internationalrivers.org/resources/independent-expert-review-of-the-myitsone-dam-eia-8129, accessed on February 22, 2018.

Zeng, X. and Gao Yongheng (2016) Short-term effects of drying and rewetting on CO$_2$ and CH4 emissions from high-altitude peatlands on the Tibetan Plateau, *Atmosphere* 7(148): 1–7. doi:10.3390/atmos7110148

Part IV

Summary and future challenges

12 Conclusions

Akihisa Mori

As an intermediate conclusion, we would like to summarize by saying that China's climate-energy policy, an outcome of its climate-energy conundrum, provokes conflicts of interest among main stakeholders, and that the technological, institutional, and political barriers in settling these conflicts have brought about the "going global" of coal, oil, gas and power industries and their CO_2 emissions.

China's notion of energy security has depended upon macroeconomic and state of enterprises reform. In this process, energy security is recognized as the appropriate mix of energies along with the way to access them, both from a geographical and technological point of view (Di Meglio and Romano 2016). The requirement to reduce greenhouse gas (GHG) emissions is reframed and added on the top of this notion, turning into climate-energy policy and achieving balance among main stakeholders: local governments with interests in their own coal industries, national oil companies (NOCs) motivated to acquire assets and resources, renewable energy manufacturers and developers who have emerged as part of a new economic growth point, and victims of air pollution and the Ministry of Environmental Protection in charge. Tightening CO_2 emissions and/or air pollution controls to gain notable improvements requires price reform and transformations of the existing energy infrastructure system, which can destroy this balance and again provoke conflicts of interest between stakeholders.

The slowdown of growth in embodied CO_2 emissions or embodied energy export before 2012, as confirmed in Chapter 2 and other recent literature (Zhao et al. 2016; Wu et al. 2016; Yu and Chen 2017), does not help resolve these conflicts. Given the energy's close association with rapid export growth, economic structural change and a tax on energy-intensive exports will have limited impact without limitations imposed on export volumes in CO_2-intensive sectors (Qi et al. 2014). However, restructuring trade may not be cost effective or realistic. It is estimated to reduce CO_2 emissions by 3.3 percent under a reasonable scenario (Tang et al. 2017), while having significant effects on employment, because CO_2-intensive sectors are also labor-intensive and export-oriented (Tang et al. 2016).

This is why change in the energy mix becomes a main measure in climate-energy policy.

Thus, the central research questions in this book examine how effective resultant climate-energy policies in China have been in changing its energy mix and

CO_2 emissions, as well as what impacts conflicts of interest between main stakeholders have on the energy mix and CO_2 emissions of China and energy-exporting countries.

Domestic conflicts and the change in China's energy mix

As suggested in the continuous decline in coal consumption between 2014 and 2016, China's energy mix is changing. Chapter 4 finds that the decline in coal consumption is a result of the transformation of China's economic structure from an industrial to service economy along with coal price reform, and that it will not be easily revert unless coal prices drop so significantly as to boost the industry again. Tang et al. (2018) reached the same conclusion, insisting that changes of both industrial structure and the energy mix started to reduce China's coal consumption significantly since 2012.

To accelerate a change in the energy mix, alternative clean energies must further replace coal consumption. The wind and solar power manufacturing sector has emerged as a new growth point, surpassing nuclear power to account for 4 percent of power generation in 2015. However, as described in Chapter 3, this trend clashes with the interests of provinces in their own coal industries and results in a large renewable curtailment and suspension of new installation and access to grid connection. As such, the wind and solar power has a minor contribution to CO_2 emission reductions at best.

Meanwhile, the Chinese government has motivated NOCs to develop domestic gas resources and acquire assets and resources in foreign countries in order to secure oil and gas and sustain economic growth. However, massive gas imports – through pipeline and liquidation – have been and will mostly be used for replacing transport fuel and coal for regional heating systems, contributing little to CO_2 emission reductions.

Nonetheless, the Chinese government perceives increasing the supply of gas as the only realistic option to achieve its goals of lowering coal dependency and carbon intensity (Di Meglio and Romano 2016). In transforming the energy mix, it employs the same strategies and agencies used for enhancing energy security.

Chapter 7 indicates that China has secured enough natural gas to satisfy the CO_2 emission reduction targets described in its Nationally Determined Commitment (NDC). It also suggests the high price elasticity of Chinese energy-intensive industries enables the government to charge only a tiny rate of carbon-energy pricing (i.e. US\$3.2–3.6 per CO_2 ton) to satisfy the NDC as well as domestic demand.

As for achieving both the 2030 CO_2 and air pollutants emissions reduction targets, however, gas should be more aggressively developed. Chapter 5 indicates that gas imports must be 3.5 times larger to meet targets, suggesting a conclusion to long-term natural gas purchase contracts with Russia for the West Siberian pipeline.

However, large imports of gas resources raise the issue of prices reform. On the one hand, the government has long offered a subsidized price to residential consumers and required energy suppliers to cross-subsidize to tame their potential repercussions of an energy price hike. As long as carbon-energy pricing has regressive distributional impacts on both urban and rural households, as analyzed in the Chapter 6, complementary measures (such as a differentiated carbon-energy pricing by type of fuel) are required to avoid energy poverty. On the other hand, such price regulations discourage both NOCs and downstream suppliers from investing in gas and infrastructure development. NOCs are reluctant to import gas at a high price, because it will drop them into deficit. This is partly why China continues to negotiate with Russia over the sales price even after the agreement on a 30-year natural gas purchase contract for the East Siberian pipeline in May 2014 after eight years of negotiation (Romano et al. 2016). However, snail's progress in infrastructure development makes the coal ban and forced switch from coal to gas likely to bring about disastrous results on residential and commercial consumers, as exemplified in the winter heating crisis of 2017.

China's trade and investment implications on energy-exporting countries

To avoid intensifying conflicts amid tightening CO_2 emission and air pollution controls, the Chinese government restricts coal imports, and encourages export of and foreign direct investment (FDI) in energy and construction industries. These measures have had significant yet varied impacts on resource-rich countries. Our findings can be highlighted as follows.

First, most of the Asian-Pacific energy-exporting countries suffer from the resource curse, though to a varied extent. The curse differs according to the country's initial industrial and trade structures, diversity of trade partners, as well as the type of its major fuel for export. Countries with high specialization in the mineral sectors of their industrial and trade structures, high trade-dependency on China, large coal exports, low preparedness for a resource burst went through deindustrialization and emerged with higher trade-dependency on China. Countries which have increased coal exports to China are hit most by the recent revival of China's coal tariff and decrease in coal consumption, as shown in Chapter 8. The resource curse is intensified by China's climate-energy policy, which accelerates declines in energy demand and worsens terms of trade, as demonstrated in Chapter 9.

Second, China's direct investment in energy resources has yielded mixed results. It has supported the coal-exporting countries of Indonesia and Kazakhstan to redirect coal exports for domestic power generation, providing an option to mitigate the resource curse caused by China's shrinking coal demand. While this serves to develop electricity infrastructure and mitigate the bottleneck to economic growth, it raises coal shares in power generation and increases CO_2 emissions. The investment also enabled Myanmar to consume electricity generated from its developed hydropower and gas fields, but at the same time brought significant losses and deforestation of land – which increase CO_2 emissions, as well as soil erosion, infertility and loss of biodiversity – reducing income for local producers fulfilling regional demand. As indicated in Chapter 11, these investments risk turning renewable resources in Myanmar into non-renewable resources for the benefit of China.

The future

The findings of this volume suggest that until exports and FDI in the energy and power sectors stop serving as a way of achieving domestic climate and environmental targets, China will not take serious measures to overcome the conflicts of interest between major stakeholders in advancing energy transformation and achieving a low CO_2 emission development. In the meantime, it continues to seek clean energy resources and outsource coal and hydropower in a way that can benefit partner countries to some extent. Contrary to the Washington Consensus that imposes a specific reform package to recipient countries, China respects the non-interference principle and seeks win-win opportunities with them (Lin and Wang 2017). However, China's FDI and resource- or infrastructure-backed loans can easily redirect the energy development pathways of partner countries toward high CO_2 emissions, as indicated in the two case studies of Indonesia and Myanmar. China's "common fate and destination" model consisting of joint venture companies with host countries as well as engineering, procurement and construction (EPC) contracts can entrench dependency on China and institutional lock-in for coal-centered energy system, incapable of moving towards a more sustainable pathway. Still, partner countries will welcome China's infrastructure finance for increasing access to affordable and reliable modern energy, regardless of the type of energy for the time being.

The findings also indicate that resource-rich countries will suffer a resource curse, unless they diversify their trade partners and industrial and trade structures, as well as develop institutions that properly manage the macroeconomic impacts of a resource boom to prepare a future burst. These measures are also essential to mitigate the risk of increasing dependency on China. Higher dependency accelerates their export and industrial specification into resources and primary goods with lower value added, making them more vulnerable to resource boom and burst.

However, diversification of already specialized industrial and trade structures imposes a far tougher challenge. The China-induced resource boom generated both technological and policy feedback effects. They entrench from changes in political costs and options (Jordan and Matt 2014), norms, policies, regulations and prevailing institutions (Verbong and Geels 2007) to state capacities and institutions to affect later prospects for policy implementation, along with the interests, identity and political participation of large groups of people to mobilize support (Pierson 1993). Such a trajectory is hard to shift considering the strong driving forces advancing them.

Besides, resource-rich countries can hardly enjoy the same positive feedback effects that China did through the emergence of renewable energies. Except a few countries, a small domestic market disables domestic manufacturers from enjoying economies of scale and enhancing market competitiveness. Feed-in-tariff can simply invite Chinese manufacturers and developers that have gained competitiveness in the world market (OECD 2017). In addition, richness in energy has often enabled countries to supply energy at a subsidized price. For fear of fierce protests from the public, governments tend to place price reform as a last priority. This prevents renewables from being competitive against conventional energy sources, thus providing rationale for energy development plans centered on conventional energy.

One of the possible countermeasures is increasing energy connectivity. Regional connectivity can bring about collective regional benefits, including: a more stable national energy supply through an increase in resource diversity, higher efficiency through economies of scale and scope, higher share of renewables by enabling the pooling of a region's renewable energy resources, and lower burdens on the environment (UNESCAP 2016).

This option may work in the Association of Southeast Asian Nations (ASEAN), which has been active in regional interconnection. ASEAN has initiated two flagship programs and an energy cooperation action plan which lists 16 projects. Central Asia, in contrast, inherits its interconnection from the Soviet period while countries are supported by China to implement major projects after achieving independence. South Asia is in the middle. On the one hand, the South Asia Electricity Transmission and Trade Project (CASA 1000) is ongoing, with backing from the World Bank and the Asian Development Bank, aiming to transfer surplus energy from Central Asian hydropower to South Asia. On the other hand, under the China-Pakistan Economic Corridor, China backs interconnection projects and energy development for – both coal and renewables – in Pakistan, with the aim of creating energy connectivity with itself and avoiding the Malacca Dilemma, while addressing the energy insecurity associated with increasing dependence on foreign sources.

Energy transformation toward low CO_2 emissions is not limited to technological and infrastructural challenge – such as high deployment of renewable energies, transformation of the electricity transmission network and management of the variability and uncertainty associated with wind and solar power. It also entails a socio-technical transition, or a non-linear shift of the current energy regime, requiring changes in not only regulations, market rules, designs and the operation of networks and systems, but also in the concept of energy security (Mitchell 2008; Verbong and Loorbach 2012). While markets can help generate feedback effects for transformation, it is only after clean energies become sufficiently competitive against conventional energies. In this process, non-market drivers are indispensable because transition provokes hard-fought inter- and intra-scalar contestations between old and new institutions, agents and technologies, all of which pose inherent limitations on rapid change (Smith and Raven 2012). Complementary measures are necessary for clean energies in order to be provided at an affordable price for all, including residents who can hardly afford the international price of energy.

It remains a future challenge to explore effective ways to minimize contestations and accelerate the transition in not only in China but also in resource-rich countries that export energy, especially coal to China.[1]

Note

1 Several works such as Delina (2017) and Mori (2018) are addressing this challenge.

References

Delina, L.L. (2017) *Accelerating Sustainable Energy Transition(s) in Developing Countries: The Challenges of Climate Change and Sustainable Development*, Oxon: Routledge.

Di Meglio, J.-F. and Romano, G.C. (2016) Introduction: From 'shaping' to 'framing' China's energy security and the example of the oil policy, in Romano, G.C. and Di Meglio, J.-F. (eds.) *China's Energy Security: A Multidimensional Perspective*, Oxon: Routledge, 1–21.

Jordan, A. and Matt, E. (2014) Designing policies that intentionally stick: Policy feedback in a changing climate, *Policy Science* 47: 227–47.

Lin, J.Y. and Wang, Y. (2017) *Going beyond Aid: Development Cooperation for Structural Transformation*, Cambridge: Cambridge University Press.

Mitchell, C. (2008) *The Political Economy of Sustainable Energy*, Hampshire: Palgrave Macmillan.

Mori, A. (2018) Sociotechnical and political economy perspectives in the Chinese energy transition, *Energy Research & Social Science* 35: 29–36.

OECD (2017) *Economic Outlook for Southeast Asia, China and India 2017: Addressing Energy Challenges*, Paris: OECD Publishing, http://dx.doi.org/10.1787/saeo-2017-en, accessed on October 10, 2017.

Pierson, P. (1993) When effect becomes cause: Policy feedback and political change, *World Politics* 45(4): 595–628.

Qi, T., Wincheste, N., Karplus, K.V. and Zhang, X. (2014) Will economic restructuring in China reduce trade-embodied CO_2 emissions? *Energy Economics* 42: 204–12.

Romano, G.C., Yin, N. and Zhang, X. (2016) Gas in China's energy security strategy, in Romano, G.C. and Di Meglio, J.-F. (eds.) *China's Energy Security: A Multidimensional Perspective*, Oxon: Routledge, 46–68.

Smith, A. and Raven, R. (2012) What is protective space? Reconsidering niches in transition to sustainability, *Research Policy* 41(6): 106–19.

Tang, X., Jin, Y., McLellan, B.C., Wang, J. and Li, S. (2018) China's coal consumption declining – Impermanent or permanent? *Resources, Conservation and Recycling* 129: 307–13.

Tang, X., Jin, Y., Wang, X., Wang, J. and McLellan, B.C. (2017) Will China's trade restructuring reduce CO_2 emissions embodied in international exports?, *Journal of Cleaner Production* 161: 1094–103.

Tang, X., McLellan, B.C., Zhang, B.S., Snowden, S. and Höök, M. (2016) Trade-off analysis between embodied energy exports and employment creation in China, *Journal of Cleaner Production* 134: 310–9.

UNESCAP (2016) *Towards a Sustainable Future: Energy Connectivity in Asia and the Pacific Region*, www.unescap.org/sites/default/files/publications/Full%20Report_4.pdf, accessed on October 10, 2017.

Verbong, G. and Geels, F. (2007) The ongoing energy transition: Lessons from a socio-technical, multi-level analysis of the Dutch electricity system (1960–2004), *Energy Policy* 35: 1025–37.

Verbong, G. and Loorbach, D. (2012) Introduction, in Verbong, G. and Loorbach, D. (eds.) *Governing the Energy Transition: Reality, Illusion or Necessity?* Oxon: Routledge, 1–23.

Wu, R., Geng, Y., Dong, H., Fujita, T. and Tian, X. (2016) Changes of CO_2 emissions embodied in China-Japan trade: Drivers and implications, *Journal of Cleaner Production* 112: 4151–8.

Yu, Y. and Chen, F. (2017) Research on carbon emissions embodied in trade between China and South Korea, *Atmospheric Pollution Research* 8: 56–63.

Zhao, Y., Wang, S., Zhang, Z., Liu, Y. and Ahmad, A. (2016) Driving factors of carbon emissions embodied in China-US trade: A structural decomposition analysis, *Journal of Cleaner Production* 131: 678–89.

Index

Note: Page numbers in bold refer to tables and italics refer to figures.

For Product Safety Concerns and Information please contact our EU
representative GPSR@taylorandfrancis.com Taylor & Francis Verlag GmbH,
Kaufingerstraße 24, 80331 München, Germany

Printed and bound by CPI Group (UK) Ltd, Croydon, CR0 4YY
08/05/2025
01864338-0003